RENAULT
The cars and the charisma

J. Dewar McLintock

W0009609

 Patrick Stephens, Cambridge

First published 1983

ISBN 0-85059-582-7

Front cover photographs: Top Renault UK Ltd.
Bottom Bruce Quarrie courtesy N.P. Slatford of Henlys.

Photoset in 10 on 11 pt Plantin by Manuset Limited,
Baldock, Herts. Printed in Great Britain on 115 gsm
Fineblade coated cartridge by R.J. Acford Limited,
Chichester, Sussex, and bound by Norton-Bridge
Bookbinders Limited, Stotfold, Herts, for the publishers,
Patrick Stephens Limited, Bar Hill, Cambridge, CB3 8EL,
England.

The administrative offices of Renault Frères at the Rue du Point du Jour, Billancourt, Paris, 1906.

RENAULT

The cars and the charisma

Contents

In the historic shed is the simple workbench where the young engineer made magic with metal.

One of the most popular of all early Renaults was the 8 hp twin-cylinder—in this case of 1911. Many are still in use.

1: From garden shed to industrial empire

It is conventional to commence any motoring history with suppositions and some-times facts, about the very first powered land contraptions. I see no reason to depart from the convention, but perhaps we can take a few short cuts, since the object is to devote as much available space as possible to things Renault, and our part of history starts at least a century after those dimly seen dawnings of automotive consciousness.

It is generally agreed that the first 'realistic' road vehicle was built in 1769 by the Frenchman Nicolas Cugnot. It was a vast, clumsy, steam-powered three wheeler intended for military purposes and is said to have taken over an hour to travel a mile. But Cugnot was a Frenchman and the French thus had a head start in motoring, which they have never lost.

Britain, however, was not far behind. James Watt, Richard Trevithick, Golds-worthy Gurney and Walter Hancock all built steam vehicles of different and often bizarre kinds, and the last-named took the horseless carriage into the realms of reality with his 'Enterprise' and 'Autopsy' steam buses. In fact his buses 'Era' and the oddly named 'Autopsy' ('See for Yourself') carried 4,000 passengers between Moorgate and Paddington in the period August–November 1834.

Many motoring historians insist that the first gas-engined 'car' (internal combustion, as opposed to the external combustion of the steam engine) was the wagon constructed by the Swiss, Isaac de Rivaz, in 1806, but others agree that the father of the gas-engined horseless carriage was Etienne Lenoir, a Belgian who built a viable prototype of a one-horsepower two-stroke engine in 1858 and had it working in a cart a couple of years later. Several examples of a 1½ hp version were made in Paris.

Lenoir was certainly a pioneer, and although his creations were under-powered and crude, he put the gas engine on the map, and set the Germans' Daimler and Benz thinking, working, making, perfecting, day and night until they had presented the first truly effective gas-engined horseless carriages, in 1865–6.

The 'German connection', however, takes us to Paris, France, 1899, for it was at the big World Fair that Benz and Daimler exhibited their cars and aroused the interest of would-be French car manufacturers in their gasoline or benzine engines. Panhard and Peugeot both adopted the Daimler engine for their early cars.

The motorcar was really arriving. Even the illustrious Emile Zola said: 'The future belongs to the automobile. I am convinced of it. At this point, it is difficult to measure the full significance of such an invention. Distances will shrink, and thus the automobile will be a new bearer of civilisation and peace. In the end, it will undoubtedly heighten prosperity . . .'

By 1896 the world had started its searing, tempestuous, almost lascivious love affair with the motorcar, which was still a frail, wilful, moody creature. In the United Kingdom, France, Germany and America, cars were being built in considerable numbers, albeit painstakingly by hand in frugally-equipped workshops in most cases. Motor racing was well into its stride and the military were already investigating the warlike possibilities of these iron carts and ponies.

The throttling effects of anti-automobile propaganda and legislation were at last being shaken off or tempered. On 14 November 1896, *The Autocar*—'a journal published in the interests of the mechanically-propelled road carriage'—started its long leading article with the observation: 'Today, November 14, 1896, is a red letter day, not only in the history of automobilism, but in that of England itself, for it marks the throwing open of the highways and byways of our beautiful country to those who elect to travel thereupon in carriages propelled by motors, instead of in horsedrawn vehicles or upon bicycles'. This was the celebration of the British motorists' emancipation, whereby he or she could travel at 12 mph instead of 4 mph and without a man carrying a red flag, far in advance of the 'fearsome monster'.

At this time, Louis Renault was 19 and he had already patented a steam boiler, after serving some time with Serpollet, the steam engineer, but his inclination lay towards the gas engine.

Most histories of Renault suggest that the man Louis Renault was a dunce at school, that he spent all his spare time learning to be a motor engineer, and that he became a successful motor manufacturer largely because his brothers supplied the commercial impetus and acumen. There is probably an element of truth in all three postulations, but only an element.

No dunce could have grasped the principles of external and internal combustion engines, transmission systems and power-to-weight ratios as he did, and there is no real reason to suppose that Renault was ignorant of normal business practices.

It is probably true that he had only a meagre knowledge of the arts and the humanities, and this made it difficult for him to be at home with the social and sociological areas of industry. It is apparent, moreover, that he had problems in forming and maintaining human relationships, although this has never been uncommon among engineers.

He was an individual with an unusually strong will, not necessarily obstinate but undoubtedly single-minded. He was certainly not a genius and was not particularly lucky, but he recognised opportunities and was never slow to grasp them. A man of exceptional personal courage, as evidenced by his successes in motor racing, he could never be considered a romanticist, although he was probably as sentimental as the next man.

Was Louis Renault, at the end, a traitor? The danger of being thus branded, during and after the Second World War, was for industrialists, an occupational hazard. Whilst some escaped the final condemnation, by luck, adroitness or absence, Renault seems to have allowed himself, almost absent-mindedly, to wander into the danger area. Whatever its views, the Régie Renault seems to prefer to forget, but the name of this melancholy man of destiny is the name on the millions upon millions of automobiles that have been, and continue to be, created in the factories and assembly plants in France and many other countries.

The garden shed at Billancourt where Louis Renault made his first car in 1898. It is there today, at the heart of an industrial empire.

A pale, rather gaunt, introvert boy, Louis Renault spent long hours in his room at the home of his relatively well-off parents, who ran a drapery and button business near the Rue de Rivoli. He devoured all literature relating to things mechanical and shirked his more academic homework. The family had a small property in what was then the countryside, at Billancourt, and when they went there, usually at week-ends, Louis was in his element, pottering and scheming in the stout shed which is still perfectly preserved.

At the Lycée Condorcet, Louis naturally failed the École Centrale examination but already had a qualified engineer's brain and it was not surprising that he should soon pass his arts and crafts exam.

When he patented his steam boiler, he was with Delaunay–Belleville and with his growing interest in the increasingly popular internal combustion engine, he would rather have worked for De Dion but they had no vacancies. In any case he was then called up for a year's military service.

Renault's service in the infantry at Chalons-sur-Marne in no way stopped him playing around with mechanisms and vehicles. In fact at an early stage he avoided tough and boring military chores by designing a system for automatically raising the targets on the rifle range. He stayed in the ranks perfectly happily, because he had no particular interest in soldiering, but with his meagre pay and a small allowance from his parents he managed to acquire his first vehicle—a ¾ hp De Dion tricycle. In this single—and to him utterly thrilling—act, he launched himself on the road of destiny.

Louis was very pleased with this tricycle and very proud of it, but its limitations were no surprise to him. It was not far removed from a motorcycle and could only take two persons in tandem. It was uncomfortable and rough to drive. The engine, however, packed a surprising punch for its size. Finishing his army call-up with relief, Renault set out to put this small engine in a simple four-wheeler—simple but sophisticated, for he was something of a purist. There followed months of sweat and midnight oil in the shed at Billancourt . . ..

An early photograph of the 1898 prototype shows a spindly, bare structure on four cycle-type spoked wheels with pneumatic tyres and a simple 'Tilbury' body for two. It had a rectangular, tubular steel frame with full-elliptic multiple leaf springs front and rear. (The Scotsman John Boyd Dunlop had invented and patented the pneumatic tyre in 1888 and by the turn of the century pneumatics were almost commonplace.)

The most noticeable things about the 1898 prototype are the almost delicate shaft drive and the indecently large and opulent split aluminium casing containing the differential. The differential was not at all an invention of Louis Renault; in fact it had been devised by another Frenchman, Pecquer, in 1828 and had been regarded as an essential feature of even the first true motorcars—the Daimler and Benz contraptions were the virtual prototypes of the horseless carriages, as the early cars were called.

On the other hand, the frail-looking final drive shaft of the first Renault car was something rather remarkable in an age when belts or chains were the normal means of transmission. Louis Renault is credited with having invented 'direct drive' and indeed his patent for a transmission system, lodged in 1899, suggests that he was claiming the use of gears instead of chains or belts as an exclusive feature, but it is more likely that the true originality lay in the use of universal joints for the propeller shaft. At the same time, Renault patented his gearbox, which was by no means the first three-speed box, but had an original system of gear-shifting using eccentrics or 'tumbler' gears, and also provided a direct top gear by means of dog clutches between the normal cone clutch and the leading universal joint of the prop shaft.

The controls of the smart little runabout, which had a fore-and-aft mounted De Dion ¾ CV engine, were a handle on the left of the steering column for gear-shifting and column controls for ignition advance/retard and accelerator; a hand brake acting on the rear wheels; and a brake pedal linked to the clutch. The steering tiller was semi-circular.

Louis Renault was a competent amateur engineer and he had all the best tools that were available, including a lathe, but it was really rather beyond his scope to make gears for the new box, and he had this done by Durands, a gear-cutting firm in the Rue Oberkampf. In the course of dealing with this firm he met the young Serre, who was to become one of his closest associates.

It took Renault about three months to make the prototype, which meant he 'burnt a great deal of midnight oil' on the project, but after all he was laying the foundation stone of an empire, although he did not have the faintest idea that he would ever become a motorcar manufacturer.

The insubstantial-looking but strangely beautiful contraption weighed a mere 1,500 kg. It also looked lighter than contemporary cars, largely because most of them had cart- or carriage-type wooden wheels and the Renault had cycle-type wheels. Indeed there was a good deal of the cycle about it, and it would certainly have been described as a cycle car in the early 1920s.

Renault may have been a wizard with mechanism, stresses and strains, cutting and filing, nuts and bolts, but he was also no fool when it came to protecting his interests—not at this time of his life anyway. He patented his direct drive in America and Germany, and successfully fought actions against people who were falling over themselves to infringe the patent, although there were still many who claimed to have used similar systems earlier than he did, and they included De Dion who never gave up the idea that they were the innovators. Indeed, even as late as 1929 they went to the trouble of digging up or inventing a Bordeaux character who had careered about in a 'direct drive' automotor before Louis took to the road. But they could not come up with a registered patent specification.

In the closing weeks of 1898, Renault constructed the body for the car—little more than a bench seat, a few floorboards and a tiny dashboard or scuttle. All this was done in the compact workshop shed at Billancourt.

Louis Renault was to celebrate his 21st birthday, but it had to have something to do with motorcars. He was not too much of a 'troglodyte' to have a 'booze-up', provided there were not too many girls around. Some chosen friends were given the rendezvous—a night spot in the Rue de Helder, a few miles north of Montmartre. It was Christmas Eve, a little early for his real birthday.

A 21st birthday party is a memorable affair for any young man. For the slightly immature yet highly talented Louis, it was almost delirious because he had chosen the occasion to launch his new automobile on this little gang of enthusiasts, not so many of whom even had an inkling that he had completed the neat little auto. Thus, on 24 December 1898, a group of intense, chattering, admiring youths gathered round the machine on the cobbled street in the cold night air. This was the new motoring! How their girls must envy them . . ..

Left to right: The 1897 De Dion quadricycle with Marcel Renault in the passenger seat, the 1898 voiturette prototype with Louis Renault at the wheel, and the first 1¾ hp model, introduced in 1899, driven by Paul Hugé.

Louis wasn't thinking about the girls much, although he had an eye for a pert pretty face, a neat ankle, a rounded figure. This was the time to show his friends what motoring was all about. He started up the puttering little De Dion motor again and it quivered in the Renault chassis with its makeshift but workmanlike body. Now was the moment of truth. Who would like a ride? 'Don't all rush at once' said Louis, with a rare attempt at humour and matey familiarity. The lads jostled each other a bit and peered and poked at the machine. More forward than the others, yet the most sceptical, the young schoolteacher Viot volunteered and climbed into the car alongside Louis.

While Marcel, one of Louis Renault's two elder brothers, regaled the rest with tales of the miracles that had gone on in that shed at Billancourt, Fernand, the other brother, simply sat and smiled, having a little less faith in the enterprise. Louis and Viot went chuntering over the stone setts and cobbles towards La Butte—the great mound of Montmartre, on top of which sits the charismatic basilica of Sácre Coeur. Anyone who knows the region will tell you how steep the streets are there, but amazingly they charged up and down the Rue Lepic, the game little engine never missing a beat, although approaching red heat . . . more soberly but still darting among the horsed carts, cabs and buses, they returned to the pub and grabbed the nearest bottle of good Burgundy, extending their euphoria in a fit and proper manner. Viot was really excited. Red faced with the cold and wine, still shivering a little, he said to Renault: 'Right old son, you've got an order. Here's your 40 louis. Get cracking'.

Renault was over the moon, but he'd seen nothing. By the end of a long, some-what riotous night, a dozen of the *copains* had pleaded with him to make motor cars for them, and quite a few had even put down a decent deposit. Renault was in business.

Business indeed had to be the operative word from then on—up to the present day and so on and on, although Louis was not to see beyond the Second World War. The thing now was for him to go into production, feverishly but skilfully at Billancourt, while his brothers attended to the finance, administration and sales. They might even make a machine for this new motor racing craze . . ..

Louis' elder brothers were content, for the 'youngster' had justified the salary they had paid him recently out of the Société Renault Fils et Compagnie—the drapery firm. Marcel and Fernand decided to set up a small motor company and in February 1899 there was a small announcement in *Petites Affiches* to the effect that a new firm, Renault Frères, had been formed with a capital of 60,000 fr, the object of which was to manufacture motorcars, that is to say, *voitures automobiles.* The registered office was at 10 Avenue du Cours, Billancourt.

The brothers envisaged a two-year plan. If things went well, 30 cars would be built. If the enterprise failed, Louis would try to get a job with one of the big car firms, and he would in any case prefer to be a designer than a manufacturer.

Louis Renault did not want to be a designer. Indeed he probably would not have made a particularly good one. A clever modifier, he was never really an innovator, as his later products showed. But he was certainly cut out to be a manufacturer.

Half the capital of the new company went immediately on plant. They bought a powerful stationary steam engine, a few lathes, milling machines, a grinder, a gear cutter and so on—the usual machine shop equipment. Louis, a bit of a boating enthusiast when time allowed, knew of a useful old boathouse on the Ile Seguin. He and his brothers and a few friends dismantled it and put it up again in the large vegetable garden at the Billancourt property. A small wooden shed was bought to serve as the office. Marcel promptly installed himself as 'managing director' and Fernand, when time off from the button business permitted, as accountant. The stores was a disused greenhouse. Ainsi Naquit Billancourt—centre of today's Renault empire . . ..

A few workmen, headed by Edouard Richet, were hired, but Louis was the most industrious of the workforce, starting always at 6 am and seldom leaving before 10 or 11 at night, with short breaks for lunch and dinner. The object was not only to produce as many cars as possible in the first six months, to show themselves and potential buyers what they could do, but to be able to exhibit and take orders at the second Paris Motor Show on 12 June 1899.

'If we sell a dozen or two before then, and get a good site at the show, they'll fall over themselves to order' said Louis to his workers and his brothers. They sold 60, in fact, but the site at the Tuileries was not a particularly good one and orders for automobiles always tended to fall off from midsummer onwards. The tally for the year was 76.

The brothers reckoned it would be a fair gamble to continue the business, because the existing buyers were happy with the product, which was proving remarkably reliable. But it would be necessary to get more publicity, and the quickest and best way to do that was to go in for a new craze—motor racing.

Renault was now making its A and B cars—both voiturettes with single-cylinder

The 1¾ hp voiturette of 1899. It could carry two people at 30 mph and would do 47 mpg on the 'urban cycle'.

Above *The famous 'coal scuttle' bonnet is a feature of this 3 CV Renault single-cylinder Aster-engined light car.*

Below *Marcel Renault at a check point in the Paris-Vienna race, 1902.*

De Dion air-cooled engines. The A-Type was a 270 cc job and the B-Type had the 450 motor. Three-speed gearboxes were used and the cars would do about 25 mph in top, 10 mph in second and 6 mph in low gear on the flat, the B-Type being better on hills and with passenger. Simple, open bodywork was standard, but a jaunty little carriage-type coupé was available. Curious little half-round bonnets were used on the A and B. It was with two of the B-types that the Renault brothers Louis and Marcel entered the Coupe des Chauffeurs Amateurs, a race from Paris to Trouville on the Channel coast, on 27 August 1899, and they came first and second. On September 1 the brothers entered the Paris–Ostend race and scored another 1–2 win, whilst on October 19 they scored the hat trick, Louis winning the Paris–Rambouillet in 2 hours 50 minutes (almost 23 mph) followed by Marcel.

The triple success really got the publicity going—most of it in motor papers, but in the nationals as well. Renault also advertised widely, with the slogan 'Always First'. By the end of 1900 the firm had sold 200 cars and they had to extend the works to cope with the demand for the little cars. It now occupied over 50,000 square feet and the personnel strength was 110.

The C-Type car was developed in time for the Paris–Bordeaux and Paris–Toulouse events. This was a more powerful version of the B-Type; although still a one-cylinder job, it was rated at 3 hp, had a longer stroke and was now water-cooled. Three cars were used as a works team and drivers additional to the brothers were Grus, Oury, Corre and Schrader. Renaults came first in their class in both races again. These were long, tough races, and Renault were proving that light cars—voiturettes—could do as well and better than the heavies. Success after success followed for Types D to J, all still with the single-pot De Dion or Aster motor except the H and J, which had twins, this being the first move into multi-cylinders. For the Paris–Vienna of 1902, however, Renault secretly prepared the first engine of his own making—a four-cylinder 3¾-litre 20/30 hp.

A few things were typically Renault about this car, in that they were not utterly revolutionary but were just a little daring, in a controlled sort of way, like Louis Renault himself—never totally the innovator, but making little jumps ahead, and usually completely disregarding anyone else's advice because he thought he knew better than anyone else and in nine cases out of ten he did.

Thus, the engine had two blocks of two cylinders and the inlet valves were automatic, whilst the cooling system involved the use of an aluminium casing around the heads. The lubrication was pressurised. Six motors of this type were made. Nominally, the designer was Viet, who had left De Dion because they would not let him make a four. But Louis stood over Viet and more or less told him what to make. He may have been right, but Renault never used automatic inlet valves again.

The last of the races in which Renault used the single-cylinder engines was the Paris–Berlin in which Louis scooped up a class win and seventh place overall. There was a considerable amount of ill-feeling over this race because a competitor had hit a child who later died in hospital. The national press in France and Germany slammed motor racing, and it was with some difficulty that the organisers of the next big event, the Paris–Vienna of 1902, got it under way at all. It was to be the most important road race so far, and the most significant victory for the Renault concern, whilst the Paris–Madrid of 1903 was to be the most tragic. The story of these great races has been told and retold so often that I need not repeat the details here, but merely summarise the events very briefly.

The Paris–Vienna started on 24 June 1902, and the course was about 1,000 miles long. There were 117 entries and three classes—voiturettes and two or three-wheelers, light cars (880–1,450 lb) and cars over that weight, which meant some monsters with 10- to 14-litre engines. This was the classic in which Louis Renault had everything go wrong but refused to be beaten, even repairing a wheel by using the rungs from a cottage chair; whilst in the later stages of the race his co-driver Szisz lay on the bonnet and poured water into a leaking radiator. Marcel Renault amazingly won this gruelling race with his quite small car at an average speed of almost 40 mph. Grus, Cormier and Lang, all driving Renaults, finished second, third and sixth in their class and Louis limped to the finish, climbing from 61st to 20th.

The Paris–Madrid, 24 May 1903, was a disaster which resulted in ten deaths, including that of the courageous Marcel Renault, who had always been somewhat happier at an office desk than at the wheel of a race car. Louis was shocked and grief-stricken, and withdrew all the cars, but the French government went further and stopped the race at Bordeaux. This was the end of road racing until 1927 when the first Mille Miglia was run.

Louis mourned, Billancourt mourned, and Marcel was buried at Passy, whilst the workers subscribed to a fund for an impressive statue which was regrettably bombed to smithereens in the 1939–45 war. But racing was not everything and the show had to go on. Fernand Renault now took the bold step of selling the drapery business and went into motors in earnest, although without the mechanical knowledge or empathy of his brother.

Accustomed now to success, and having acquired trophy after trophy, Louis seemed henceforth to channel his drive and ambition into acquisition of another kind. Marcel had willed his share of the business to his mistress, Suzanne Davenay. Suzanne was a simple, good natured girl who loved luxury. In effect, Louis said to her 'Look Suzanne, a nice girl like you doesn't really want to mess around with a motor business. It's not worth much anyway and the motor industry's in a dicey state. Let me look after your share of the business and I'll set you up in a ritzy apartment, with a useful income, and what's more you can have one of our new cars.'

Left *Louis Renault checks in at Bordeaux in the notorious Paris-Madrid road race in 1903, in which his brother Marcel was killed.*

Right *Indestructible little twin-cylinder Renault engine of 1905-6, with Bosch magneto ignition and Renault carburettor.*

Not in the least interested in commerce or industry, the pretty lady gladly accepted. Louis was now on the way to taking over the business.

Fate seemed determined to cast him as a Croesus. They had all known that Fernand was not strong and he suddenly fell ill and deteriorated rapidly. In 1909 he died, but Louis had already bought him out at the bargain price of eight million francs. Louis was now the eponymous 'hero' of the Renault empire.

In the meantime, since the drama of the Paris–Madrid in 1903, the Renault range of cars had been extended to comprise voiturettes and light cars of 7 to 40 nominal horsepower. Louis had given up racing temporarily and spent a lot of time reshuffling the models as well as designing, inventing and patenting where possible, eg, dismantlable spark plugs, hydraulic shock absorbers, a gas-operated starter motor, etc.

Models included the 8 hp, twin-cylinder taxicabs which gained a monopoly in Paris and became familiar in London; the little two-pot 10 hp N-type; a 14 hp four which was derived from the Paris–Vienna cars; and four-cylinder 20 and 35 hp models. The 14 hp was one of the most successful of all early Renaults and with minor modifications was kept in production for many years. Introduced in 1904 it was the first model to have the radiator behind the engine—while magneto instead of accumulator ignition was introduced for this and other cars in the same year.

Louis showed a renewed interest in racing in 1905, entering a car in the Gordon Bennett Cup, with Ferenc Szisz, his former mechanic and co-driver, as contestant for this important event. The car was a 90 hp four with a speed of about 100 mph. Unfortunately, Szisz did not qualify, since he gained only fifth place in the eliminating trials. For the first time Renault had used a water pump, and it failed. In the following year, however, Szisz covered himself and Renault with glory by winning the first-ever French Grand Prix over the Le Mans course. The 100 hp car was fitted with Michelin detachable rims—a historic invention which was a step towards the detachable wheel, and eliminated the dreadful business of taking off a damaged tyre and putting on a spare one. The big red Renault ran faultlessly in the hands of its inspired driver, who covered the 780 miles of the race at an average speed of 63 mph. Melting tar apart, it had been a classic race which brought back road racing, yet at the same time inaugurated circuit racing.

After Fernand's death, Renault Frères ceased to exist, its place being taken by Automobiles Renault—the title itself indicating the extent to which Louis had adopted the despotic role. In the meantime, the firm had gone into the commercial vehicle business and Louis was exploring further areas of possible conquest, including that of air space.

Louis may have been shy and gauche, but this did not prevent him from being rather a playboy. Thus he had a country mansion, Herqueville, a hunting lodge, a mistress and a yacht, and was greatly interested in aircraft and sailing. With such a strong enthusiasm for matters marine and aerial, what more natural than that he should commercialise his technical knowledge in those fields? He already had the germ of the idea for what is today Renault Marine, and now he turned to aviation, building his first aircraft engine, an air-cooled V8 of 60 hp. Mounted in a Maurice Farman biplane and piloted, oddly enough, by an air ace called Renaux, in 1911 it won the Michelin Cup and 10,000 fr for the first airman who could fly from Paris to the strange volcanic Puy de Dome and land on top of it! Anyone who has seen the Puy must appreciate the nature of the feat.

On 11 October 1906, the Chevalier de la Légion d'Honneur was conferred on Renault—a mark of the government's regard for the motor industry as well as of the man. The company was now becoming established almost globally and certainly in those 'other worlds' America and Russia. What was known as the Renault Selling Branch in New York was budgeting to sell 1,200–1,500 chassis in 1909 and was convinced that racing would help. Accordingly they entered a 35 in the prestigious New York 24 hours. Knowing the track was largely of dirt and cinders, the drivers Raffalovich and Basle fitted light mudguards at the last minute and this helped them to win the event by covering over 1,050 miles in 24 hours. This helped to spread the Renault gospel in the New World.

What was it like to drive those old cars? Well, first it must be remembered that traffic density was low even in busy places like the suburbs of London, Manchester, etc. Traffic could be quite busy in a city centre, yet tailbacks as such were virtually unknown. If, on a fine Sunday, motorists had to come down to a crawl for a few miles on, say, the Brighton road, it made national news. Week-day traffic jams were rare, and soon unsnarled by one competent, firm-handed bobbie. If you wanted to come out of a side road, or turn right at an intersection, you hardly had to wait—there was a long interval between vehicles. A great deal of what traffic there was, was commercial—lorries, horse-drawn vehicles, delivery vans, brewers' drays, steam wagons, motor tricycles and messenger boys on pedal trikes and bikes. The car owner was rather a special person, who was either rich or well-off in the middle class manner, or he was a professional man such as a doctor or a dentist, barrister or high-class accountant. If anything went wrong with the motorcar, he either had to be wealthy enough to take a bus home and send out his handyman to mend it, or he had to know more or less how to deal with things himself.

It was no fun to have to take a tyre off, mend a puncture and put the whole thing back again; if you were lucky the car had detachable rims or wheels and a spare. It was easy to get at the engine and all components and there were no complications. No cars were particularly reliable, but you could mend things easily provided you were prepared to get dirty and bad tempered and lose a great deal of time. Spares were cheap, or you made them in your workshop, if you were a 'serious amateur'.

Above *As early as 1900, Renault had introduced a 'Conduite intérieure' (saloon) model. This example, with spider seat, is, however, of 1909 vintage.*

Right *Something very trendy in body styling . . .. The double coupé creation is on a Renault four-cylinder 20 CV chassis of 1907.*

Below *In 1909 Renault were already into the commercial vehicle field with the 20 hp 3 ton and other models. The car is a contemporary Renault voiturette.*

The typical engine was a side-valve with four cylinders cast in pairs, but the twin-cylinder was also popular on small cars. The clutch would be of cone type and the gearbox a three- or four-speed unit, without synchromesh of course, so that you had to double-declutch for every change down. Ignition would be by magneto or battery and coil, or a combination of the two. Petrol would be gravity-fed and the oiling system of splash or low-pressure type.

I was not even born then, but it was only a year or two ago that I was able to drive a 1906 20–30 hp Renault—this was one of the Beaulieu Motor Museum cars which Lord Montagu had lent me. It was a very low mileage car for its age—a mere 40,000 miles having been covered in all those years—so its performance and general feel were authentic for the era.

The car's specification was as follows: 24.8 hp four-cylinder side-valve; 100 × 140 mm bore and stroke; 4,398 cc; high-tension magneto; a four-speed gearbox; foot brake acting on transmission, hand brake on rear wheels; half-elliptic front, half-elliptic longitudinal and transverse rear springs. This model was current from 1905-1910 and cost about £660 for the chassis.

This particular car has been beautifully restored; it did not need much mechanical restoration, but was a little neglected externally. The Museum did a wonderful job, lovingly revarnishing the woodwork and repainting the 8 ft high carriage-type body in dark blue coach paint with immaculate gold lining.

I was present at a ceremony in 1980 when the restored Renault received a hackney carriage licence—one of only two in existence for veteran cars, I believe. It was a couple of years earlier that I had driven the car.

What surprised me was that the old car had so much power. When you put your foot down, there was an instant response from the big low-stressed cylinders, although torque and power tended to fade if you tried to get high revs in an intermediate gear. Those old motors peaked at about 1,500–2,000 rpm. You seemed to be able to hear the individual engine beats. There was a large, daunting quadrant-type gear shift and of course double-declutching was *de rigeur*. The gears fairly sung and whined, not quite drowning the deep burble of the engine. There were no chains to thrash, but the back axle made a sound like an underground train. Brakes were so good that you had to be careful, and the steering needed lots of muscle. Everything shook and vibrated a lot, but my lady assured me that the ride in the closed-off luxurious saloon was comfortable, if suggestive of a trampoline.

The Renault brothers had always had an eye on the activities of other motor manufacturers, and not least those in other countries. They had been quite glad to see Britain at last catching up on the scene and saw the possibilities for reciprocal trade, which started in a small way very early on. Now Louis Renault, alone in his direction of the destiny of the multi-million franc concern, focussed his prophetic gaze even more clearly on the overseas industries and markets.

Britain looked a natural. Germany he looked at sideways, and Italy's artistic engineering interested him, as well as their success in racing. Most of all, however, he was interested in the American scene and this obsession was to haunt the Renault organisation like a kind of unconsummated passion throughout its history. Not only was Renault interested in the mechanical aspects of the progress of the motorcar in America, he was impressed with the idea of mass production and followed the fortunes of Ford with keen interest. Visiting the Ford plant, he found himself much in sympathy with Henry Ford and was utterly fascinated by the Model T 'Tin Lizzie' although regarding it as somewhat precocious in design. It was at this time,

Celebrities have always been attracted to the marque. Maurice Chevalier was a 'natural' for the 20/30 hp limousine.

between 1905 and 1910, that he came to the firm decision to produce relatively small or medium sized motorcars of as good quality as possible but in the quantities that would meet the demands of ordinary people. He accordingly made a full scale study of mass production and the complicated labour relations associated with it and started on the long hard road of industrial control—and sometimes lack of control when turbulence was too pronounced or when he lost his temper.

At the same time, Louis Renault kept his eye on the drawing board and his hands, figuratively speaking, at the bench. He was fascinated by the raging controversy over valving and induction—whether to have side or overhead, automatic or positively actuated or even sleeve valves, for example—and even ordered a sleeve-valve prototype to be made. He decided that the gilled tube radiator was old-fashioned and should be replaced by the honeycomb type, and he had rear suspensions redesigned, using both lateral and longitudinal springs. Importantly, too, Renault introduced his first six-cylinder engine, although this was a competitive measure, largely inspired by S.F. Edge's successful Napier in Britain. Louis was not keen on anything complicated—he was rather sold on Ford's airy dictum: 'Simplicate and add lightness'. By 1907, the typical Renault had a chassis with pressed steel channel-section side members, raised at the rear to allow springing-articulation and provide for a low centre of gravity for the whole car.

In the period from 1908 to 1912, several new models were introduced. They included a 7–8 hp twin with 75 × 120 mm bore and stroke and three-speed gearbox, selling at 4,650 fr, which was very cheap; a 9 hp twin (80 × 120 mm); a 10 hp four-cylinder car with 70 × 110 mm bore and stroke and a monobloc instead of two blocks of two; and an 18 hp six, of 80 × 120 mm bore and stroke. At about this time, Renault started making bodies to special order, having previously offered only chassis. A year or two later, there was a range of standard bodies. At the end of 1910, incidentally, the personnel strength at Billancourt was 3,000.

In the matter of mass production, the mistake that Renault at first made was to try to apply the principle to too wide a range. He was, in effect, visualising quantity-production lines for a dozen models, from 8 to 40 hp. Not surprisingly, all kinds of things went wrong on the lines and in any case this new 'automation' was decidedly unpopular with the workers, who at first did not seem to appreciate that they were going to make cheap motorcars for themselves as well as the 'toffs'. So Louis experienced his first strike and felt extremely hurt by this intransigence. It was soon over, after some diplomatic handling of the workers by trade union officials and Renault was able to introduce at least some elements of the Taylorism (science of automation) initiated by Ford. But he lost his personal faith in the workers and became even more autocratic.

Since this book is mainly about cars—the Renault cars of nearly 90 years—it is not appropriate to devote more than a few lines to the firm's military achievements in the First World War, but it is certainly worth recording once more (it has been done so often) that for an important action in the Battle of the Marne, General Gallieni commandeered all the taxis of the Compagnie des Fiacres de Paris—the 8 hp Renaults so familiar in Paris and London. Under General Manoury, 12,000 men, half of whom had 'taken a taxi' to the front, flanked von Kluck with vigour, and made a useful contribution to a battle which gave France the relatively quiet winter of 1914 in which to build up strength. The little Renaults became affection-ately known as the 'Taxis de la Marne'.

Renault made important war contributions in producing aircraft engines. The 200 and 300 hp Renault aero engines were made in great numbers, mainly to power the Breguet warplanes which secured mastery of the air over the Hun. Other significant Renault efforts included the production of munitions, transportation units, gun tractors and, of course, the famous Renault light tanks of which 1,200 a month were being churned out by the end of the war, and which had been engaged in 4,400 actions.

In the course of the 1914–18 war, some minor modifications were made to the Renault cars, but the numbers produced were in any case small. Of the three or four thousand cars that came off the crowded, jostling lines, all were destined for the military. For the duration, motor manufacturers were forbidden to sell cars to civilians. Louis Renault ignored this ban only once, and received a sharp rap over the knuckles from the Minister for Munitions.

'Well, that nonsense is all over,' said Louis Renault after the signing of the Armistice. 'We can get on with making motorcars again, as well as lorries, buses, tractors and plane engines.' He dismissed the war as he had greeted it—as a waste of time and a stupid mistake on the part of politicians and generals.

But the politicians and generals did not dismiss Louis Renault in such a cavalier manner. Indeed, his citation for the Légion d'Honneur said that he had made a most important contribution to the war effort, as indeed he had, especially with the tanks and aero engines.

Above *Surely the daddy of all GT cars. This 40 hp grand tourer of 1912 was a six-cylinder car with 100 × 160 mm bore and stroke.*

Below Les Taxis de la Marne. *In 1914 General Gallieni used 600 Renault 8 hp taxis to transport fresh troops to the battle of the Marne.*

Logo used on Renault light tanks after the 1914-18 war differs somewhat from today's diamond symbol.

Louis was 41 and probably the most respected and powerful motor manufacturer in Europe. He had built up a vast production complex at Billancourt, with a steel foundry, three iron foundries, an aluminium foundry and a brass foundry. There were rolling mills and press shops and a great general machine shop of 110,000 sq ft. The assembly shops occupied 360,000 sq ft. A year or two later, Renault was to form the Société Anonyme des Usines Renault, of which he held 98 per cent of the shares.

In the immediate post-war years, Renault found himself with a thorn in his flesh, in the form of what he called 'that little Yid from Javel'—Andre Citroën. Andre was already also an important and respected motor manufacturer, although not quite in the same league. The amazing thing is that although Citroën was already a well-established industrialist in the sense that he had a gear-cutting business, he did not start making motorcars until after the war, when he came out with a sleeve-valve 4-litre (to be taken over by Voisin) and a 1.3-litre side-valve four-cylinder, examples of which, with their distinctive disc wheels, flared wings and pointed radiator, can still occasionally be seen in and around remote French farms. Moreover, André Citroën, like Louis Renault, was in love with American mass production methods, and adopted derived methods on his own lines. In 1920, Citroën made 12,000 units of his one-model range while Renault, with a diverse range, produced 18,500.

The illustrious Renault 6 CV (8-9 hp) was introduced in 1922 as a competitor to the Citroën 5 CV, and was in production until late 1927 with progressive improvements including four wheel brakes in 1924. This is a 1925 tourer.

Naturally, Louis Renault was jealous of his rival and his 10 cv four, launched in 1919, was deliberately aimed at Citroën's general-purpose car. Incidentally, this was left-hand drive, like the Citroën, and this was the first time Renault had offered the *direction a gauche* which became the norm in France.

Renault's new 10 cv actually had an engine of just over two litres capacity, being a long-stroke motor and cheating the horse-power formula then used in France, to the benefit of the owner. It was a conventional monobloc engine with single camshaft side valves in place of the T-head arrangements popular up to that time. The car had a Dynastart or Dynamotor—an advanced component consisting of a combined dynamo and starter motor. These were used on many cars of the era and of later vintage and worked very well. Being in constant engagement, the starter function was smooth and completely silent. Magneto ignition was used, the instrument being across the front of the block, and driven by helical gearing from the camshaft. The carburettor had a mixture device controlled by the driver.

Renault had designed a simple, popular model in the general conception of the Model T Ford, so he supposed; but of course, he should have done it much earlier—for example, by modifying and mass-producing the twin-cylinder of 1905. But now there would be no more of those delightful, faithful little 'taxis of the Marne'; the last was the taxi Type FD of 1920, in fact.

Perhaps Louis Renault had missed his chance to be the Henry Ford of France, but at least a valid form of quantity production was introduced for the new 10 cv and the car emerged looking a neat, handsome affair, with its obligatory coal scuttle bonnet, rather frail looking mudguards and toylike disc wheels. At least the wheels were detachable and one could now have a spare wheel!

Citroën meanwhile decided that one model was not enough and he introduced the illustrious little Cloverleaf three-seater. I recall, as a child, occupying the third seat of one of these open coupés, behind my mother and the local doctor, and he was as thrilled as I was with the new car, which fairly buzzed up the steep Wimbledon Park Road. Like all the Cloverleafs, it was in buttercup yellow.

What Louis did then, to put the 'little Jew' in his place, was to bring out his 6 cv Type KJ, which was the 8.3 in the United Kingdom nomenclature. It was a compact, sprightly four-cylinder, of 58 × 90 mm bore and stroke, giving a capacity of 950 cc. This later became the Type NN so familiar to collectors of vintage cars.

Features of the KJ included inclined side valves and adjustable tappets, submerged oil pump, lateral radiators allowing a smooth bonnet line, magneto ignition, Dynamotor, three-speed gearbox in unit with transmission tube, semi-elliptic front springs, a single semi-elliptic transverse rear spring, and Hartford shock absorbers. The car could be right- or left-hand drive, according to the buyer's wish. The body was a three-seater, open or closed, in the initial series, but it was not long before four-seaters appeared with proprietary bodywork, and the later NN was, of course, normally a two- or four-seater. the KJ had a detachable cylinder head, an innovation in those days, making decarbonising much easier.

In 1923, the first models designated Sport were introduced. These had a sleeker bonnet line, flared wings, aero-type screens and various other accoutrements of the more extrovert cars of the era, for, of course, we were now entering the gay twenties, when the girls wore cloche hats, had short skirts, flesh-coloured silk stockings and high heels, when 'chappies' wore flying helmets in open cars as well as aeroplanes, when the King opened the Wembley exhibition and Lindbergh flew the Atlantic alone, and there was a general strike which shook financial empires.

By 1927 the 6 CV had become the NN and cost £180 in Britain in this touring form. Today it is a coveted collector's car.

So in 1923, there were sports and touring models in the range—the latter still with the open or saloon bodies, although a rather strange-looking *coupé de ville* was available, and generally used as a cab. The Renault logo had now appeared in its circular form, on the front of the bonnet.

In its various forms, the 8.3 (6 cv) went on until 1929. In 1924 the Type MT had four-wheel brakes and was available in four standard types of bodywork—three-seater 'torpedo', in open, closed, cabriolet and cab form. In 1925 came the NN four-seater variant, with longer wheelbase and bigger tyres, and this became one of Renault's biggest successes, and one of the most durable of all cars of the era. Today, one can see delightfully preserved little NNs at veteran and vintage car meetings and *concours d'élégance*, etc, and they are extremely reliable and economical machines which must be a good investment. If I could buy a vintage car, that is the one I would seek.

In 1926 the driver M. Bertrand took out an NN and drove 10,000 miles round the Miramas circuit in 203 hours—an average of 49 mph, stopping only to refuel.

So indestructible did the NN appear to be, that this was the car chosen by Georges Estienne to cross the Sahara as 'an ordinary tourist', in January 1927. All kinds of trans-Saharan expeditions had already taken place with special vehicles, and there were already Renault buses doing the crossing regularly, following earlier expeditions with the special six-wheeler 13.9 'routiers du desert', but this was the first time a standard, small, open tourer had been used, without any supporting vehicles or follow-up. Estienne's trip of 11,000 miles was completed without any mechanical breakdown—even without changing a plug.

The 8.3 compensated, in general, and for some years, for the losses suffered as a result of the rather mediocre 12, 15 and 18 cv cars, whilst the 10 cv was a steady seller. Then there was the 40 cv—better known to the British as the '45'. This was in the exotic class, for the wealthier buyers, and deserves some separate consideration.

First, however, let us look at the overall picture of the Renault set-up in these

The majestic, monstrous, much-loved Renault 45 in torpedo-bodied form. Introduced in 1921, it was a great contender in the luxury market. This is a 1923 Scaphandrier (torpedo).

years. To further his new aim to dominate Citroën and indeed the European motor industry by producing in mass quantities, Louis Renault needed to extend the already vast plant. He therefore acquired the now famous Ile de Seguin in the Seine. Billancourt, in fact, had become veritably a small town by the late 1920s. Louis Renault had not only been a master of the strategy of acquiring property piecemeal, but during the Kaiser war, it had been necessary to extend the works greatly to produce munitions, and the government had sanctioned the incorporation of complete streets. It seemed natural enough to acquire the use of the Isle de Seguin, and build a handsome new bridge from the 'mainland'. The joint tenants of the island were Louis Renault and M. le Comte de Lambert, the latter a veteran aviator and the first man to fly around the Eiffel Tower.

The whole Renault complex at Billancourt was roughly the size of Chartres, a town with about 22,000 inhabitants, but Renault had around 32,000 at Billancourt. They were not inhabitants, not so many of them anyway, but they worked long enough hours and pretty well lived the job in those days of work satisfaction and limited greed for money and leisure. Chroniclers of the day said there was a good spirit at the firm. Picard, father of the epic Model 4 CV that was to come in another 15 years, was not so sure. He said conditions at the factory were lamentable and Louis Renault was a tyrant whose absolute authority could make employees' lives a misery.

Evidently Renault got results, however. Writing in *The Autocar* at the time, Maurice Sampson said: 'Perfect cleanliness prevails everywhere; there is not a spot of oil on the black and white tesselated floor, along which a woman could walk in her most elaborate evening clothes and shoes and not collect a stain on either'. He was talking of the engine shops, but his picture of the drop-forging area was a little different: 'In an atmosphere of heat, glare and flame, workmen with almost tigerish energy are heaving, pulling, struggling with immense blocks of white-hot metal, thrusting them under the great drop hammers which crash down and force the heated metal into a die . . .'.

2: Little Sixes and big Eights

The early Renault six-cylinder cars deserve some separate consideration, and even the Renault *aficionado* is apt to forget that Louis was an early entrant in the lists for the 'perfect six' and produced 18/25 (24 hp) and 40/50 (37 hp) cars in 1910, following the tentative 50/60 hp of 1908–9. Meanwhile, of course, there were six-cylinder Renault commercial vehicles and buses.

The big 45 of the early 1920s was successful but expensive and the design team, in an endeavour to produce a cheap, popular six, came up with the Monasix, a 12.5 hp car, in 1927. If the 'Mona', as it was popularly known, was overbodied and sluggish despite its 1,500 cc engine, as many have stated, it must be remembered that Renault were not alone in their optimistic enthusiasm for the small six and in Britain the Austin, Daimler, Lanchester, Morris and Wolseley concerns all had limited successes with such units in the late 1920s and early 1930s.

In 1929–30 the Monasix was improved slightly and the company claimed that when running at the same speed and pulling the same weight as the Renault 9/15 four-cylinder, the Mona would give the same fuel consumption or even better it, with a smoother performance.

In their promotional material they kept harping on this economy but made no great claims in the matter of speed or power, confining themselves to vague statements about 'rapid acceleration' among other qualities. They were enthusiastic, too, about the factors of durability and reliability, which it is difficult now to challenge. That few of these cars remain may be simply due to the fact that relatively modest production figures were attained because of sales resistance to these new-fangled tiny sixes. Moreover, they were expensive to produce and maintain—one of the reasons why the type has made little headway even today.

The company claimed: 'The name of Renault guarantees the Monasix's quality and capability for hard work. It will never wear out or lose its usefulness.' They pointed out that the engine was the same as that used in the six-cylinder Paris taxis, although they did not say how many of these there were.

The engine of the Mona, which was housed in the same chassis as the tough, immortal, 8.3, was a long-stroke motor—58 × 93 mm bore and stroke—which was all the rage in those days, partly because of nominal horsepower formulae. Small units of this kind did not need to have the cylinders cast in two threes, like the 45, but could conveniently be monobloc, as in this case.

By 1931, the radiators of all Renaults were at the front of the engine, cooling was thermo-syphon. Water pumps were not always necessary in those days, although

Above *Guillon, Garfield and Plessier (left to right) with the streamlined 45 at Montlhèry.*

Right *Cockpit of the racing 45—in this case a faithful replica.*

some earlier Renaults had cooling systems dependent upon pump circulation, and with a cooling fan on the flywheel rim.

The clutch was described as being very progressive—of the single-disc type, exerting no thrust on the crankshaft. It could be easily dismantled without touching the engine. Quite a number of cars of this era still had cone clutches, which were comparatively crude.

The three-speed gearbox was in unit with the rear-axle torque tube, with a cardan shaft between it and the clutch. The actual drive shaft was inside the torque tube, which took up driving thrust and torque reaction. This system was necessary because of the use of the single transverse spring at the rear, as on the 8.3. Four adjustable dampers were fitted.

At first the Monasix had magneto ignition, the unit being driven from the front of the camshaft, but later models had a coil and distributor system.

The gear lever was a stout upright 'stick' emerging from the exposed selector tower in the middle of the floor, and alongside it was the equally robust handbrake. In those days it was always considered that the gear lever and handbrake should be as near to each other as possible, although in this case, as in some others, they were so near as to get in each other's way.

The single screen wiper was suction operated, with the small manual handle which was obligatory from early days in France. An admirable feature was that the neat central instrument panel was hinged for easy access to the wiring, etc.

Coachwork on these cars was of traditional composite construction with ash framing and mild steel panelling, the standard body being described as 'low and roomy, with four wide doors with pockets in front, and four comfortable seats facing forward'. The open version of the car, ie, the tourer, was fitted with a front screen of adjustable angle and a vee-type screen in front of the rear passengers, and there were the usual detachable side screens of celluloid, bound with leather. A nice touch, not uncommon in those days of almost obligatory do-it-yourself, was a complete tool kit housed neatly under the driver's seat.

The Monastella was offered concurrently with the Monasix, but this model was simply the same car with a slightly more luxurious body available as a four-seater saloon with fixed or drop head, or as a two- to three-seater drop-head coupé.

More remarkable, and lesser known, was a version of the Mona known as the commercial saloon—a Renault-built and not custom-built body, but somewhat in the nature of a special order. Outwardly it was the same as a normal saloon, but, as the firm themselves put it, 'the only difference, hardly noticeable at first sight, is that the top and bottom halves of the rear panel are hinged to open outwards. To transform this into a commercial vehicle, the rear door is opened, the rear seats are taken out, the fittings removed and a moveable floor is slipped into position. The dimensions of the compartment thus revealed are: height 3 ft 5 in; length 3 ft 6½ in; width 4 ft 1 in.'

There was also a commercial tourer in which the rear panel and top part of the hood opened out. This must surely have been the mother of all hatchbacks. This was available from 1926 on the 8.3 and 13.9. There are five examples in the UK.

By 1931 only the Monastella version was listed, in the UK at any rate. It was the 'baby' of the range, which also included the Vivastella, Nervastella and Reinastella. A latter feature of the car was a mechanical servo for the brakes, whilst a useful feature was one-shot lubrication for the chassis, operated by a pedal. The specification was generally enhanced.

The Vivasix was introduced in 1927, when there was a vogue for the small six-cylinder car. By 1931, it had the radiator at the front.

In 1927 the Vivasix was introduced and it went on sale to British buyers at £345, 'including bumpers', as the distributors George Newman and Co. of London's Euston Road said. The car was offered alongside such models as the 9/15 four-door saloon at £185 and the 14/45 four-door at £245. The Vivasix was a 3-litre of nominal 21 hp and the company somewhat ingenuously stated that this unit was well tried and that Renault had been perfecting it for nearly 20 years, but presumably what they meant was that the company had started making sixes long, long ago . . ..

The Viva, it was stated, was designed for those motorists requiring a fast, roomy, comfortable car which could be fitted either with five- or seven-seater coachwork taking trunks and luggage as well. One has to remember that cars did not have boots in those days, although these came into use a mere two years afterwards.

Renault claimed: 'Although capable of terrific acceleration, the Vivasix can be driven at a walking pace in top gear, should town or village conditions make that necessary. The great resource of power is evident when, at a touch on the accelerator, the car leaps forward from a mere crawl.' It all sounds rather dramatic, but a 3-litre car of the era was really quite a powerful animal, and sixes could give one a noticeable shove in the small of the back, although not even remotely in the same class as today's V6 2½-litre Renault.

The Vivasix was made in four forms—the five-seat torpedo, the five-seat saloon, seven-seat saloon and five-seat sports saloon or berline. The use of pressed steel panelling was still in an early stage of development. Up to the middle 1930s the carriage-type wood framework was used, with either steel or plywood and fabric covering, the latter being the Weymann body. Instead of being panel-beaten, the metal was now being pressed into shape by giant machines, but the wood framing was still retained. Later it would give way to metal framing and would eventually disappear altogether with the coming of integral construction, as used on the Juvaquatre in the late 1930s.

The Viva chassis was similar to that of the Mona, but the wheelbase was 10 ft 2 in and body space 8 ft 7 in, so it was a bigger car. There was also an option of a seven-seater body, on a 10 ft 2 in wheelbase chassis.

The standard bodies were quite luxurious and elegantly trimmed. The four wide doors had roomy pockets, the windscreen was adjustable and there were sun visors and an interior mirror. The rear screen was fitted with a blind operated by the driver; such a thing would be useful today, when it is customary to irritate the driver in front by keeping the headlamps on 'dip' at night, even in traffic.

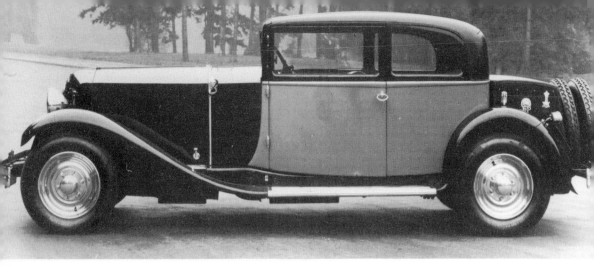

Originally the Rena-huit (Renault 8 cylinder) the 7,125 cc top-of-the-range car of 1928 became the Reinastella in 1929. This is a 1930 model with Weymann body.

There was a handsome metal footrest for rear seat passengers, and on the seven-seaters a rug rail on the back of the front seats. There were no car heaters in the 1920s and it was quite normal for passengers to use travel rugs.

Just as there was an up-market version of the Monasix, known as the Monastella, there was a super Vivasix called the Vivastella, and on the model it was possible to have a five-seater saloon, seven-seater drop-head limousine or a variety of drop-head sports saloons, three/four-seat drop-heads with dickey seats, or coupés of *limousine de ville* type.

By 1930, the starter and generator were separate units on this and other Renault models. One must tend to lament the passing of the Dynamotor of that era, but reliability was not of the highest order and if anything went wrong, you lost both starting and generating.

The Vivasix had four-wheel brakes, of course, in common with all Renaults since 1925. There was a vacuum servo. Assisted braking was nothing new to Renault, the '45' being fitted with a mechanical servo years earlier.

Standard suspension was on the Mona—semi-elliptics at the front and a single transverse one at the rear—except that the seven-seater version had the single transverse spring and two cantilever springs at the rear, presumably to cope with the extra weight. For 1931 there were the same improvements as for the Mona—ie, height reduction, lower centre of gravity, etc, and there were new sports bodies.

This was a good period of Louis Renault's life. He was starting to shake off the Citroën competition. He must also have been starting to enjoy life more freely on the social side, being less addicted to the workshops and more to the 'boardroom' and all the perks that went with being Mr Big. It is said that the Mona was named after a 20-year old beauty who worked on the production lines at Billancourt . . .. But Renault had married the sophisticated Christiane Boullaire in 1918 and she did much to make him into a man of the world, so perhaps it was not too much of a sin to name a car after a pretty maid. I do not know whether Mrs Renault ever had a Monasix, but she certainly had a nice little 10 cv all-weather tourer in 1927, and a Vivastella Berline in 1935.

Diamonds are a girl's best friend. One wonders who put the idea of the diamond logo into Louis' mind, but whatever the source it happened at this period, the circular motif on the bonnet being replaced by the familiar lozenge which was to impart corporate identity for so many years.

In 1932 a more sporty version of the Vivastella was introduced. This was the Primastella, of 3,180 cc and 16 cv, and it was in production until 1934.

Of all the cars that ever came out of Billancourt, none can have been as charismatic as the great 45. Merely to look at it was to feel in the presence of brute power, yet its style and elegance mellowed the effect.

There are not many of these cars still in existence and the 45 (or 40 cv as it was classified in France) has come to have almost a mythical character, although you will occasionally see one at a vintage car meeting or *concours d'élégance*, or may visit a motor museum where an example dominates its surroundings.

The model virtually dates from 1921, although it was derived from earlier models. Its grandsire—or is it *grande dame?*—was perhaps the car that more truly deserves the description 'monumental' for it was Louis Renault's first six-cylinder car, the 50/60, which was all of 9½-litres and saw the light of day in 1908. This big six was, like the 45, a side-valve machine, although Renault had filed patents for a sleeve valve at this time. The more obvious predecessor of the 45 was the Type CG 40 cv six of 1911. This was the model which received the honour of being the first official motorcar in the Elysée Palace for the exclusive use of the President. It was not at all unlike the 45 and the coal scuttle bonnet was longer than on any other Renault models except perhaps the four-cylinder, 40 cv cars which set the pace in early road races. But, of course, the big radiator was a separate and somewhat ugly excrescence between bonnet and scuttle. Later it disappeared behind panelling with louvres but Louis Renault insisted on keeping the rear-mounted radiator right up to 1928 on some models.

It was a car of character, often purchased by people of character, including celebrities like Betty Carstairs, Sacha Guitry, Sir Henry Segrave, and Commander Burney, designer of the R101 airship and Burney streamline car. The test staff at Renault's London works used to take them out on the Kingston by-pass and it was not only a great sight but a great treat for the ears if one came across this phenomenon because many of the early ones were fitted with silencer cut-outs, which the testers would use with great glee. But the car would be burbling, not screaming, because it would be doing only about 3,000 rpm at 85 mph.

Bodies for the big car were, of course, custom built. This was the car for the wealthy, and Renault had never had any intention of mass producing it. Louis' idea was to emulate the idiom of Isotta Fraschini, Hispano Suiza, even the Mercedes 36/220 and the bigger Bentleys.

The 45 was offered in two wheelbases—12 ft 6 in and 13 ft 1 in—and the presidential cars were naturally the long ones, as were many of the examples with exotic bodies such as boat-decked *sedanca de ville* creations or the imposing torpedo-tonneau.

The engine, even for a car of the middle 1920s, was frankly outdated and only its low efficiency, giving smooth and relaxed running, and its simplicity, saved it from being a somewhat ludicrous lump. The cylinders were in two blocks of three; the earliest 40 cv had a capacity of only 7½ litres but the 'real' version introduced in 1921 was a 9-litre machine, with bore and stroke of 110 and 160 mm, detachable heads and seven-bearing crankshaft.

Ignition was by magneto and fuelling by a horizontal, twin-barrel Renault carburettor feeding two separate inlet manifolds, although there was a single exhaust manifold, all these being on the near side. On the off side were the coolant pipes to the rear radiator, an affair which, with its 12 gallon capacity, more or less lay astride the rear cylinders. The flywheel had enormous fins. At the front end were the Dynamotor and a large oil cooler. The radiator could be isolated in cold weather.

The car was never an easy starter, either on the button or the vast starting handle, which even had a second low speed as well as the direct swing. Multi-grade oils did not then exist, of course.

In 1923, *The Autocar* tested a good example of the model. It had evidently been shipped to England from Billancourt after being at the Salon and was an open tourer in vermilion. Acceleration figures were quoted and that for 10 to 30 mph, using the gears, was 6.4 seconds. The same speed range in top gear (about 3½:1 ratio) needed 7 seconds, which is about what a Renault 14 would do today, if one could persuade it to pull away from so low a speed. The testers described the car as a thing of beauty to handle, its springing as exceptional and the seats as very comfortable.

The enthusiastic reporters were also full of praise for the braking system which embodied Louis' historic mechanical servo driven off the gearbox and which was, I understand, copied by Rolls Royce, albeit legally, as they paid royalties.

The splendid car took the Surrey Hill of Newlands Corner quite fast and without effort in its high top gear and had to be restrained on White Downs Hill, since it clearly wanted to zoom up at an impossible pace. Petrol consumption was recorded as an aristocratic 10.4 mpg at a steady speed of 30 mph, the tank holding sufficient, however, for 250 miles.

In 1925 they tested a Weymann fabric saloon. In the gears it went to over 40 mph in second and over 60 mph in third. Acceleration from 10 to 30 mph in third took 5.6 seconds but for some reason the top gear figure was 10.4 seconds. At 60 in top the big motor was idling at 1,800 rpm and the testers are reported to have achieved a comfortable 80 mph on a private road, the speed limit being 20 mph on all public roads in those days!

In 1924 Renault made it a part of their now aggressive sales and promotion policy to attack a few world records, using the 45 which in its hoydenish way was quite a fast lady. A youthful engineer and head of the proving department, R. Plessier, was put in charge of this enterprise; his assistant and co-driver being Garfield, an American race driver who worked in the Renault test shop. The Montlhèry race circuit, a few miles from Paris, was opened for competition purposes on 4 October 1924, so this was a suitable venue for their attempts in May 1925. They used a L'Avocat and Marsaud-bodied four-seater, covering 107 miles in the first hour and broke the world records for 500 km and 500 miles, the latter at an average speed of 97.84 mph. In June they broke 17 world records, among which were the 12 hours at 100.39 mph and the 24 hours at 87.65 mph. They could have done better but for a nut which came adrift and shattered some fan blades, causing overheating and repeated radiator refilling.

In September the records were snatched back by a Bentley, which notched up a speed of 94.95 mph for the 24 hours, although it managed only 97.46 mph for the 12 hours. Still interested in the value of racing for promotion, Louis ordered a fresh attack. This time, a special streamlined saloon version was made, with a fabric-covered body of semi-aerodynamic shape, which hardly rose above the height of the enormous bonnet, so that Plessier, Garfield and the spare driver Guillon could see the way ahead only through a slip of glass a few inches in depth and very narrow, since this was the single-seater body which, incidentally, weighed only 150 lb. The whole car scaled over two tons, despite its aluminium bonnet, wire wheels and absence of mudguards. The front of the familiar Roman-nosed bonnet was cut away to offer maximum cooling to the big motor, which did not dissipate its heat readily, but the Renault diamond logo was prominent on the central strip that remained.

Originally it had been intended that the 75 cm wide body should be a tandem two-seater with mechanic sitting behind the driver but no takers were found for the rear seat . . .

Pit work was very good, a team of 14 being employed, eight of whom were tyre changers. Tyres had to be changed every hour and the driver had a rear-view mirror focussed on the rear tyres so that he could see when the rubber started to disappear! About 100 tyres were used. On the second day all the Michelins were used up earlier than expected because of hot weather and for a few hundred kilometres they were replaced by Dunlops because it was Sunday and no Michelins were available. This is why contemporary pictures showed the car with Michelins on the front and Dunlops on the rear.

The pit work being so good, the shortest stop took only 52 seconds, although on average, including 'catching up' time, three minutes were lost in each hour. After many practice runs, during which Garfield upped the 100 km record to 117.275 mph, they made the main attempt on 10 July 1926. The three drivers covered 2,587 miles in 24 hours at an average of 106.53 mph, also breaking all records from 500 to 3,000 miles and from 1,000 to 4,000 km. Louis' piece of automotive exotica had really arrived, and as a piece of promotion not only for the 45 but for the whole range, this had been a most effective exercise. This was the first car to exceed 100 mph for 24 hours. On the last lap they speeded up to 119 mph to demonstrate that the car was not getting out of breath.

There are still a few Renault 45s in collectors' hands, like this beautifully kept tourer.

3: Into the exciting, threatening years . . .

The year 1928 was a prestigious one for Louis Renault and the company. The new Ile de Seguin factories had been built following the visit of Renault and Serre to Detroit, and modern production methods were in force. The range had been extended to comprise four-, six- and eight-cylinder models and with certain modifications these would be the basic production cars until the introduction of the Juvaquatre just before the war. Production rose by 40 per cent in 1928.

The extent to which Louis Renault had been influenced by his visits to America, and by close studies of the American scene, was strongly evident from the restyling that started in 1932, when bonnets and body lines were unashamedly Americanised. Citroën was doing the same sort of thing, although already planning the startling mechanical individualism that has characterised the marque ever since. It has been said that Louis did not really want to be a leader of industry and was still wrapped up in ideas for the drawing board, and that his heart and mind lay in the workshops, but one wonders if he was all that receptive to new ideas or to mechanical ingenuity. Certainly he missed a trick when he turned down an idea submitted by André Lefèbvre, a young employee in the drawing office. This was for a 7 cv with front wheel drive. Renault would have nothing to do with it. Lefebvre took it to André Citroën. It became the illustrious *traction avant*.

When Louis Renault said: 'Look, Lefèbvre, I'm all for revolutionary ideas provided they work, but this thing of yours is ridiculous' he may well have lost a few years of progress and it was not until the advent of the Renault 4 in 1961 that there was a front-wheel-drive Renault car. Now they are all front-wheel-drive except the specialised 5 Turbo and Alpine 310. So are most other cars.

However, Renault was not entirely old-fashioned, otherwise he would not have put so much faith in the six-cylinder models. Now he had pushed his new addiction to the multi-cylinder a little further by introducing the eight-cylinders. It was time for a new top-of-the-market Renault. The 45 had served its purpose well, but was now embarrassingly outdated. Its successor was the Reinastella—a 7.125-litre car and the last of the Renault giants for a long time to come. The 90 × 140 mm bore and stroke gave it a 41 cv rating and it was a 100 mph car under suitable conditions. It had the distinction of being the first Renault to have its radiator at the front of the engine, the rest of the range shortly following suite. Accordingly, all the cars had new radiator shells—flatter and with louvres—and these evolved into the Americanised Chrysler-type shells within a year or two. The Reinastella was now, and for eight years to come, the great luxury car of the range, with the Reinasport as

Above *Reinastella with cabriolet body by Million Guiet, a quality custom body builder.*

Below *Pretty car, pretty lady . . .. The 'Reina' was always much admired by women, especially if they were publicity-conscious.*

a sporty variant. Of these cars, Renault said 'Adoptées par toutes les élites, elles permettent les plus incroyables moyennes sur les parcours les plus difficiles'.

The company made much of the fact that these big cars could be driven by the frail sex (who were really no more frail in those crazy days than they are now with all their exploits) and it was noted that 'driven by women, the Reinastella has given a brilliant proof of its qualities in a great road competition, the Ladies Paris–Cannes Rally, which included various tests of regularity *(sic!)*, flexibility, brakage *(sic)*, starting, slow running and acceleration'.

In 1930, the smaller straight eight, the Nervastella, was launched. This was really a smaller version of the Reina, with a 4.24-litre motor and it at once made its mark by storming successfully through the tough Rallye du Maroc. The three Nervas took the first three places after covering the 440-mile circuit at an average speed of more than 74 mph.

With the 4.24-litre engine of similar type (later 4.825), the Nervasport was launched in 1932 and it was intended as a 'poor man's Reinastella'. It was in a stream-lined Nervasport that four drivers covered 5,000 miles at Montlhèry at an average of 102 mph in April 1934. This was the world 48-hour record and they took nine other records in the process, including the 4,000 and 5,000 mile records.

In spite of strikes and disputes in the early thirties, Renault continued to prosper, their penetration in the motor industry in France being 26.1 per cent in 1932, 26.4 per cent in 1933, 31 per cent in 1934 and 35 per cent in 1935. In 1933, while industrial crises were raging, Renault even managed to sell 4,500 Viva taxis to a large Paris cab operator who employed Russian immigrants as drivers; some of them were still in service in the late 1950s!

Citroën, meanwhile, had gambled all on the front-drive . . . and lost. The car later became a great success, but its introduction came too late to save 'the little Jew, Le Petit Citron' as Louis variously and half-lovingly called him. Michelin bought out the ailing concern, Louis Renault having turned it down. Motoring and other historians still violently disagree on the matter of whether Louis was being altruistic or whether the idea of taking on the *traction avant* as well as a bankrupt company scared the hell out of him . . ..

At this time, Louis Renault was, according to contemporary reports, already beginning to show signs of strain and ill-health, although nothing particularly alarming was diagnosed. Moreover, the first signs of the aphasia—speech difficulty—which became acute in the late years of the 1939 war, had already appeared. But Louis was still a little car-mad, if not mad in any other way. He consoled himself with a beautiful Reinastella with *coupé de ville* body. Presumably Christiane was allowed to use it, although she had her own 'small' car, a Vivastella.

In the early 1930s the big sixes and eights had a strong appeal to women of character as well as to the male celebrities of the time. A delightful contemporary publicity picture showed the immortal Gaby Morlay with a Reinastella at the *Concours d'Élégance de Femina* in 1934. The wonderful Josephine Baker (Le Bakaire), black cabaret star who died a few years ago, had a Nervastella Grand Sport in the 30s.

The 1932 Nerva with the new engine of almost 5 litres had a rating of 32 hp when it was marketed in the UK, as against 28 hp previously. Both the Nervastella and Nervasport had notable rally successes, as well as making their mark in record breaking and track racing.

In November 1933 the model was simply designated as the Straight Eight in the

A Nervasport of 1934—otherwise known as the Speed Six.

UK, selling at £545 in coupé form. The big, muscly, side-valve engine was rubber mounted, which was just about all the rage by then, following Yankee practice. Citroën had to be different, of course, and I recall that the very early *traction avant* had helical springs for vibration dampers and mountings.

Centralised lubrication, as in the case of several other makes of car, had been abandoned and the old grease gun system brought back, Memory again serves me well, because I remember at least one of my vintage cars having central chassis lube systems which had been abandoned, the owners having substituted grease nipples.

A free wheel clutch was a new feature. Free wheels were popular at this time; Rovers kept theirs for many years. They were just one-way clutches in the transmission line and if you took your foot off the throttle the engine idled as though in neutral and you could coast down hills. Gear changing was easier too. You saved gas but the system could be potentially dangerous and so there was usually a control for locking the device, as on the Renault.

By now the Reinastella was being phased out and in fact the appellation Stella had disappeared from the British catalogues. The smaller eights continued to go under the prefix Nerva in France for a few years, the car that really took the place of the Reina being the Nerva Grand Sport—a 5.4-litre car with the new 85 mm motor with an alloy head.

In 1935, the Renaults were all managing to look like Chryslers or other American cars. Specifications included enterprising things like thermostatic choke, throttle-coupled starter, umbrella-handle handbrakes and gear shifts. On most bodies now the boot was enclosed, there was a separate compartment for the spare wheel and there were only vestigial running boards if any at all. The rear wheels often had those trendy and infuriating covers known as spats.

In the UK in 1935, the Renault concern had just reopened the Acton works. In 1932-3 they had had to close it and go back to Fulham, because there was a

'Art deco' interior of a Celtaquatre of 1936.

trade recession and imports were discouraged. They were listing their models simply as fours, sixes and straight eights in 1935. They were as follows: 12 hp, four-cylinder Airsport saloon, Airline saloon, two-seater drophead coupé, and four-seater drophead coupé: 13.9 hp, four-cylinder Airline saloon, two-seater and four-seater drophead; 24 hp, six-cylinder Super Six saloon, two-seater and four-seater drophead, short chassis; 24 hp, six-cylinder Super Airline saloon, Big Six five-seater, Big Six seven-seater limousine (long chassis); 32 hp, eight-cylinder four-light saloon, two-seater drophead coupé, four-seater drophead coupé (short chassis); 32 hp, eight-cylinder Super Airline saloon, five-seater saloon, seven-seater limousine (long chassis). Prices ranged from £189 to £585. There was a choice of 80 coachwork colours and 52 upholstery materials, leather or cloth.

The new closed models had a luggage compartment—a kind of rudimentary boot—within the body, so that the fitted suitcases could lie snugly therein, but it must have been something of a struggle getting them in and out, as the only access was via the rear seat squab, which hinged upwards. How many of today's motorists can recall the relief with which external access to the boot was greeted in those far-off days? With Renault, as with most other makes, this was to come within a year or two if it had not already arrived and in a few cases there would be both inside and outside access.

The 12 hp (1,463 cc) four-cylinder car, called the Monaquatre, was the basic breadwinner for Renault in these years. In 1935 came the Celtaquatre, with a more modern, still more Yankee body but the same engine, which developed 34 bhp at 3,400 rpm.

The Primaquatre was another best seller, this being the 17.9 in the UK, and in 1939 a Primaquatre Sport was introduced, with a 2,383 cc motor and a longer body in berline, cabriolet or coupé form. The Novaquatre was another variation on the Prima theme, being a more economical 2.4-litre car. Also in 1939 came the Suprastella—a 5½-litre straight eight which replaced the Nerva Grand Sport and was a big prestige car.

It is often said that in the immediate pre-war years, Louis Renault was not in the least interested in the possibility of war, did not even believe that it could happen, and hated the idea of being in any way involved in politics, either industrial or governmental. But it is difficult to see how he could have avoided involvement; his design staff must have been working on military vehicle, tank and aircraft projects in some form, just as in Britain secret work was going on in automotive and other design departments. Possibly this was one of the reasons why the pre-war Renault car designs were relatively unoriginal. Even the Juvaquatre's front end was cribbed from the Opel Kadett, according to many experts. Some French journalists are said to have asked Louis Renault 'Comment l'Opel-t-on?' when seeing the Juva for the first time . . ..

I have never been able to decide whether the pre-war Renaults were good-looking cars or not. To me they all, except the Juva, of which one saw few in England, seemed to have a curious 'going uphill' look. The flashy lines tended to slope from front to back in a way which was unfamiliar to critical British eyes. They had almost a raffish look. I always recall the car used by the English columnist Godfrey Wynn— a pale blue, open two-seater which was a familiar sight in Pimlico and Fleet Street— and thinking that it was tawdry and flashy compared with, say, an open Alvis. Yet those pre-war Renault fours were in reality tough as old boots and not a little 'agricultural'.

French, yet so American . . . a 1937 Celtaquatre convertible.

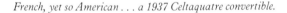

The Primaquatre of 1935—a 2-litre 4-cylinder, also called the 17.9.

Of the 12 hp touring saloon, Renault said in their promotional material in 1937–8: 'It is hard to believe that five or six passengers can travel in comfort in this attractive 12 hp saloon, until you realise that the rear seat is 4 inches wider than the measurement recently quoted by *The Motor* as being ideal for large cars'. General equipment of this model included the following: safety glass windows and windscreen, chromium plated bumpers front and rear, built-in luggage compartment fitted with suitcases, new-type tubular framed front seat, twin screen wipers, direction indicators, inside mirror, driver-operated rear blind, ashtrays, dashboard cubby hole with door, wide-opening windscreen in case of fog. Additional on the de luxe model were a sunshine roof, hydraulic four-wheel jacks, luggage grid, folding table in rear, anti-draught front windows, sun visors, arm rests all round and travelling rug . . ..

The opening windscreen, four-wheel jacks and rear blind are things that could be very useful today. A few British cars were fitted with built-in hydraulic jacks in that era; to raise the car one simply pressed a button; the system was fail-safe, and there were no disasters or comic incidents with them as far as I know, although the possibilities are obvious.

Renault made much of the roominess of these cars. The old running boards—a feature of most cars until the 1930s—had been abandoned and a wider body was consequently possible. There was supposed to be room for three adults in the front of the two-seater coupé, and it had a neat dickey seat. Obstructions in the front compartment were minimised by using an umbrella-handle handbrake and designing the gear lever in a contorted shape which displeased the purist but worked quite well.

The 17.9 models were very similar in specification, but the braking system included the Renault mechanical servo, and the battery was a 100 amp/hour unit, although still six-volt. The starter was operated by a foot switch. Both models had a three-speed gearbox with silent second. Transverse rear leaf springs were still used.

These four-cylinder units were still side-valve and the 12 hp was even a two-bearing crankshaft engine, but they were evidently very sturdy, if not lively, the 17.9 hp car having a maximum speed a little in excess of 65 mph. A four-cylinder, 2½-litre car was somewhat unusual in the UK at that time but it had advantages in easy maintenance and good running economy.

The Juvaquatre was a different animal together; although the little 1,000 cc engine was still a side valver, it had a three-bearing crankshaft and the main and big-end bearings were of shell type and not white-metalled like the bearings on the larger fours. This was the first all-steel monocoque (integral) bodied Renault and it was fitted with independent front suspension, although both front and rear suspension used leaf springs of transverse type. The body was roomy for a small car, and relatively rigid despite the large doors which, incidentally, were hinged at the front, allowing a narrow door pillar and obviously being safer than doors that opened at the front.

The British version, known as the Renault 8, was equipped with proper leather upholstery and there were two large suitcases supplied as standard. One of the popular motoring magazines of the time recorded an acceleration figure of 26 seconds for 10–50 mph, a maximum speed of over 62 mph and fuel consumption of 36–40 mpg. The new car was obviously comparable with the Ford 10 and Standard 10 of the time, whether or not it was in an image similar to that of the Opel Kadett. My own view is that the latter was inferior to any of them, although very inexpensive and fairly brisk in performance.

1939 . . . the mood was what, at that time, they called grim and gay. We young people were sad and glad—sad because the good times were clearly over for an unpredictable time, glad because there was a great and awful adventure ahead and a way of life to be fought for. Some of us were saddest because motoring, as we knew it, was over, although we would get our hands on some machinery if it killed us, which in many cases it did.

On August 13 and again on August 20, 1939, I drove between the Gare du Nord and the Rue de Turbigo in a taxi. It was my honeymoon. The taxi was a Vivasix, driven with absolutely traditional élan by a bearded giant in a cabby's cap. It was really my first and last physical involvement with Renault until ten years later. During the war, at the other side of the world, I often read the motoring magazines and wondered whether I ought to spend my gratuity on a Ford 10 or a Renault Juvaquatre, but in the event I could not afford either, and committed the folly of acquiring a 1932 Hillman. It was a few more years before I bought the first of nine Renaults.

4: Out of the darkness, into the sun

There is a popular, ill-founded, indeed totally erroneous idea that the designer of the Volkswagen Beetle, Ferdinand Porsche, had a hand in the design of the Renault 4 CV. As a matter of fact, anyone who takes the trouble will find that Porsche had a virtual prototype of the VW in his workshops as long ago as 1933 and it was very nearly taken up by NSU, as described in that significant work *The VW Story* by Jerry Sloniger (Patrick Stephens Ltd).

The early prototypes of the 4 CV could be said to resemble the Beetle, but the same thing might have been said about the Morris Minor or the Dyna Panhard, come to that. After all, even that 'toy' car the Fiat Topolino was beetle shaped. Anything that had two doors, four wheels and a beetle shape was not necessarily designed by Ferdinand Porsche, whose genius, after all, lay in engine and chassis design. Beetle shaped cars were the result of the increasingly popular study of aerodynamics, on the industrial scale. The 4 CV, of course, never went into production with only two doors. The firm's market researchers advised that few Frenchmen would ever buy a two-door car, which was somewhat odd, as several earlier models, including the Juvaquatre, had been available in two-door form. (It is interesting to reflect that the two-door Renault 5 has been a best seller, although the four-door version was also introduced to meet popular demand.)

However, there is still a certain amount of mystery about the conception of the Quatre Chevaux. Porsche's interest, apart from the purely academic, can be dismissed, but there is doubt about whether Louis Renault played any useful or realistic part in the development of the car.

According to Edouard Seidler in *The Romance of Renault* (Edita SA) Louis Renault started thinking about a 'peoples car' in 1940, during a mood of recrimination over his pre-war lack of progression in design, not to mention lost ground after the 1914–18 war. Seidler says Renault visited the Berlin Motor Show in 1938 and was impressed by the KDF (Kraft durch Freude) which later became the VW.

Renault, according to this author, was received at the Chancellery and brought home with him a complete file on the new German car. He adds: 'He was fascinated by its all-steel body mounted on a platform chassis with the engine at the back. "You must make me a car like the one the Germans have" he told his planners.'

Undoubtedly Renault visited the Berlin Show and was received by Hitler, the meeting being arranged by Francois-Poncet, the French ambassador. He also probably brought back from the show a Press pack, or something comparable, and he was probably quite genuinely, but somewhat superficially, interested in the VW.

Not a relative of the Volkswagen, but an early prototype for the Renault 4 CV.

The two-door prototype with disc wheels.

Four doors and the spider-type wheels bring the 4 CV near the production stage.

By 1958-9 the Baby Renault had slotted wheels and a 750 instead of a 760 cc engine; also three bonnet strips instead of four.

Of the meeting with Hitler, the writers Jacques Borgé and Nicolas Viasnoff (*Renault, l'Empire de Billancourt* published by EPA), state that it was brief and superficial and that Renault saw before him a conciliatory man who could not possibly want war. Tartly, they add: 'Louis Renault rejoint le camp des pro-munichois'.

Seidler suggests that Renault subsequently gave instructions for the development of the car to Edmond Serre, head of projects, and his deputy Fernand Picard, a former Delage engineer, as well as to Guettier, a transmission expert, and Berthaud, a stylist. Borgé and Viasnoff, however, suggest that Serre and Picard worked on their own initiative, and secretly, right from the start, having perceived that France and probably the world would want a cheap, small, economical car after the war. They also suggest that as a result of stress and a monumental row with his nephew Francois Lehideux, who was trying to get control of the business, Louis Renault at this time started to deteriorate physiologically and to disassociate himself from development work—'. . . Il est incapable de prevoir l'avenir et se désintéresse de son bureau d'études . . .'

It appears that Renault's health deteriorated quite rapidly and that aphasia had set in quite severely in 1940–41. Aphasia is confusion and difficulty in speech which can result from brain malfunction, either organic or functional, eg, as a result of stroke or by reason of a mental illness such as schizophrenia. On the other hand it can result from wrong dosage or abuse of medication.

Picard, in his diary for 1941, describes Renault as being almost inarticulate, and looking exhausted, as well as seeing idlers and thieves everywhere. To add to all this he was 'under the domination of a 23-year old girl who was making him lose what little control he still possessed'.

Picard, however, does state that Renault made a surprise visit to the development department in May 1941 and caught him and Serre with a wooden mock-up of the engine for the 4 CV.

'We saw Renault a little way away, his hands in his pockets with the thumbs outside, an attitude familiar to him. He looked at us . . . Serre blushed like a child caught at fault and spluttered several words. Le Patron came up and jostled us. Without a word, he walked round the model of the motor. Then, taking his hands out of his pockets, he began to caress it with concentration, as if it was a work of art.

"It's beautiful. What is it?"

Serre, embarrassed, explained:

"In his free time, Picard has designed this little overhead-valve motor for the Juvaquatre or, eventually, for a small rear-engine car, if you wanted us to make one. We've made this model to give us an idea of it. But we can't go any further. We haven't the right."

"Not the right? How bloody stupid."'

Louis Renault, thereupon, said they should make three engines. They started on the project, and also on the structures of two cars. Meanwhile, Renault production was confined to two types of commercial vehicle and certain marine engines, by order of the Germans. Francois Lehideux was at this time made Secretary of State for Industrial Production and exercised even more control over the motor industry. Somehow, by the end of 1941, the first prototype of the 4 CV was in existence and in February 1942 the engine was on the test bench. At the same time, the factory managed somehow to start on a new study—that of an 11 CV intended to succeed the Primaquatre.

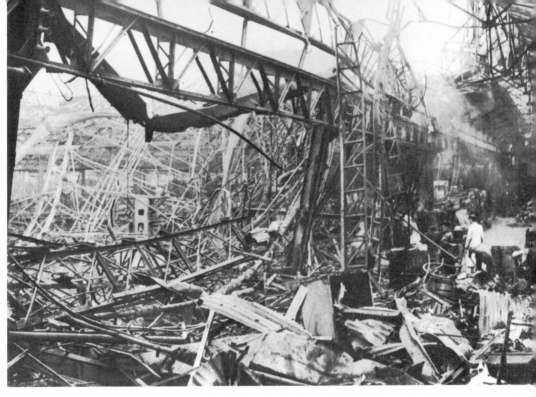

Allied bombing devastated the Billancourt installations in the Second World War, and their rehabilitation was almost miraculous.

In March, Parisians heard the thunder of heavy aircraft then the terrifying sounds of high explosive bombs blasting into the offices and workshops of Billancourt, seemingly for an eternity. The RAF did heavy damage to the Renault installations for the first time, but miraculously missed the prototype engine of the 4 CV, which continued running on its test bench.

Louis Renault was shocked by the raid, which completely destroyed 1,500 machine tools and damaged another 1,500. Of the already reduced work force, 463 people were killed.

After clearing up, work resumed remarkably soon, and by September the factory was producing 70 commercial vehicles a day. The body of the 4 CV was made up in aluminium, and painted sea green. At the same time, the post-war Primaquatre was at the design stage—a car with an American-style body and a four-cylinder, 2-litre engine.

The Baby Renault had its first road test over a route in the Bois de Meudon in January 1943. It performed quite well, and buzzed along at over 50 mph, climbing the Côte des Gardes smartly with four people in it. Seidler states that the car was not green at all, in the following terms:

'This achievement begat another hardy legend, namely that Prince Albert von Urach, a director of Mercedes–Benz who had been appointed commissioner in charge of the Renault works, found the green prototype too showy and stopped the trials; so Serre had the machine painted black as a precautionary measure. The truth is that this first prototype of the 4 CV had been black from the very start, and if von Urach ever actually noticed it round the works all he did was to advise the drivers to show a little more discretion.' One result of the first tests, incidentally, was the decision that the car should have a three-speed gearbox instead of the four-speed used experimentally.

Whatever von Urach did in the way of controlling the determined engineers, Louis Renault himself seemed oblivious to any interference and by now he was undoubtedly getting out-of-touch with reality. He did have the good sense to keep one of the prototypes at Herqueville, however, which is just as well, because devastating bombings of the factory which took place in September 1943 could easily have removed all trace of the 4 CV.

One or two favoured members of the Press tried the prototypes 'off the record'. The distinguished French motoring journalist, Charles Faroux, evidently had a thrash around with Christiane Renault and they ended up in the ditch.

As a result of the works tests, the iron pistons were replaced by alloy ones, the timing gear was strengthened and the oil pump improved. Late in September there was a comparative test of the 4 CV and the new Primaquatre prototype, with Auguste Riolfo at the wheel of the latter and Picard driving the former. Louis Renault watched the two cars closely and decided in favour of the Primaquatre, ordering the tooling-up forthwith. Nevertheless, the 4 CV project went on in the development shops, with a steel body in place of the aluminium one and still with two doors. Riolfo tested it over the Route Napoleon, with a 17-stone passenger, and it went well.

The factory was bombed again in December. Renault the firm and Renault the man were both badly shaken. By July the factory was closed, but Louis visited it regularly, walking the lines like a man in a trance . . ..

The story of the dramatic deterioration of Louis Renault has been told many times over, and with infinite and confusing variations. Today, as far as the Régie is concerned, the file has been closed, even if it surely lies open in some drawer with the Renault family. Was Renault a fool, traitor, mental invalid? Did he truly mean well, and was it all too much for him? Was he too weak and ingenuous to resist crafty usurpers? It was unlikely that we shall ever know. His last appearance in public was on 28 August 1944, when he attended the funeral of a director of the company. In September he was arrested for collaboration and sent to Fresnes Prison. In a month he was dead, perhaps as a result of beatings by his guards.

The name Renault lived on. There was no longer any person of that name at the controls, but Renault will always be the name on the cars, trucks and great industrial equipments that spew out of the factories of the greatest industrial group in France. The name of the man who henceforth took the helm was Pierre Lefaucheux. This was the name of the man and this was the name of a vast new factory for the mass production of new light cars. This time Lefaucheux, not Renault, would gamble everything on the voiturette!

Lefaucheux it was who, over a period of 10 years, gave back life and a future to Renault, at the expense of his own life. It was perhaps incongruous that he should be killed by a karate chop from his own brief case, but quite in character that at the time he should have been fighting a skid on black ice in a Frégate. For Lefaucheux was a fighter and if ever Renault needed a fighter, it was then.

It is difficult to imagine that this man was not really a car enthusiast, as some have suggested. True, he was an industrial engineer and did not have Louis Renault's empathy with cams, gudgeons, spigots, gear wheels and the like, but he owned a Viva Grand Sport and knew all about the uses and appeal of the motorcar for business as well as pleasure, and he was a keen camper and canoeist.

Lefaucheux was made provisional administrator of the works in October 1944. He was 46—a vigorous yet thoughtful and reasonable man who had been 'Major Gildas' in the resistance movement and was married to a dynamic woman who was a member of the Paris Committee of Liberation. She had snatched him back through the German lines after he was arrested, at the very time that the allied invasion had been launched.

Within days of his appointment (he was later to become President Director General) he decided that the 4 CV was to be the machine that would put Renault in the big league, but he opted for four doors, since he himself had had difficulty in

The man who rebuilt Renault. Pierre Lefaucheux, reluctant hero.

The 4 CV assembly line at Billancourt, in 1956. Over 800,000 had been built.

getting his large frame into the back of the two-door. To the factory's personnel strength he added 4,000, bringing it up to about 21,000, or half the 1939 strength. Now they were making about 40 lorries a day. By the end of 1945, about 12,000 vehicles were produced, but only about half a dozen were cars.

In January 1945 the firm was nationalised, the State acquiring the entire property except the private assets of the Renault family, which included Herqueville, certain properties in Paris, yachts, farms and overseas assets. The agreement was signed by De Gaulle, who said 'The Régie is my child'. Other signatories to the instrument forming the Régie Nationale des Usines Renault were Robert Lacoste, Pierre Mendes-France, Alexandre Parodi and René Pleven, respectively Ministers of Industrial Production, National Economy, Labour and Finance.

The Régie was given civil and financial autonomy but placed under the authority and control of the Ministry of Industrial Production. It was to be run by a President Director General, Lefaucheux, who was assisted by an administrative council and a central works committee. Now Lefaucheux could really get on with the business of putting the Baby Renault into production, or so he thought, until he found that it was first necessary to win a war against the unruly elements in the factory.

Lefaucheux had all sorts of trouble in those early days, and it is interesting to note that he more than once crossed swords with Pierre Dreyfus, who was then Inspector General of Industrial production, and later became Lefaucheux's successor.

For months he had to deal with all sorts of quarrels, accusations, prohibitions, expulsions and a great deal of general bitching and settlements of grudges and old scores, but in the end his tact and force of character won the day and they were able to get on with the business of making motorcars. In November 1945 he came to a definite decision to series-produce the 4 CV and totally abandon the 11 CV. He proposed that the 4 CV be exhibited at the Paris Motor Show, that cars must start coming off the lines in the summer of 1947 and that agents must get 300 before the show of that year. By the following summer output should be 130–150 cars a day and production must reach 300 a day before the end of 1949. His idea then was to call the car the Regina or Reginette. Not all his work force had faith in the idea. One of them, the Director of Work Study, even commented: 'You are tooling up for the production of 300 cars. You might do better to make a machine to sell them . . .'.

The 4 CV never belied its looks of rugged capability.

Lefaucheux did not suffer fools gladly; in fact he did not always suffer geniuses with benevolence. This was especially the case when the government invited Porsche, then 'on parole' in France, to advise on the future of the 4 CV. Angrily, Lefaucheux wrote to the Minister to say that he resented this intrusion, saying 'Je ne crois pas que la valeur technique du professeur Porsche soit supérieure à celle des ingénieurs du bureau d'études de la Régie'.

The car was shown to the Press in September 1946 and in October it was presented at the Salon. It had externally mounted trafficators and was painted sand yellow, since only ex-Afrika-Korps paint was available at the time! People accordingly called it the 'little butter pat' when not describing it as a bug, flea or cockroach.

So the car that put Renault back on its feet was launched. But there was no question yet of selling it. The production lines were not yet ready, although they were planned—on the style of American installations which Lefaucheux and Picard had visited in June 1946, thus following the example of Louis Renault.

But 1946 was an important year, because the production of private cars started again at Billancourt. The Régie, in fact, produced 8,500 cars out of 30,000 made in France that year. They were exclusively Juvaquatres, in saloon and small van form. The Juva had hydraulic brakes of Lockheed design, hydraulic shock absorbers and a 38-litre petrol tank in place of the 22-litre one fitted to the pre-war Juvaquatre. The spare wheel was inside the boot—essential in those days when thefts of scarce tyres were common. The Juva was on the market—mainly for export—until 1949 in saloon form, and an estate version was available right up to 1959.

In 1947 there were strikes and nasty scenes at Billancourt, and Lefaucheux was frequently frustrated and saddened by the inability to produce to capacity. Nevertheless, 25,000 commercial vehicles and over 18,000 cars, still Juvas, were made in this year. More importantly, the revolutionary transfer machines were installed at the 4 CV shops, and production of the Baby started at last. At the 1947 Salon, the car was this time a reality rather than a mock-up, and orders could be taken. It was also simultaneously launched in 300 French towns with all the appropriate razzmatazz of publicity and public relations. People fell over themselves to order it, and delivery delay rose to one, then almost two years. There was, of course, a thriving black market.

Lefaucheux's wildest dreams were being realised. Production rose to 300 cars a day in March 1949 and in 1950 the 100,000th Baby left the lines, the daily output being 400. The 500,000th car went to an ecstatic owner in April 1954. The 4 CV was in production until 1961 and it was the first French car to reach the magic million production figure.

The idea of an 11 CV Primaquatre was, as we have seen, jettisoned by Lefaucheux, although Louis Renault had been so much in favour of it. At the end of 1947, however, Lefaucheux had a rethink, and since Picard was playing with a different kind of 11 CV he more or less gave him his head. The result was a proto-type based very much on a scaled-up 4 CV.

(These scaling-up and scaling-down exercises do not often seem to be successful. One recalls the Lagonda Rapier which was a scaled-down Lagonda 2-litre. It was not a successful car. The BMC 1100 was, however, virtually a successful scaled-up Mini.)

Called the 108, the prototype was a 2-litre, rear-engined car in the same image as the Quatre Chevaux, even to the 'funny' wheels and Beetle shape, bumpers with prominent overriders, etc. It did not look right, somehow, and they had all kinds of troubles with it. Lefaucheux lost his patience with the whole exercise and decided that what they wanted was a front-engined car. He would be competing with the front-wheel drive Citroën 11 CV, which led the market in that sector, but neither he nor Picard wanted front-wheel-drive—it was almost a point of honour. To get the desired flat floor, however, the designers came up with a horrific design of lowered prop shaft and floating differential demanding three universal joints between gear-box and differential and four between differential and road wheels!

The car went into production earlier than originally planned—indeed in a great hurry—because in view of the situation in Korea, the government planned to prohibit the production of new vehicles from January 1951. The Frégate was presented at the Palais de Chaillot in November 1950, six months earlier than scheduled, which was probably why it had so many teething troubles. In fact, a lot of people thought it never was much of a car, and I tended to agree. Its engine was inspired by the 4 CV and had wet sleeves, but the camshaft was low and the pushrods long and whippy. The car had independent suspension with helical springs.

The car never seemed to have enough power and it felt lumpish and heavy to drive, although it was very comfortable and luxurious. Many attempted improve-ments were made between its introduction and 1957, when Frégate sales were dropping dramatically. As a last fling, the Régie introduced the Transfluide version—France's first automatic, in effect, although automatic clutches had been options on the 4 CV and other cars such as the Citroën 2 CV and DS.

Even the Transfluide was not a true automatic, since, although it had a torque converter with the usual three elements, this was mated to a normal clutch operated automatically by a small servo, and a classic three-speed gearbox—not an epicyclic as used in full automatics. The system worked quite well, but the car was under-powered even with an up-rated engine, and one had anxious moments when over-taking or climbing steep hills.

The engine—of 2,200 cc—developed 80.3 bhp at the SAE rating at 4,000 rpm and had a compression ratio of 7.5:1. Maximum torque was 124 lb ft at 2,500 rpm. The speed range ratios were: reverse 2.52; town/road 1:1; mountain 1.62:1 and

Manoir estate version of the Frégate.

'exceptional' 2.28:1. Fuel consumption was claimed to be 11 litres per 100 km (21.38 mpg) with a cruising range of 500 km (310 miles).

I tested one of the later Transfluide cars for the magazine *Motor Industry* and was not able to give it a particularly good report. It was extremely heavy to drive, tiring over long distances and even more so in town traffic, largely because of the heavy steering and pedal actions of clutch and accelerator. I have no doubt that it was a well-built and durable car, but that was not necessarily what the world wanted at that time.

Renaults got up to all sorts of larks to try to popularise the Frégate, including a record breaking Cape–Algiers run in nine days and North Cape to Cape of Good Hope in 16 days.

The factory sold about 10,000 Frégates in 1958, which was only half as many as they had sold in 1956, so the model was not by any means a great success. Many people, including farmers and taxi operators, preferred the Colorale, a tough, no-nonsense estate or pick-up, which was derived from the pre-war Primaquatre. Except for the Ford V8, it was the last side-valve engined, mass-produced car in use in France. From 1953, however, it was fitted with the 11 CV Frégate engine. Between 1952 and 1957 about 28,000 were sold.

Frégate Transfluide automatic transmission saloon.

It is interesting to note, in passing, that whilst the saloon Frégate did not look at all like a scaled-up 4 CV, once the 108 project had been abandoned, it did look rather like a large version of the Dauphine, which was still to come. The Dauphine could only be regarded as a scaled-down Frégate in the sense that the body shape was similar; there was obviously a strong continuity of ideas in the body design team's efforts, but the Dauphine was to emerge as a derivative of the 4 CV, mechanically.

The car in which Lefaucheux met his untimely death is said to have been a special souped-up version of the Frégate. It still cannot have been exactly a fireball, and the handling was never anything special. The Frégate probably served its purpose—to allow Renault to compete to some extent with Citroën in the medium-sized family car sector and to help to meet the demand for a good work-and-play car, for the camping and leisure craze was already well into its stride in Europe, with the Germans and French leading the way.

One of my last recollections of the model was in the course of an ascent of the St. Gotthard pass in the late 1950s. On one of the countless steep, tight, hairpin bends I was balked by a Swiss in a new-looking Frégate. In the middle of the bend (and in the middle of the road) he appeared unable to select any gears at all and after a long time, when a queue of cars had formed in each direction, the rescue service hitched him up and spirited him away. He and his family looking desperately unhappy.

Even if the 'Baby' was not, strictly speaking, innovative, it was out of the ordinary and had its own particular charisma, and what could quite justifiably be described as 'bijou charm'. (Citroën not so long afterwards introduced a weird British version of the 2 CV called the Bijou, but it had little charm and was less of a jewel than a lump.)

When on the staff of the British motor journal *Motor Industry*, I had the good fortune to carry out and write a road test of one of the earliest 4 CVs to be introduced to this country. It was a pleasurable experience and I was most impressed by the little car—in fact it was this that set me on a kind of Renault road, whereby I subsequently bought no other make and became involved with the activities (though not the fortunes) of this concern for many years.

I recall that a young salesman took me for a spin just before I took the car away from the Acton premises, and he was wildly enthusiastic about the little machine, although himself the owner of a splendid Ford V8 coupé. As a *tour de force*, he explained to me that this little Renault was like nothing else he had driven because 'you could just turn it at right angles as quick as you like at any speed'. He promptly did just that at about 40 mph on some waste ground near the factory. I was ready to understand that he meant turn it at right angles on its longitudinal axis, when to my relief and amazement we made the impossible turn like a fairground dodgem car, all wheels firmly on the ground and without a hint of roll from the body. This flat cornering ability was one of the outstanding features of the model, which enabled it to be such a wonderful subject for artists of road and track who thrashed it successfully to victories in notable events.

The following are a few quotes from my road test report, of the 760 cc 4 CV, which was by then being assembled at Acton.

'The impression left by a severe test gives no room for doubt that at its price of £409 12s 9d (including purchase tax) here is money's worth for any class of user. Many, indeed, would feel that certain of the 760's qualities, such as handling and ease of maintenance, are far beyond price.

Maximum speed under test was 56 mph on a very slight down grade, but a fair distance was needed to reach maximum under certain conditions. What is more important, however, is that 50 mph is always within reach and that 45 is a comfortable fast cruise.'

I also stated: 'Steering is describable only in superlatives. The car can be thrown about in a most astonishing fashion and seems to inspire more confidence the more it is gyrated . . .'.

I said that the car was comfortable, but, looking back, I can only assume that there must have been some very uncomfortable cars around at that time. I tried a few 4 CVs in later years and found the ride harsh almost beyond endurance, although the seats were always quite good and there was a remarkable amount of space in the car considering its modest external dimensions. In this and other respects, it would be quite reasonable to consider it the first true mini, because the Fiat 500 and the several bubble cars of the era were toys by comparison.

My test included the observation: 'One lifts the rear bonnet and behold—the lovely little power pack is exposed on a tray, as it were, for the delight of the technician. More ambitiously one disconnects things, lifts the rear of the body well aloft and wheels out the axle, power unit, etc, in a compact mass.' Without removing the power unit, incidentally, one could if necessary fit exchange cylinder liners and piston–con–rod assemblies.

It was years before I could afford to buy even a secondhand baby Renault—a 750 and not a 760—but I made sure I got a good one. It was, in fact, one of the rare cabriolets—truly a little gem, in light grey with simulated pigskin upholstery.

You can still see the occasional cabriolet in France—usually in tatty condition. There must be one or two still in Britain, and my own car 'VPC 4' must be around somewhere, I am sure. Originally it had a neat canvas hood in beige, but this deteriorated and I had a good quality heavy PVC hood in royal blue fitted. Generally speaking the 4 CV was reliable, but as on this car, the final drive could get out of adjustment and become worn, a fault which I had rectified. Overheating could be a problem if the cooling system was not in good order.

Even in the 1950s, self-service fuel stations were hardly known and it was always wise to keep an eye on a petrol pump attendant who was filling a 4 CV. The radiator filler cap was more prominent than the petrol filler cap and you could finish up with some petrol in your cooling system, although usually an errant pump hand would get a steamy surprise when he or she took off the wrong cap. On the other hand, I knew of a case where an owner with an overheating 4 CV pulled in to a garage, and asked for a can full of water. The brisk attendant picked a full can up from the forecourt island, whipped off the petrol filler cap and had half a gallon of water in the fuel tank before the owner realised what was happening . . ..

One of the car's endearing features, to the enthusiast at any rate, was the tiny gear lever—like six inches of knitting needle with a marble on the end. Because the 4 CV had a nice gearbox, this was a joy to use, although synchromesh was only on second and top ratios of the three-speed box. You could finger and thumb the lever through the ratios. It is doubtful if Renault ever matched that silky shift in any later gearboxes.

There were interesting details about the car. The lights and horn were operated by a neat steering wheel stalk—unusual in those days—the flasher switch being on the wheel hub. The starter motor and choke were operated by twin 'ringpull' levers, one on each side of the central handbrake. Thus there was no key start, although there was the combined ignition switch and steering lock, on the column.

Early cars had the 760 engine with 55 mm bore and this model was the R 1060. Later, the bore was reduced to 54.5 mm, bringing the capacity down to 750 and this car was the R 1062. Engine, transmission and suspension were imported from France for the UK models and the body panels were welded, painted and trimmed in London. Battery, ignition components, fuel pump, wiring harness and direction indicators (of the semaphore type, recessed in the body) were British made.

The main features of the car were the rear engine, driving forward to a unit gearbox and differential, and the independent all-round suspension with coil springs and swing axles.

The three-main-bearing, overhead-valve engine did not have any revolutionary features, but was sophisticated, compared with other small family car engines, in having wet cylinder liners flanged at the bottom and spigoted in the crankcase with a copper gasket so that the liner stood proud of the top of the block by about 0.005 inches. The crankshaft—a very sturdy unit which made tuning of these engines safe—ran in steel-backed, white-metal lined shell bearings which could be changed, in an emergency, with the engine in place. Big ends were direct white-metalled and small ends bronze-bushed for floating gudgeon pins. Pistons were invar-strut, solid skirt type in aluminium alloy. Pistons and liners were supplied as matched assemblies for renewal if required. Big ends would pass through the bores if required, but it was considered best to withdraw liner, piston and connecting rod as an assembly.

Countless private owners maintained their little 4 CVs themselves in those days, even carrying out major overhauls without difficulty. I knew a man who could whip the power unit out in 20 minutes without special equipment. Changing the cylinder liners was an easy job for a reasonably competent amateur. Decarbonising (seldom necessary at all) was child's play.

The wheels of the earlier series of 4 CVs were interesting, because of the method of attachment. Very early motorists may recall the detachable rim, used on many American cars, and the system used on the Renault was not without similarity. An unusually large brake drum and hub assembly was used on the 4 CV and this was in the form of a spider, the ends of the arms of which bore the wheel studs. The wheel itself was more of a rim than anything else, and was held to these studs by the usual wheel nuts. Later cars had the conventional type of wheels. The original system seemed to work quite well, and presumably it was not retained because it was more expensive. In the same era, similar wheels were used on the Dyna Panhard, which was a small, air-cooled car competitive with the Renault.

A peculiarity of the steering system of the 4 CV was that it had return springs. It was advanced for the time, in being of rack and pinion type, instead of the more usual worm type, and this gave precise steering with absolutely minimal lost motion. Rack and pinion steering was not unfamiliar to British motorists, the Morris Minor having such a system. The use of return springs, which actually shoved the steering back to the central position, was, however, not only unusual, but somewhat barbaric. It worked very well, and the steering was light despite the fact that the driver was working against the spring every time he steered. If one turned the wheel and released it in an unguarded moment, however, the effect could be quite dramatic, for the rack centred itself very smartly.

A feature of the body of this remarkable small car was that the front doors were rear-hinged—that is to say, the door opened at the front. This had not been unusual in earlier cars of many makes, but might have been regarded as a retrograde feature in a car of such advanced design. However, the system seemed to work quite well. I once had a front door blow open. The check-strap broke and the door slammed back alarmingly but no damage was done. I could, I suppose, have fallen out with astonishment!

Because this engine was so sturdy, it was a natural for 'hotting up'. Various accessory and component manufacturers in France and Britain offered parts and kits for performance tuning, eg, special induction manifolds, replacement carburettors, streamlined exhaust manifolds, special silencers, etc. There were even special cylinder heads, but the most popular and dramatic way of gaining extra power was to raise the compression by having some metal shaved off the existing head, in time-honoured fashion. Special camshafts were sometimes fitted, but made little sense except for competition work, as they spoilt the slow running. When the Dauphine engine came in, people would slip a Dauph' engine into the 750 with excellent results, but of course that was rather 'cheating'.

An enthusiast for the 750 was John Bolster, the distinguished motor sport enthusiast, writer and Francophile, who wrote in the following terms in the magazine *Autosport* in 1955, when commenting on the special competition version (1063) of the 4 CV:

'. . . The competition car has two pairs of rear shock absorbers, and coarser teeth for the rack and pinion, to give quicker steering. The brakes are also larger.

A great deal of work is done on the engine. It has an iron block with wet liners and this is standard, but the light alloy cylinder head has larger valves and ports. The crankshaft has standard size journals, but these are most carefully radiused into the webs, which are of increased section. The connecting rods are of light alloy and the pistons are domed. The sump has double the normal capacity and the oil pressure is raised. There is, of course, a special camshaft.

The most impressive under-bonnet feature is the literally enormous twin-choke, pump-type, downdraught Solex carburettor. Curiously enough, both chokes feed all four cylinders. The exhaust system is an outsize "bunch of bananas". Apart from that the engine is indistinguishable externally from the standard article.

The normal wear for the 4 CV is a three-speed gearbox. It definitely needs no more, owing to the tremendous low-speed punch of the engine. However, the 1063 motor naturally operates in a higher band of revolutions than the series production, at the expense of the bottom end. Accordingly, two proprietary gearboxes have been made available—the four-speed Fapram and the five-speed Pons-Rédélé.'

Bolster said his own 4 CV was a much more mildly turned car, ie, with a 32 mm pump-type carburettor in place of the standard 22 mm one, on an Autobleu manifold. (Autobleu offered all kinds of 'goodies' for 4 CV owners in those days.)

He requested a test of the works car, and Renault's competitions manager, François Landon, put at his disposal a 1063 which had won its class in the Mille Miglia. Bolster's own car, he thought, gave about 28 bhp against 21 bhp for the standard car; the works machine produced 42 bhp at 5,800 rpm on a compression ratio of only 8.2:1.

The 1063 said Bolster, was like a small racing car to handle. On the Montlhèry road circuit he found the acceleration away from bends was most impressive. There were no long straights on the circuit but he was able to exceed 6,000 rpm in fifth gear at two places on each lap.

He found that even moderate engine tuning improved the handling of his own

By 1964—the date of the Dauphine seen here—two million had been made in seven years, and production was 10,000 units a month.

car, and the extra power of the 1063 was a great help when flinging the machine through a series of bends. The ride was harder than normal but the wheels stayed glued to the road over the worst bumps. The high-geared steering was 'a useful safety measure when one had exaggerated rather seriously'.

He used the banked track for maximum speed and the lap speed turned out to be 85–90 mph, which meant a maximum level road speed approaching 90 mph. As far as acceleration figures are concerned, he quoted 0–60 mph in 15.6 seconds and the standing quarter mile in 20.8 seconds—figures which would not disgrace a 2-litre car today.

I had a great deal of fun and quite a lot of mileage out of my 4 CV, and kept it in as nearly original condition as possible. It had lovely white-wall tyres bearing the Renault name: the Régie made their own tyres for a few years. When they began to wear I knew I would not be able to replace them, so I had them retreaded. For some reason I still have the fifth tyre; I think I was having it retreaded at the time I sold the car.

The Quatre Chevaux was a tough little nut. I had not had the car long when a minor disaster overtook it. I had parked it in a street in Hammersmith and was just walking away when I noticed a coal lorry with perilously bulging sides approach. Just as it passed my parked car, a lump of its nearside gave up the ghost and there was a cascade of coal, the black diamonds fairly rattling off the defenceless 4 CV. Surprisingly, the cabriolet top was hardly grazed, and there were pock marks over much of the paintwork, but there was not a single dent on front or rear bonnets. I put in a reasonable insurance claim and rectified the damage myself, with pains-taking brushwork and much rubbing down and polishing.

The cabriolet top, which was a substantial hooped fabric affair fitting on to the body sides and screen, was so strong that for a long time I carried a small boat on a roof rack perched on top of the hood. Finally I got tired of the harshness and noise of the hard-worked little machine and decided to have a change, particularly as I had been doing road tests of the new Dauphine and was hooked on it. The 4 CV was surprisingly difficult to sell; I think I took £125 for it. Today it would be worth £4,000 or what a wealthy collector would pay for it.

You could have a sliding sunroof on a Dauphine, although not necessarily for this purpose . . ..

I bought a grey Dauphine with over 20,000 miles on the clock. It was a dream after the willing but fussy, loud-mouthed little 4 CV. The engine felt like a small turbine, there was hardly a trace of vibration and the ride was soft and smooth. Handling was excellent and I have never understood why it had a bad name on that score, although rear-engined cars demand respect.

The suspension was softer than that of the 4 CV all round, and this allowed a greater degree of roll. Whilst this conferred greater comfort, it also meant that a rear wheel would tend to tuck in if one cornered more than usually enthusiastically, this tendency being aggravated by the swing-axle suspension and the weight of the rear-mounted engine. Sideways gravitational effects are always more interesting with a rear-engined car but on the other hand, rear-wheel traction is good because of the weight over the axles. What all this adds up to is that if you corner violently, break-away will come in suddenly and you have to have exceptionally good reactions to correct the slide and avoid disaster. The same considerations applied to the VW Beetle, but for some reason any disasters with Dauphines seemed to attract more attention than with the Volkswagens. The Dauphine had some faults but personally I do not think bad handling was one of them, unless by bad handling one means incompetent driving.

Certainly the model had a tendency to rust badly, although no worse than the 4 CV or certain other contemporary small cars. The panelling was relatively thin and in those days paint processes were not particularly good, whilst body designers did not always avoid water traps as conscientiously as they might have done.

Opinion was divided on the matter of whether the Dauphine body design was aesthetically satisfactory. My own opinion was that it was a good looker and certainly aerodynamically good, but some people took exception to the arrangement for providing air flow to the rear engine compartment, via a curious slot in each side of the rear quarters. Some went so far as to describe the Dauphine as 'the car with the built-in accident', implying that from birth it had a bash in each side . . ..

One good thing about the car was that if you *were* so unfortunate as to roll it, you had a good, strong turret top to take the crunch.

5: Dreyfus and the Dauphine affaire

The hour, they say, finds the man. Certainly this had been the case with Lefaucheux and now, again, a leader of exceptional ability was to be found in the small, slim, charismatic figure of Pierre Dreyfus who succeeded him in March 1955, having for a considerable time been Vice Chairman of the Board of Directors and a member of the Administrative Council of the Régie. He was about 48 and totally different from Lefaucheux in stature and personality, but with the same rapier-keen brain and utter dedication to the fortunes of the Renault empire.

Dreyfus knew all about the 5 CV—the future Renault Dauphine which Lefaucheux and the design team had been enthusiastically babying along on paper and to the prototype stages—and he had no hesitation in carrying on and intensifying these efforts.

In the factory, the new car was at first called the Corvette but somebody must have told them that there was already an American car—the Chevrolet Corvette—with the same name, so the name Dauphine was adopted. The word means 'wife of the Dauphin', and the Dauphin was the eldest son of the ruler of the region of the Dauphiné—in particular the son of Louis XIV. Dauphine, on the other hand, also means a female dolphin, so one has an interesting choice of origins.

The new car was presented to the Press in April 1956. It was said that it had been christened at an informal dinner not long before that, when somebody had said 'If the Renault 4 CV is the queen of cars, surely the new model should be the Dauphine'.

Left *Pierre Dreyfus—motor man* malgré lui.

Right *A Saviem (Renault commercial vehicle) carrying its clutch of 'offspring' on its back.*

The sleek, compact machine—bigger and more practical than the 4 CV but still child's play to drive and economical in every aspect—was an instant success. There were no teething troubles, although the model was progressively improved in the usual way. After all, the Dauphine had been gestating since 1952, and its creator, Fernand Picard, had himself tested the '109', as the prototype was called, over tough routes in Spain. As with the 4 CV, the Régie launched the Dauphine on a brilliant sporting career at once, this having a dramatic effect on sales.

The Dauphine had a ten-year career which was brilliant, tempestuous, costly, profitable, disastrous and altogether historic. A million Dauphines were made by February 1960, ie, in four years, which made this a European 'first'. By 1963 some two million Dauphines had been made. The monthly production at Flins was approximately 10,000 a month and there were as many as 2,600 variants of the basic specification to meet the demands of customers all over the world.

At first the car had the 'starfish' wheels of the 4 CV, with the characteristic five chrome nuts at the rim, but in 1957 the conventional wheel was adopted. In the same year, Renault offered the Ferlec automatic clutch, a great help in traffic and quite reliable and inexpensive. The 845 cc motor was up-rated in 1959 from 30 to 32 bhp and a year later the famous Aerostable suspension designed by Gregoire was introduced and helped a great deal to stabilise the skittish rear end as well as impart greater comfort.

The Ondine appeared in 1961. This was a luxury variant with a four-speed box, reclining seats, special wheels, etc, but it was in production for only two years. It was followed, however, by a special export version in 1964; this had the disc brakes of the R 8 and an all-synchromesh four-speed gearbox.

The lovely-looking Floride coupé, with 40 bhp Dauphine engine, appeared in 1960 and was instantly coveted by collectors and enthusiasts as well as countless pretty ladies. Frua-styled, it was offered as a coupé or a cabriolet and was graced with a 51 bhp motor by 1963, this Floride S being virtually the mechanical prototype of the R8, with its 956 cc five-bearing engine.

The Floride became the Caravelle in 1963. It had the 1,100 engine and was thus the first Renault to have an engine over 1-litre capacity since the demise of the Frégate. It was available in two versions—fixed head coupé and convertible. A detachable hard top was available for the soft-top. There are still quite a few of these cars about—much prized by their owners and worth a great deal of money if rust-free. Renault still had not mastered the corrosion problem in those days.

In the course of the Dauphine's career, the high-performance engine expert Amédée Gordini joined Renault's competition department and was responsible for the introduction of the Dauphine-Gordini, which sold well in all markets including the UK. It was a four-speed car with a mildly tuned engine (37 bhp) and cosmetic equipment such as slotted wheels. Later, it had the 40 bhp Floride engine, and was in production until 1964.

It is of more than passing interest that the R8 was chosen for Renault's introduction of electro-magnetic automatic transmission, in 1955. Although neither this, nor the Transfluide system used on the Frégate, were automatics as we understand them today, the system used on the R 8/10 was fairly effective and was one of the earliest applications of auto transmission for a small car. The DAF belt-drive automatic was in production in 1958 but was not refined for some years.

In the R8 system there was neither a fluid coupling (as used on the early preselector Daimler and Lanchester cars in conjunction with an epicyclic gearbox)

French police used 4 CV and then Dauphine 'Panda cars' in black and white.

nor a hydraulic torque converter, because it would use up too much power with so small an engine. Instead, there was an electro-magnetic clutch, which used iron filings as the equivalent of a fluid. Smooth action of the coupling was due to the progressive increase of a magnetic field, transforming the metallic powder from a pulverised into an integrated state. Gear shift was by means of an actuator which embodied a selector operated by an electro-magnet system and a small electric motor. There was over-riding control by means of a three-button control on the fascia. Used by an intelligent driver, the system worked reasonably well, but was not entirely reliable, and Renault owners had to wait until the introduction of the Renault 16 TA in 1969, before a truly automatic system was available. A 'real' automatic system for small cars was not offered until 1978, when the Renault 5 was equipped with a transmission similar to that of the 16.

Despite its sporting successes and a few finishes in long-distance rallies, the Dauph' was never a round-the-world type of car, but people did quite interesting things with the model from time to time. A French woman, Michèle Ray, distinguished herself by using one for war reporting. Her aim was to reach the 17th parallel by the ancient mandarin road between North and South Vietnam in a Renault Dauphine (as far as I know, perfectly standard) after six months of operational reporting with the American Forces in Vietnam. In February 1967 she was captured and kept prisoner for three weeks. The attractive woman—a former Chanel model and an amateur race driver—wrote an account of her adventures in *The Two Shores of Hell* (John Murray). Here is a tiny sample: 'Then I really got stuck in the mud, with the wheels skidding round and round. I tried to explain that we must put some branches under the wheels. So at last they set me free. I got down and helped them lay the brushwood. For the first time the Viet with the bayonet met my eye, gave me a faint smile, then quickly turned his head away . . . .

. . . While I drove—the others were running behind as fast as their legs would carry them—I hunted for my American Press card and hid it under the floor mat. I was afraid of being taken for a spy. I would like to have left a note as well, but that was impossible.'

That was very much an individual effort, but it was a veritable army of men who, in England, distinguished themselves, not very honourably, by adopting the Renault Dauphine as the means of launching a taxi war. Thus arrived the mini cab, now a respectable and universally accepted means of public transport, albeit grossly expensive within most city limits. In the early days there were many savage battles between the established licensed cabbies and the freebooting newcomers; and that the latter should use Renaults was a little ironic, since such wide use was made of Renault taxis in the formative years of the legitimate taxi companies.

A man called Captain J. Edwards, of Surbiton, Surrey, distinguished himself in the 1960s by taking an alligator about with him in his Renault Floride, which was one-upmanship of the highest order. His hobby was collecting tropical fish and reptiles and he toured England giving lectures on the subject. With him went Trudy, the 4 ft South American caiman alligator.

At first there was a problem. Every time he braked at all sharply—easy enough to do if you have disc brakes all round—Trudy either got thrown under the seats or round the driver's neck. Edwards said 'I was almost knocked out several times by the whip of Trudy's tail and I soon realised how dangerous this was. But apart from the road safety aspect there was also the important fact that by the time I reached the lecture hall, Trudy was in a pretty mean mood and this made lecturing rather difficult.' This was understandable, because the caiman alligator is known as one of the fiercest and most mean-tempered beasts in the animal kingdom.

The problem was solved by approaching Britax, the well-known seat belt people, who came up with the 'you know it makes sense' answer—a special seat belt for the somewhat victimised creature.

The Régie spared no effort to keep the Dauphine in the public eye, and their public relations department were very much on the ball. When the Queen and Duke of Edinburgh visited France in April 1957 they were naturally invited to tour the Renault plants. The Queen signed the visitors book at Flins and was given a small present—a gleaming pale blue Dauphine. It had, as a matter of fact, been assembled on the production lines at the Acton, London factory and was shipped out to Flins for the occasion. This Dauphine, which had special leather upholstery and chromium-plated wire wheels, was used by the Queen and Duke at Balmoral for a few years and was still at Buckingham Palace in the late 1960s, when I was interviewing the Equerry in connection with my book *Royal Motoring*. He told me the people in the Royal Mews all cordially loathed the Dauphine because it was always going wrong, but it was after all used as a staff hack. However, it was replaced by a Renault 4, which gave faultless service.

Many people think that the famous factory at Flins, on the banks of the Seine some 25 miles west of Paris, was expressly built for the Dauphine, but the truth is that Lefaucheux was thinking in terms of units rather than particular motorcars when he went looking for a piece of land in 1948-49 and the Dauphine was still just an idea being tossed around in the design shops. The Frégate and the 4 CV were destined for mass production at Flins although there would still be some produced at Billancourt. Lefaucheux found his bit of land—a vast area with excellent communications by road, rail and river—and work started on the building of another limb for Renault in 1950, the first cars leaving the lines at the end of 1951.

Both the building of the factory and the introduction of the Frégate were accomplished with almost hysterical speed. One of the reasons was that the military authorities had threatened to appropriate the Flins site since there was war in the East and they were short of supplies. As we have seen, there was a lot wrong with the Frégate and it was never quite rectified, but despite the rush to occupy and equip Flins, it turned out to be a model factory and was ideal for the production of the Dauphine.

By June 1958 they were turning out Dauphines at the rate of over 20,000 a month. I visited Flins around that time and was amazed to see the neat little cars coming off the assembly lines about every 45 seconds and being driven straight off for a brief road test, at a speed that might have dismayed their customers. The Flins plant, of course, was a pressing, welding and assembly plant. The Dauphine and other engines were made at Billancourt, where the transfer machines and other tools for the 750 had been set up at great expense. Transmission units were made at Le Mans, where Renault had had a plant for some time.

The Flins factory became the Pierre Lefaucheux plant and at the entrance to what is now, to all intents and purposes, an industrial town, there is a simple memorial to the man who had the courage and foresight to gamble on the 'little butter pat'.

The pert, seductive Dauphine was a mistress whose influence took Renault to the heights of fame and success, but there is a familiar characteristic of mistresses which enables them to plunge a victim to the depths of despair and finally ruination. This is what might easily have happened with this seductress. In fact Renault might never, 20 years later, have been in a position to call one of their models—the Renault 20—the seductress as they did in a TV advertising! They might have been out of business.

With the Dauphine, the Régie was for the first time exporting half its production, and Dreyfus had ordered an onslaught on the American market which was proving to be highly successful at first. The 4 CV sold well enough in the states and it was assumed that the Dauphine would have a great sales future. At the start of 1960 the millionth Dauphine left the lines and in July 1961 the last and 1,105,543rd 4 CV left Billancourt. Between those times, something went very wrong with Dauphine sales in the USA.

America was in recession and its own motor industry was in trouble. One way in which it tried to remedy this state of affairs was to make compact cars, which became to some degree competitive with European family cars. Sales of Dauphines dropped sharply, not only because America did not wish to import large quantities of small European cars any more, but because the little Dauphine, quite tough by European standards, turned out to be inadequate for poor climatic conditions or hard usage in America. The early cars were fitted with a stupid 6-volt electrical system, and in any case an 850 engine with three-bearing crankshaft was hardly up to the sustained high mileages knocked up by many Americans. Dreyfus was virtually in danger of 'getting the boot' at this time of crisis! Fortunately he had allies in high places, and even De Gaulle supported him, in his distress.

Dreyfus solved the problem by cutting production dangerously—there were strikes and protest marches—but he knew just how far to go. He also sent a hatchet man out to America and slashed viciously into the dealership network. As to the thousands upon thousands of Dauphines rotting in import parks, they would just have to rot, although matters were improved by dropping prices dramatically.

The débâcle was the result of a multiplicity of factors: the hasty planning of the export drive, the loose nature of the dealership network, the mechanical unsuitability of the car for the particular conditions, the recession, and the tough competition from Volkswagen. Factors that saved the day were the swift, ruthless action of Dreyfus and his hatchet men, the Régie's strength in other markets, and the introduction of such models as the Dauphine-Gordini, Ondine and Floride/Caravelle, before the advent of the Renault 8/10 and Renault 4.

Licking his wounds, Dreyfus concentrated on meeting the demands of the European market, before returning to the struggle to topple Volkswagen's superiority in the American market. Looking a little way ahead, he had already

Above left *You could get to faraway places cheaply with a Dauph', which would do 50 mpg on a long run.* **Above right** *Renault Gordini De Luxe of 1961, with 40 bhp version of the Ventoux 850 cc engine.*

commissioned prototypes for the new models.

Meanwhile, the Régie had its fingers in many pies, including the commercial vehicle, tractor and machine tool industries, with which we are not concerned in this account. In October 1960, a co-operative agreement was signed with Alfa-Romeo, and the Dauphine was assembled at Pomigliano d'Arco, near Naples. The 4 CV, incidentally, was still being made under licence by Hino in Japan. Renault had assembly plants in Belgium, the UK, Brazil, Mexico and Argentina.

Renault had a strange flirtation with the US concern American Motors in 1961, whereby the Rambler Classic 6 compact car was assembled at the Régie's plant at Haren in Belgium. It was distributed by Renault in France, Belgium, Holland, Austria and Algeria as the Renault Rambler. This arrangement did not last very long, but collaboration with American Motors has been renewed in recent years.

One thing is certain, 'right up to the end' the Dauphine and its variants retained their charm and in most cases continued to give a fine performance and excellent service unless caned and maltreated in the manner of which the Americans were unfortunately guilty, and in the hands of whom even the VW was by no means infallible. The Renault PR people continued to cash in on the little car's appeal. In mid-1960, the father of Peter Townsend's wife gave his daughter a white 'Dauph' for her 21st. (Townsend, incidentally, owned a Frégate when he was courting Princess Margaret.) Man and wife team Trevor Howard and Helen Cherry presented a Floride to a competition winner in Colchester. Otto Brandenburg, pop star, bought a Floride, etc, ...

I had the opportunity to try many Dauphines other than my own, and wrote several road test reports on them. These Press cars were nearly new, of course, so it was not surprising that very little ever went wrong with them. On the other hand, cars that have done only four or five thousand miles have not loosened-up or settled-down to optimum performance. They always said that Renaults never developed their full power until they had done 10,000 miles or over. I don't know how true that is; if it is true, it is probably not exclusive to Renault.

Above *Pretty car for a pretty girl, although less flamboyant than Bardot, who also posed in Florides.* Below *Caravelle 4-seater fixed-head coupé and Floride Spéciale 2-3-seater convertible. Both cost about £1,200 in 1962.*

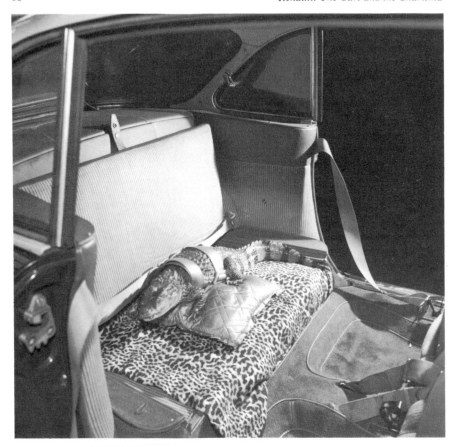

Every alligator knows it makes sense to belt up.

I also tried a Floride and a Caravelle or two. My favourite was the Caravelle Convertible of 1963, which was no longer really a Dauphine variant. Indeed, the 956 Floride and Caravelle and the 1100 Caravelle were the 'missing links' between Dauphine and R 8. The 1963 car had the 1,108 cc, five-bearing engine which produced 55 bhp SAE at 5,100 rpm and of course it had the four disc brakes. The gearbox was a four-speed unit with a nice close ratio between third and top. In '63 the car cost £975 including purchase tax and you could get a detachable hard top for a modest sum. It was very much a 'bird-bait' type of car, cosmetically, yet it had quite a useful performance and did not really deserve the 'sheep in wolf's clothing' tag given by some of the hearty types. The engine, incidentally, was derived directly from the Estafette van unit and was the ancestor of today's 1,100 and 1,300 cc engines used in the smaller Renaults.

The ladies loved the Floride and Caravelle, which looked at once impudent and opulent, as well as being essentially French, even if designed bodily by an Italian. It was no hardship for Brigitte Bardot to sit prettily at the wheel of a Floride when asked to do so by the Renault PR boys, and she made a wonderful picture.

6: A change of ends for Renault

Disaster and success, joy and despair, tough as a tigress, frail as a butterfly, the Dauphine spewed out of Flins until the end of 1966. A few 4 CVs were still being made, mainly in Japan, and the Frégate had had its day eight years earlier. Renault were virtually offering a one-model range. 'But we shouldn't be thinking that way any more' said Dreyfus. Volkswagen might be successful in emulating Henry Ford but it was a risky business. You could rely on vast production of one model for ten years, then the thing became obsolete and you were lucky if you could suddenly produce a viable substitute out of the hat.

'We'll have one dynamic new model', said Dreyfus, 'and while it is meeting the new demand—it must—we'll be planning the rest of a range'. It was 1956 and he already had the R 3-4 in mind.

The better, perhaps, for not being an engineer, he saw clearly what the public wanted in the new decade ahead, and he was certain that it had to be simple and cheap, yet practical and tough, and not necessarily at all pretty like the Dauph', yet in every way more of a motorcar than the 'Deuche' as the Citroën 2 CV was popularly or unpopularly known. He was enough of a motor man to know, moreover, that the rear-engined car had nearly had its day. For this model the tail would never wag the dog, never mind how cheerfully or willingly, and the Renault 8, still to come, would be the last of the rear-engined, mass-produced cars, with its variants. He was thinking of the 8 as well as the 4. It would be easier to develop the 8 and 10, for they would be based on the Dauphine, although in a completely new image, which, in fact, initiated the 'Euro shape' which is even now almost *de rigeur* in three-box (front boot, passenger space and rear boot) cars today.

The design staff already had the R 4 on paper, but in the new Estafette van, launched in 1959, the firm played a very clever trick by including elements not only of the Sierra engine, which was to power the R 8 1100, but of Renault's first front-wheel drive, which is a feature of almost all today's models of the marque.

Briefing his design team, Dreyfus said: 'What I want you to come up with is a holdall on wheels—a travelling bag that can go anywhere without feeling self-conscious. It must be tough as a rhino and cost a lot less to run. People will go to church in it, will go camping, will commute to the office, will make it a livestock carrier, a shop, a wedding car, a passion wagon . . .'

Never have there been more prototypes for a Renault. There were two-, three- and four-cylinder jobs; open, closed, half-open, steel and fabric bodied jobs, even a kind of beach buggy. Citroën knew and laughed, or got hopping mad. Finally

Renault settled for the very configuration that we know today—the five-door boxy little doxy that is 20 years old and still revving and raving it up all over the globe.

Pierre Dreyfus very nearly had his chips during the prototype tests in Sardinia, when, accompanied by the young test chief, he took the wheel on a mountainous route and left the road on a loose-surfaced, hairpin bend. Bouncing down the precipice for a metre or two, his progress was arrested by a large rock . . ..

The new car was initially available in France as the R 3, with 603 cc engine and the R 4 with 747 cc unit but the 603 did not tempt the market. There was also the R 4 L, a version with six instead of four windows and in fact this became the definitive version, simply called the 4 L in the UK. It is chronicled that when the car appeared at the 1961 show, General de Gaulle, who opened the Salon, took a good look at it and moved on to Citroën, where he asked how things were going. François Michelin, boss of Citroën, said things might be a lot better if Renault were not copying them. But of course this was perfectly unreasonable, because the R 4 was much more of a motorcar than the 2 CV, and it still is although both have their applications and devotees.

The introduction of the 4 in September 1961 was indeed timely, because the company's production had dropped from nearly 550,000 units to 400,000; work hours were being cut and strikes were occurring. The R 4 was to put Renault virtually back on its feet, although the new marketing strategy and the launching of the Floride S and Caravelle helped enormously.

The launch of the car that was to become fondly known by countless individuals and families in Britain as 'Noddy' (after an Enid Blyton characterisation) was a giant PR exercise. In Paris 200 or more of the cars were virtually given over to the public, who could drive them with reckless abandon and simply leave them anywhere for the company to pick up. There were test cars also available at dealers' premises all over Europe. People very quickly got to know and love this rather ugly little duckling.

Not only the first front-wheel-drive Renault car, this was the first of all cars to have a cooling system of completely sealed type and it was remarkable also in having a chassis that needed no greasing at all—none of that old drudgery with the pressure gun. To say that it had a chassis is, as a matter of fact, somewhat of an understatement for it had a stout underframe and an overall steel deck as well; with the body bolted on, this made for a very robust structure indeed.

In the UK there were two models—a saloon, and an estate car which differed little—and other versions were to be seen in almost every country of the world in ever-increasing numbers as owners discovered the go-anywhere capabilities of this remarkable maid-of-all-work.

In November 1961 the Fourgon 6 cwt van was introduced, using the same mechanical basis as the car. This proved equally popular and still does today, a new and more powerful version having been introduced only a year or two ago when the Renault 4 GT L was launched.

On 3 March 1964 the half-millionth 4 L saloon came off the lines at Billancourt; in the same period 64,000 Fourgons had been built. Lined up three abreast they would have stretched nose to tail from the Southampton Renault UK import depot to Edinburgh, where Louis Renault appointed his first overseas agent in 1901. Today, over seven million of this stoic, amusing and highly economical model have been built and production is running at nearly 1,600 a day.

In the early years of the Renault 4, there were four engine types, the most basic

The original Renault 4, with tubular chairs and bumpers, and a 750 cc engine.

being rated at 3 cv. Having a capacity of 603 cc it naturally produced a modest 23 bhp at 4,500 rpm and did not appeal to many people. There were two 747 cc engines with outputs of 27.6 bhp at 4,500 rpm and 30 bhp at 4,700 rpm, these having a fiscal rating of 4 cv, and there was the 845 cc, 30 bhp engine rated at 5 cv. All these were three-bearing-crankshaft engines with wet cylinder liners, aluminium heads and overhead valves, and all were derivatives of the 4 CV (Baby Renault) engine which had been built in prototype form as early as 1942, and which was adopted and adapted for the Dauphine, Floride, Caravelle, Estafette, etc.

For the R 4 and Fourgon, the rotation of the 'peanut pusher' (the popular works name for the unit) was reversed so that owners would not have to turn the starting handle in the wrong direction, which is interesting since the starting handle was eventually and regrettably abandoned. Eventually, of course, the Renault 4 was to use the 1,100 cc, five-bearing engine, which it now has.

Three types of gearboxes have been fitted, ie, three-speed with non-synchro first gear, three-speed with all synchro, and four-speed fully synchronised. The very crude, very effective umbrella-handle, fascia-mounted gear shift was used for all models. For many years 6-volt electrical systems were used; a false economy which infuriated many owners and dealers, as was the case with the Citroën 2 CV.

Steering has always been rack and pinion, and the earlier cars had the curious return spring, as on the 4 CV. Suspension was, and is, a truly excellent system, independent all round, with torsion bars, hydraulic shock absorbers and anti-roll bars. When people first saw those spindly torsion bars, they imagined them snapping like sticks of celery, but a breakage is almost unknown.

Things that made the R 4 a winner were the four doors plus big tailgate, the excellent headroom and the versatility of the whole thing. 'Give me a holdall' Dreyfus had said, and that was what he and several million customers got. 'Great', he said, 'now we can start thinking about more genteel but no less practical cars to sell alongside Noddy'.

With four or even five passengers seated, there was ample space for 17 cu ft of baggage behind the back seat in this little money-saving machine. With rear seat folded, on the estate version, this became almost 50 cu ft on a flat floor about 4 ft 6 in long. The early saloons had tubular-framed, cloth-covered seats and you could take out the back seat for camping, etc, or just to make a big load space. Perhaps this was just a gimmick to infuriate Citroën, who had quick-detach seats on the 2 CV, but Renault, rather regrettably I feel, discontinued it.

An excellent feature, retained for many years, was a well-made, plastic-textile sun-roof in two sections, so that virtually the whole roof could be open to the sky. It was an extra, but inexpensive.

I was among the countless people tempted by this perky little baggage and although I still had my Dauphine—now with 40,000 on the clock and going strong—I could not resist the proposition when Acton offered me a 4 L with a mere 7,000 miles to its credit. It had been the managing director's second car and was rather a special example in light blue with black leather upholstery and a Philips radio.

I did not even bother to take a test run. After all, I had attended the UK Press launch at Wentworth Park and had thrashed one of the cars around a 'forest section' after a rather splendid lunch. When I collected my own car from Acton, I decided within minutes that it was dreadful—almost unbearable, in fact. The engine noise level was so high that I had to use full volume on the radio to hear a music programme, and first gear was so low that the motor was screaming its heart out almost immediately after get-away. What I had not allowed for was the 747 cc engine and the low gearing which the designers had deemed necessary for the power transmission; but as I grew familiar with the little beast I made allowance for its shortness of breath and peculiar gear ratios, and was quite charmed by the absence of vibration even when the revs were indecently high. Moreover, it never looked like failing, even on the 1 in 4 hill which I was occasionally required to ascend at that time, and its front-wheel drive conferred astonishing benefits on muddy tracks and in snow or icy conditions. This was one of the many plus features of the Renault 4, ie, that many people found they could operate under conditions that would normally require four-wheel drive. The effect of a power train that pulls instead of pushing has to be experienced to be believed, although, of course, today most owners have never known anything else.

Certainly I was charmed by the chore-horse qualities of the little car and I made good use of the detachability of the rear seat, as I was a dedicated seasonal camper. The folding roof was a joy for three-quarters of the year, but the Dauphine was the only Renault I have had which did not have a sun roof of some kind.

Not to have to bother with any grease points or with any demands from the cooling system made my motoring life much easier, whilst the remarkable economy of running was much in keeping with my life style.

Despite its use of the 4 CV power unit and gearbox, the 4 L bore no resemblance to the Baby Renault, which I remembered mainly for its eager performance, rough running and harsh suspension, although it had a much flatter ride. The frantic but smooth 4 L gave an armchair ride and you could corner it on its door handles, which in fact was obligatory if you were in a hurry, or what passed for a hurry within the capacity of a manic little donkey.

Somebody at the factory said 'Stick with it. This model can only get better.' Perhaps as a rebound from an earlier experience with a secondhand, very early Citroën Light Fifteen, I believed them, and they were right. My Citroën put me off the Light Fifteen for always, yet it was modified to become a best seller.

Acting on a hunch as well as my 'mature' judgement and this Renault man's advice, I put up with the 750 4 L for another few months, and consoled myself with the thought that I was one of the first people in the UK to own a historic car. What I should have done was to have cocooned it and bought something else, because it became far more historic than anyone might have imagined, but I traded it in for a new 845 cc 4 L. This was the first new car I had ever owned and I will never forget the thrill of my first run, although for most of my adult life I have been accustomed to testing new or nearly new machinery.

After the 750 version, the 850 was a dream, especially as a new car. A new car has that special quality of being immaculate, like a perfectly crimped and turned-out cherry pie, a primly painted brand new garden barrow, a maiden prepared for confirmation. Everything is, or should be, crisp and fresh and quiet yet full of promise. Noisy timing gears or tappets or pistons simply do not exist, if the men on the assembly lines have done their work as intended by its creator, who is the supremo of the design department.

The engine, of course, was still the 'peanut pusher', but bored out from 54.5 to 58 mm with the same 80 mm stroke, and with a slightly enlarged inlet bore, these modifications giving it a developed horsepower of 32 to 4,500 rpm and maximum torque of 50 lb ft at 2,000 rpm. The gearbox was the same as on the 750 but a higher final drive was used. This power/transmission pack gave the car a totally new character. Perhaps, considering it objectively, it was noisy, but the noise was a pleasant, meaningful one with some quality of serenity, unlike the eldritch rasping and shrilling of the 750 used on the early 4 L. The power delivery was quite astonishing, giving first class acceleration and an indicated maximum speed of 85

'Ten per cent? You've got to be joking.' Nubar Gulbenkian, multi-millionaire, eyes a Renault 4 at Earls Court.

mph, although this probably meant about 73 mph as these speedometers were always optimistic. But it would keep up that speed all day.

By 1963 the R 4 had overtaken the Citroën 2 CV in sales figures, and Dreyfus's faith in the 'Noddy car' was justified. People had realised that this was not a crude, tinny agricultural device, but a proper car, in which one could, if expedient, go to the ball or the embassy; in fact, one's lady might very well be a great deal less rumpled and creased than if she were taken in a taxi and she would be able to get into and out of the car with much more grace, because of its tall, wide-opening doors. Disabled people found the little car a boon, and it was a perfect camper, as Jacques Tati demonstrated in his epic film 'Playtime'. When General de Gaulle was introduced to the car, he commented 'That should be a real money spinner for you, Dreyfus'. He certainly hit the nail on the head, for it was this model that pulled the Régie's chestnuts out of the fire at a critical time.

In the spring of '63, the R 4 Parisienne had been launched in Paris with the collaboration of the journal *Elle*. This was a standard model, but with a special cosmetic attraction in that the body could be in a tartan finish or a kind of imitation canework. This rather appealed to me. I had always been fascinated by the basket-work finish on the special London taxi used by Nubar Gulbenkian, the oil baron, who was a keen car fancier rather than motorist. When Acton introduced a do-it-yourself kit of imitation basketwork for the Renault 4 they offered me one, as well as a set of prissy wheel trims. This was my consolation for not getting a discount on my purchase of the car. Renault were always very tight-fisted in such matters. One could, as a motoring writer, get a reasonable trade discount on most other makes, although it infuriated the dealers. But Renault were almost calvinistic in their approach to this and similar matters.

I applied the basketwork material carefully, and it made the car look very smart and interesting, although my R 4 was white and it would have looked better on a black car. The stuff was tough, and took all sorts of knocks, yet was easy to clean. It was like a kind of extra thick Fablon, and looked as good when I sold the car four years later.

In 1967, to bring it in line with competitive cars (although not the 2 CV) the Renault 4 was fitted with a four-speed gearbox of fully synchromesh type. The ratios, compared with the three-speed, were as follows:

	4-speed	3-speed
Gearbox ratios	3.80, 2.06, 1.36, 1.04	3.80, 1.84, 1.04
Overall ratios	15.68, 8.50, 5.61, 4.28	15.68, 7.60, 4.28

At the same time, the car received a face-lift, with a new grille surrounding the headlamps and bearing the diamond logo. The bumpers were not only sturdier, but were of an interesting half-round section. The first 4 L had had tubular bumpers, and these were replaced by curved-channel section ones, which gave way to the new stouter blades still used. Renault dropped the starting handle rather surreptitiously round this time, but the bumper continued to have a hole for it. Some people spent their life savings on a Renault 4, only to find that they could stick the starting handle (which was also the wheel brace) through the hole in the bumper but there was no starting handle dog to engage. But the van still had a handle and dog, and those in the know just bought a dog (still listed as a spare for the van) and fitted it on the front of the crankshaft.

Internally, the old tennis ball gear lever knob (it really was a very satisfactory

Launching the R 8 in America.

Napoleon was never so beautiful . . ..

The boxy shape of the 1100 was trend-setting.

fistful) was replaced by a kind of inverted pistol grip. This, too, annoyed many traditionalists but it was actually a justifiable improvement.

The four-speed shift was not entirely satisfactory because fourth gear was 'out on a limb' and difficult to engage if you were not thinking. Also, the three-speed had such a useful second gear that one hardly needed a third. Later they used the gearbox of the Renault 6, which made it all much better.

In 1968 the Renault 4 cost £543 including purchase tax. A de luxe version was listed at £558 and a sun roof cost £20. Today it costs over six times as much, and is slightly improved.

In the years when the Renault 4 was establishing itself as a way of life for millions of people round the world, other exciting things were happening to the Régie and its range of automobiles.

Annual production rose from 461,100 in 1959 to over a million in 1969, in which year more than half the total production was exported. By 1970, the Régie was France's leading enterprise, the third largest motor manufacturer in Europe and the seventh in the world.

In 1962 the Renault 8 was introduced, with all the appropriate razzmatazz, including being suspended from a helicopter flying over the Statue of Liberty. This was the first-ever mass-produced car with disc brakes all round. The still current Dauphines and Caravelles were similarly equipped. Flins was extended once more, having more than doubled since 1956 and grown more than four-fold since 1954. The R 10 followed the R 8 and by 1970 more than a million and a half of the two had been made.

But the big sensation came in 1965, with the launching of the Renault 16—a futuristic hatchback which was also a luxury 'limousine' to the middle-income buyer to whom it made the strongest appeal. This was the car which was to take Renault into a whole new area of marketing, following Dreyfus's policy of extending the range. For the 16, a great new factory was built at Sandouville near Le Havre in the record time of 18 months.

In addition to their production record in France, Renault assembly and manu-facturing plants in 28 countries produced a further 295,000 vehicles in 1969. In countries such as Spain and Belgium, the production of Renaults was higher in that year than the total production from Billancourt in 1939.

Factories at Flins, Cleon, Sandouville, Choisy-le-Roi and Orleans had now been added to the rebuilt and enlarged Billancourt and Le Mans works. There was a technical centre at Rueil and a test facility at Lardy. The area of the factories had now reached ten million square metres and personnel strength was over 85,000. New establishments were being constructed at Douai and Dreux and (in association with Peugeot) at Douvrin-la-Bassée (engines) and Bruay (gearboxes).

To consolidate their position in the European automotive scramble for supremacy, Renault and Peugeot decided to share a bed in 1966, signing not exactly a marriage certificate but an article of association, an agreement to live-in amicably and profitably. To the co-operation established for research, purchase and manufacture of certain common units would progressively be added a wide common production effort for basic elements: engines from Douvrin, gearboxes from Bruay and bodywork from a Renault-Chausson plant at Maubeuge.

Pierre Dreyfus, in 1968, said 'I have high hopes that Renault and Peugeot will one day manufacture, one for the other, more than 20 per cent of all the basic elements of their respective vehicles'. He did not foresee that Peugeot would buy out Citroën ten years later; three in a bed was not what Dreyfus had had in mind at all.

In 1970, a *Sunday Telegraph* feature writer asked Dreyfus 'Is it because Renault is State-owned and Peugeot private that there is not a full merger?' Dreyfus said 'No, we want confidence to grow. The more we live together the more we know each other.' Evidently Renault never got to know Peugeot well enough, although today they still co-habit successfully and at least share common engines and gearboxes for some models.

To quote Edouard Seidler, (*The Romance of Renault*, Edita, Lausanne):
'While the elite of the automobile and industrial world of Paris mused over the incredible news of an alliance between Renault, the company claiming to conduct experiments in socialism, and Peugeot, that epitome of a capitalist family business, Pierre Dreyfus was peacefully in the country, in Normandy, in his garden. He was happily enjoying a quiet, sunny Saturday afternoon and indulging in his favourite occupation—doing nothing and watching the trees grow.' It is a slick, rather pleasing comment, but I would be surprised if it is apt. I can imagine Dreyfus enjoying doing nothing, but I think his mind would be furiously active and the trees would be seen only subconsciously.

The Renault 8 and its derivatives, the Renault 10 and the R 8 Gordini, were the most advanced and successful rear-engined cars ever produced by the Régie, if one excludes the Caravelle as being hardly a mass-market model. The 8 and 10 series were certainly not tarted-up Dauphines. Dreyfus knew the shortcomings of the Dauph' series and he was not going to allow any of that kind of business again. Yet the first of the 8 series, introduced in June 1962, were not without the teething troubles to which most mass-produced cars are subject, eg, water getting into the body, hot starting troubles, screeching brakes, brake fade, etc, and the hierarchy commissioned the designers to produce the R 8 1100 (known as the Major in France). This really was a superb car. The R 10 was to all intents and purposes a long-nosed version of the same car; the purists turned up their supercilious noses at it but it probably made more sense than the snub-nosed 8 for family purposes, and from an aesthetic viewpoint. Where competition work was concerned, of course, the R 8 in 'S' or Gordini or other souped-up form was the only version to be considered.

Apart from the four disc brakes, the single most important feature of the later

Caravelle, 8 and 10 series, was the five-bearing crankshaft engine, which first appeared in 956 cc form and was later up-rated to 1,100 cc. It is interesting to consider the evolution of Renault engines, and their family inter-relationship.

We have seen that the 4 CV engine was developed to provide an 845 cc motor for the Dauphine, with stronger crankshaft, (58 instead of 54.5 mm bore) and a 28 mm carburettor; it developed 27.5 hp at 4,250 rpm. In the works rally cars, it was developed to give 55 hp and from it was derived the later 48 hp motor for the listed Dauphine versions. Developed in the meantime, the Dauphine-Gordini engine was a separate entity with special head and its output was 33 hp at 5,000 rpm.

The engine for the earlier Renault 6 models was the final evolution of the 845 cc unit. It developed 34 bhp at 5,000 rpm and had a 32 mm carburettor.

The new five-bearing-crankshaft engine designed for the Floride S and the R 8 was very similar in general design to the 850 three-bearing unit, although surprisingly the use of five bearings enabled it to be actually shorter, because it was no longer necessary to have so much space between cylinders 2 and 3.

The combustion chambers were redesigned to give higher compression ratios in the R 8 and derivatives, and also to provide for the larger intake charges. The combustion chamber roof was inclined to modify the flame front and control the speed of combustion, and the valves were parallel but inclined. As in the three-bearing engine, a high camshaft (driven by chain) was used in order to minimise inertia stresses of the valve gear. Keeping in mind always the idea of a short, robust structure, the designers came up with 72 × 70 mm stroke/bore dimensions for the 1,100 version, despite the currently popular practice of making engines over-square.

The 1,100 first appeared on the Estafette van, whilst the Floride S, and then the R 8, had the 956 unit, the bore of which was reduced to 65 mm for fiscal purposes. Output was 42 bhp for the R 8 and 45 bhp for the Floride. Both had a 32 mm carburettor, but the Floride had a higher compression ratio. The following year the Floride was renamed the Caravelle and got the 1,100 motor with 8.5 compression ratio. (Compression ratios on the R 8 and Floride S with the 956 engine had been respectively 8.5 and 9.5.)

The Caravelle's 1,100 engine had an output of 47 bhp, but two years later it acquired a double-barrel carburettor and an output of 51 bhp for the Caravelle S. In 1964 the 1,100 motor was adopted for the R 8 and a little later for the R 10. The R 8 S had the Caravelle S engine with 9.5 compression ratio, and gave 53 bhp. It is interesting to note that even in this advanced form, the five-bearing 1,100 engine weighed only 7 kg more than the 850 unit of the Renault 6. In fact the specific weight per hp for the R 8 S was only 1.75 kg compared with 2.58 for the R 6 850.

The Renault 10/1300 and Renault 12 engines which came a little later were still derivatives of the 956/1,100. However, in order to take the bore to 73 mm without production problems, the inter-cylinder axis was modified to 85 mm for all cylinders, whereas in the 1,100 it was 83 mm for cylinders 1-2 and 3-4 and 87 mm for the dimension between 2-3. In the form used for the Renault 12, the 1,300 cc engine, with 77 mm stroke, gave 54 bhp with a 32 mm carburettor. This was only marginally greater than the power of the R 8 S but the mid-range torque was considerably greater and the engine had a vast tuning potential.

In all its forms, the R 8/10 series proved extremely successful. The snub-nosed 8 in standard form was luxurious yet economical and quite 'cheeky' transport; the 8 S and the Gordini 1100 and 1300 were exciting and seductive; the R 10 was the 'grand tourer' among small cars.

Right *Jaeger auto transmission on Renault 8. On left: 1a—press buttons for selection; 1b—governor; 1c—relay box; 2 and 6—secondary throttle; 3 and 5—magnetic coupling; 4—actuator. On right: 1—press buttons; 2—governor; 3—relay box; 4—secondary throttle; 5—actuator; 6—coupling.*

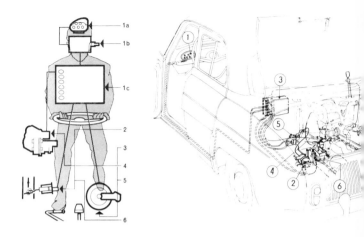

Right *Caravelle/Floride 950 cc engine with five-bearing crankshaft, which replaced the three-bearing 850 of 1962.*

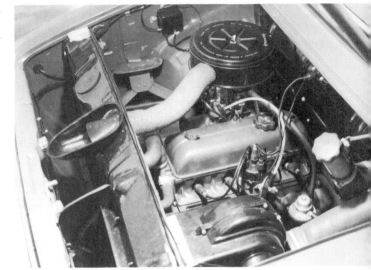

Below *Dreyfus with four beauties —the oldest on the left, the youngest on the right.*

The Renault 1100 (Renault 10 on the continent) was a long-nosed version of the 8.

I bought a low-mileage, pale yellow 956 cc R 8 from a dealer and had three years of good, uncomplaining service from it with only minor parts replacement. I had more trouble with door handle gear than anything else and even that was minimal. The unusually smooth and silent shutting of the doors was probably obtained at the expense of reliable mechanism. The squeaky brakes never bothered me much. Nearly all earlier disc brakes squealed and screeched. Even Mercedes told their customers they would have to live with it.

I used that car for several runs the length of France, usually to camp on the Riviera. It always went like a bird. Sometimes, on motorways, the red temperature warning lamp would come on and off, now and again, or flicker for a few minutes, but nothing dramatic ever happened. The R 8 had the same sealed cooling as the R 4. Possibly the fan belt, which drove water pump as well as cooling fan, was on the slack side, when everything was very hot. The car was unusually comfortable, with superb seats not repeated on later R 8/10 series, unfortunately. Like all rear-engined cars, it was affected by side winds but one became used to this. Handling was otherwise of a very high standard and the high-performance variants did very well in rally events.

It never occurred to me that I needed more power than the 956 cc engine would provide, but probably I am not very demanding. Eventually I just felt like a new car and liked the R 8 so much I opted for another one—a new one this time—and by then the R 8-1100 as well as the R 10 had come in.

Even Renaultphiles are apt to forget that the 1,100 motor was first fitted in the Renault 8 Major and Caravelle 1100 in 1963 and in the 8 Gordini in 1964. The standard 8 stayed at 956 until 1967, when the R 8-1100 was introduced. Alongside was the Renault 1100, called the R 10 on the continent.

Market research, an activity in which Renault were always very strong, had indicated that many owners wanted more luggage space. To increase the capacity of the boot by 25 per cent called for a change in design with the minimum increase in overall size. The Régie's design team achieved this within a length of 13 ft 9½ in which was only 8½ in longer than the R 8.

When the R 8 was given its bigger engine, it became one of the cheapest and best 1100s on the market at £648. There were other improvements, or at any rate changes, eg, a new fascia finished in simulated wood and instruments with attractive circular dials, whilst the steering wheel had trendy and rather self-conscious spokes simulating perforated metal. Renault claimed better seating but I think this was a PR fantasy. I bought my new car as soon as I could and it was only the seating that disappointed me very mildly, because the upholstery was in coarsely-grained black PVC and I missed the soft red trim of the previous car. I think it was a foam-backed material that they used on the 956 but it gave the effect of genuine soft hide.

Again, however, my R 8 gave sterling service and I would run it down to St. Tropez or Stes Maries without doing anything but putting petrol in. On a long run these cars would do anything up to 50 miles to the gallon, and they used no oil. I never had any rust problems and the only notable replacements were silencers and brake pads. The car was always very quiet as long as the silencer was in good condition and I think it even became fractionally quieter when I had a folding sun roof fitted.

In the meantime—in autumn 1964—Renault had announced what they called 'a startling new Renault'. This was the R 8 Gordini and since France had had the 1,100 unit in the R 8 for some time, the power unit of the new car was based on that unit. The new model was described as a 105 mph luxury saloon. They stated: 'The famous French racing-car designer Amédée Gordini, known by enthusiasts all over the world as "The Sorcerer" has collaborated with Renault engineers in the design of the engine of this new competition model'.

Modifications to the all-independent suspension resulted in the lowering of the car by two inches. Sets of double shock absorbers were fitted at the rear, and the 10.2 inch front and rear disc brakes were given servo assistance. The rack and pinion steering was higher geared than on the standard models, resulting in less turns from lock to lock, which was a matter of importance to rally drivers and saloon car racers.

A special cross-flow, light-alloy cylinder head was fitted, with hemispherical combustion chambers and the fuel supply was by two twin-choke Solex carburettors. A racing pattern 'bunch of bananas' exhaust system was used for rapid extraction of the exhaust gases. Compression ratio was 10.4:1 and power output 95 bhp at 6,500 rpm, which was 90 per cent more than the standard R 8-1100. The new car weighed only 80 lb more than the standard machine, despite the extra equipment. A fully synchromesh, four-speed gearbox with central floor change was used and the rear axle ratio gave 16.3 mph per 1,000 rpm in top gear.

The new model was distinguished by its big headlamps and colour scheme of French racing blue ('le bleu de France') with two broad, white stripes across the top of the car from end to end. Upholstery was in black vinyl. Instrumentation included an electric tachometer and the electrical wiring was so arranged as to make it easy for rally enthusiasts to fit extra lighting, etc. Rally-type compressed air horns were fitted. Traditionalists will be delighted to know that the car still had a starting handle, although it was never easy to start even the standard R 8 on the handle.

The R 8 Gordini 1100 ceased to be produced in 1967, by which time 2,623 had been made, and it was replaced by the 1300 with 71 × 77 mm bore and stroke. Billancourt turned out 9,600 of this more potent model, sales being boosted by the introduction of the Coupe Gordini saloon car race series.

The new car was distinguishable at once by its extra twin headlamps inboard of the main lamps. It was, as always, in French racing blue with the white go-faster stripes. Mechanically, it differed in some respects from the 1100; the larger engine apart, it had a five-speed gearbox, all synchromesh. Details are as follows:

Final drive by bevel gear with 4.125 ratio (8 and 33 teeth) or as an option 3.78:1 (9 × 34) or 4.57:1 (7 × 32).

Gearbox ratios	Speeds per 1,000 rpm
1st : 3.61	4.6 mph
2nd : 2.37	7.0 mph
3rd : 1.70	9.8 mph
4th : 1.30	12.8 mph
5th : 1.03	16.1 mph
Rev.: 3.08	5.4 mph

The clutch was a 7.1 inch unit in place of the 1100's 6.3 inch component and it had a needle race bearing. Electrical equipment embodied a 40 amp alternator. A supplementary fuel tank was located in the front bonnet, along with the Bendix Hydrovac brake assister and the compressor for the air horns.

The 1,300 engine, with its compression ratio of 10.5:1, pushed out 110 bhp at 6,750 rpm (gross SAE rating), maximum torque being 91.8 lb ft at 5,000 rpm.

In the Renault magazine *Autoworld* of April/May 1967 there was a report by rally star Roger Clark, who tried the first Gordini 1300 to reach the British market. The following are excerpts:

'For a start, the 1,255 cc twin-Weber engine has a lot more torque than the old 1,108 cc Gordini. 147 cc doesn't sound a lot but it means a lot, and you feel it right away on acceleration. The figures show what she can do—0 to 30 in 3.5 seconds mean (3.2 best) is a healthy getaway by any car and although I couldn't get a maximum speed figure for obvious (blue-coated) reasons it is clearly well above 100 mph—I would say about 110 mph.

The Renault 1,100 cc five-bearing engine which has been used in so many forms.

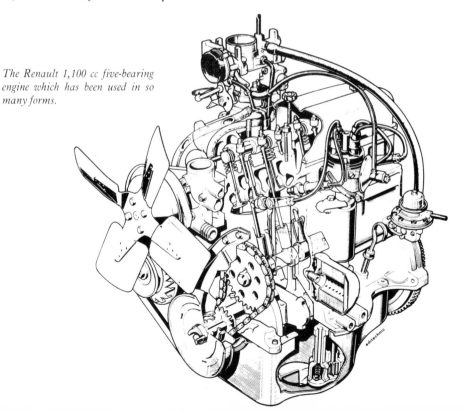

'The Sorcerer'—Amédée Gordini.

The gearbox has five speeds, and though still a bit stiff the change is just right—very quick right through—and the ratios ideal, though the five-bearing crankshaft engine is so flexible you don't have to keep changing unless you're in a hurry. We pootled along behind a lorry at about 25 mph in a 40 limit area as smoothly as you like and I suddenly realised we were in fifth and going uphill, with never a niggle.

Pushing the car hard through open swinging Buckinghamshire lanes, with lots of rain and puddles about, I just couldn't fault its handling. This boxy little bomb really goes; it hangs its tail out just nicely, but always controllably (those rear-engined breakaway fears are right out-of-date nowadays) and the car sits down beautifully. It is two inches lower than standard by the way and has stiffer springs—but you would hardly know it, the way she rode through those bumpy lanes.'

In the same issue there was a note or two on the Gordini by Sylvia Osterberg, a successful rally driver, in a report by Graham Gauld, who said: 'We met her in Karlstad when, with deep snow lying around, we jumped into the factory Gordini she was to drive on the Swedish Rally and spoke about the Monte Carlo Rally in January, when she won the Ladies Award for Renault. First of all I asked her how she felt driving a small rear-engined car, compared to the bigger front-engined Volvo she had been used to.

Her reply was: "I find no problems with the Renault because the car is not so heavy and I think it is easier for a woman to drive. The car I am driving on the Swedish Rally is a new one and not the one I drove to Monte Carlo." '

Gauld suggested to her that the first part of the rally had been fairly easy but she explained that the pop singer Johnny Hallyday, in his Mustang, caused a lot of trouble because the fans mobbed him at the controls.

In September 1968 came the Renault 8 S. This was described by Renault at the time as 'the young sister of the rally-winning Gordini 1300' but it would have been fairer to have described it as an up-rated version of the standard R 8 with cosmetic attractions. It had the 1,100 engine with one twin-choke Weber, giving it a 60 bhp output at 5,500 rpm, and torque of 70 lb at 3,000 rpm—an increase of some 30 per cent over the 'cooking' version. Renault claimed a maximum speed of over 90 mph.

An echo of the 'little butter pat'—the 4 CV—was seen in the adoption of yellow (actually Belgian racing yellow) for the introductory models of the car, although five other colours were later available. Externally, the car was identifiable by the four headlamps, as on the Gordini 1300, and the interior was notable for special upholstery, honeycombed in the centre sections of the seats to give extra comfort and coolness.

It is worth pausing to consider what sort of a man was this Amédée Gordini. What he was *not* was an Alex Issigonis. He could never have done for Renault what Issigonis did for BMC (forerunner of British Leyland). He was not a car designer, he was a mechanic with good theoretical as well as practical knowledge; Louis Renault would have approved of him.

Gordini was born in Italy but left for France when he was 20. He had been a mechanic since he was ten; in 1922 he was fortunate enough to be allowed to work on the heroic cars such as Hispano-Suizas, Italas, Bugattis, etc. At the age of 21 he built his first car, a 'bitza', from parts of an Isotta and an old Bianchi engine which he had managed to get back into working order. One of his early moments of glory came when he got his hands on a Hispano engine which he tuned as much as he dared. (There is a lot more in tuning than just adjusting an engine; it means rebuilding with many modified and improved parts.) He put the tuned motor in a special car of Tazio Nuvolari, the little chap later known as 'Il Maestro' but at that time just a keen motorcycle racer. The Nuvolari–Gordini car was timed at 143 mph at Brooklands.

Gordini set up his own workshop at Suresnes, on the outskirts of Paris, not far from Billancourt. He employed five mechanics and specialised in tuning, but soon took time off to show that he was quite a competent race driver too. Driving a Fiat 6 CV which he had waved his magic wand over, like the sorcerer he already was, he covered the 500 metres of the Mont Valerian hill climb in 27.45 seconds.

In 1934 Simca cars—really Fiats under a new name—were introduced into France and Gordini, fancying the design, modified one of these cars and entered the Bol d'Or, a historic car race. He was victorious over the MG, Amilcar and Salmson cars, which were strongly favoured. This marked the start of his career as an ace tuner as well as an able driver. Gordini joined the ranks of the 'greats', with star performances in the Spa 24 hours, Rheims, Algiers, the Bol d'Or again, etc. In 1938 one of his cars won its class in the Le Mans 24 hours and in 1939 he himself drove one of his cars to victory in the same event, with José Scaron as co-driver.

After the war, Gordini rounded up his mechanics again, but this time at 69 Boulevard Victor, near the Porte de Versailles. In 1945 the accomplished drivers Wimille and Sommer drove for Gordini, but the sorcerer was not yet ready to hang up his helmet. He built a single-seater race car with a Simca 1100 motor and carried off the Grand Prix de Marseille of 1946, in front of two powerful BMW 2-litre cars driven by Sommer and Eugene Martin. In 1947 he improved his team of road racers and things really got going, but now he left it to others to do the actual driving, and concentrated on the wizardry of getting every last gramme of power out of any engine he or his mechanics touched.

Now he was giving his cars to 'names' like Scaron, Prince Bira of Siam, Sommer and Wimille, and even to a certain ex-bus driver called Juan Manuel Fangio . . .. In France he also entrusted cars to young Turks like Manzon, Trintignant, Simon and Behra, all to become ace grand prix drivers.

Still cleaving to his tiny but eminently tuneable engines, Gordini was beginning to trail in the slipstreams of the powerful Alfas, Ferraris and Maseratis and by 1952 he had had to start using 1,200 and then 1,500 cc units, but this was still not enough. He then cloistered himself and his chief mechanic day and night for a while and came up with a new 2-litre motor—a six-cylinder unit with overhead camshafts. This engine went into sports racers of several types and was up-rated, as required, to 2,300 and even 2,500 cc capacity, and the supremacy of even Ferrari was being challenged. Soon, Gordini created an entirely new 3-litre engine—a straight eight—and continued to gain honours. In 1953 he was made a Chevalier of the Légion d'Honneur and in June 1966 was further honoured by being made an Officer of the order.

In 1954 Mercedes decided to start racing again and even the big boys—Ferrari, Maserati, Lancia, Jaguar and Aston Martin—had to make greater efforts. Gordini was already doing all he knew but financial problems were becoming more and more acute. Nevertheless his man Behra drove like a fiend to win the Grand Prix at Pau at the start of the season. The Press gave Gordini his due and even talked of whipping up a public subscription to help him to continue, but nothing came of it.

The Sorcerer continued to get a win here and there but the small struggling company really started to get into deep waters and in 1957, with a heavy heart, Gordini closed the doors of his workshop after putting the dust sheets on the diminutive blue single-seaters.

If anyone thought Amédée had given up, they were a long way off the mark, however. Within a few months he was working for Renault, who had summoned him to put strength and life into the Dauphine and, as we know, the Dauphine-Gordini was presented at the Paris Show in 1957 and was an instant success. That was the start of a long association with the Régie and, in particular, with Alpine, which scored so many successes at Le Mans and in other events. The name of Gordini was also associated with the Renault 8, 12 and 17 and, most recently, the special version of the Renault 5. Gordini died in Paris in 1979, at the age of 79, his mission in life accomplished.

7: Renault's truest trendsetter

The Renault 16 was 'something else', quite literally, because there was not another motorcar quite like it. It also marked the re-entry of Renault into the larger car field, from which they had been absent since production of the somewhat unlovable Frégate ceased in 1960. The determination of the compact, diminutive Dreyfus had resulted in the birth of a big compact car that would be seen over almost all the habitable earth within a few years and for many years to come. Everywhere, still, today, you can see Renault 16s. They are exactly the same shape as the first examples of 17 years ago, but they do not look in the least old-fashioned because they are distinctive.

Renault quite rightly said: 'The Renault 16 is a limousine in all the accepted senses of the term. First of all because it completely fulfils the final definition of this word, with its four doors and six side windows, and also even from the very first impression the vehicle looks spacious, designed for long-distance journeys and has simplicity, combined with an air of dignity.

Even before getting into the car we can see that the occupants of the rear seats have plenty of legroom well clear of the front seats. The external dimensions are, however, within the average figures for European cars in the 1,500 cc category, but the passenger compartment is very large and well lit, thanks to the three windows on either side and the sloping rear light.

The Renault 16 comes in three versions which differ by the body trim. The De Luxe model has a single bench seat at the front, the Grand Luxe models have two separate front seats and in the Grand Luxe (reclining) the squabs are moveable and can be lowered to the horizontal position to form travel beds.'

Dreyfus was utterly determined that the 16 was going to be a winner—that it was the perfect car to serve as flagship to the multi-model range essential to the new vigorous sales policy of the Régie. Accordingly the preproduction cars were not only thrashed mercilessly by works testers but their reports were studied carefully and as many as 250 detail modifications were made before production. In particular, the brakes were improved, with different linings and a different rating for the pressure limiter. Crown wheel and pinion teeth were modified for greater silence and the timing case was altered with the same object, whilst the scuttle was given a special sound-proof wall.

Dreyfus was taking no chances. Even after the production lines were in working order and a few hundred cars were coming off, he delayed the launch of the car and lent 400 of these early examples to staff and friends so that they could try them

Above *One of Renault's most advanced and trend-setting models —the versatile 16 TL.*

Right *Renault 16 driving compartment—modernistic but practical.*

under workaday conditions and report any hang-ups. (One wonders whether that was a cold winter in Paris, because when the cars reached the mass of buyers one of the complaints was that the heater was work-shy.)

The first car released for sale came off the lines at New Year 1965, only a couple of days before the Press launch at Juan-les-Pins. Truly was this another historic day for Renault. By the following spring they had sold 65,000 in France, 11,000 in Germany, 3,000 in Holland, 3,500 in Belgium and 2,500 in Sweden, Switzerland and the UK.

The engine had a family resemblance to the epic Quatre Chevaux and Sierra units, but was otherwise completely new and advanced, and of course the gearbox was new, and operated by what appeared to be an anachronism—a steering column shift. That gear shift, however, was an educated one, and proved to be one of the best of the many excellent features of the car. The seating was superb for a car in its price bracket (£888) and the big tail door and convertible rear seating were major selling features. The generator was an alternator, which in those days was found only on a few specialised cars. It conferred the benefit of a high charging rate at low engine speeds, and was more reliable than a dynamo. The heater and ventilation system was sophisticated and even if it did not please everybody at first, it was progressively improved.

As far as the engine was concerned, the Renault engineers elected to use an aluminium cylinder block in order to save weight. The wet-sleeve system, as used on the other Renault engines, lent itself to the use of an alloy block. With big production runs, the aluminium units would not be any more expensive than cast iron blocks because shorter foundry times would compensate for the greater expense of the material. The weight saved on the engine amounted to about 15 kg.

Features such as the alloy head, combustion chambers with sloping roofs, parallel sloping valves and, of course, the use of a five-bearing crankshaft, followed the tradition of the Sierra (Renault 8) engine. The camshaft, however, was pushed up as far as it would go without being an actual overhead camshaft, and it operated very short pushrods, so the inertia stresses were kept to the minimum possible without using overhead cams.

It was necessary to keep the length of the unit to the minimum and to this end, as on the R 8, the stroke was longer than the bore—the respective dimensions being 81 and 76 mm, giving a capacity of 1,470 cc. The fully sealed cooling system, as on the other models, was retained, but on the 16 it was supplemented by an electrically driven fan of thermostatic type, a feature which was to be adopted on other later models in the range.

The camshaft was in a channel at the top of the block and the tappet housings, which were mushroom shaped, were machined directly in the head. The camshaft had four journals in direct contact with the head. Only the front bearing, nearest to the water pump drive, was circular. The other three were open towards the top and their effective contact area was a little more than a semicircle. A double roller chain was used for the drive from the crankshaft to the camshaft, with a sprung tensioner pad.

A vertical shaft drove the oil pump and distributor. The oil pump housing was machined directly in the lower half of the block; it had a cylindrical shape as the pump rotors were eccentric.

Cooling water passages surrounded only the top half of the cast cylinder liners, which were a push fit in the block. The lower flange was sealed with a paper gasket

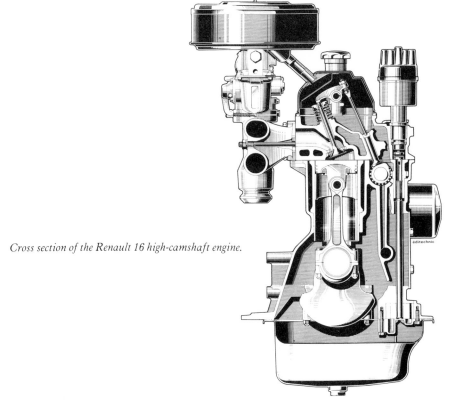

Cross section of the Renault 16 high-camshaft engine.

and the top with a Reinz-type gasket, so that as on the other Renault models it was a simple matter for a competent amateur or professional mechanic to renew liners and pistons. The engine was meant to take a thrashing if required; on bench tests of prototypes they were required to do 15 hours at 5,500 rpm on full load—the equivalent of 1,500 miles at 94 mph—also 100 hours at very low temperatures.

Dry weight of the engine was 203 lb, the power–weight ratio of the unit being 1.47 kg/hp, and that of the whole vehicle being 15.7 kg/hp. Piston speed at maximum engine speed was 15.4 m/s. Maximum power available at the clutch was 58.5 bhp (DIN) at 5,000 rpm and maximum torque 78.11 lb ft at 2,800 rpm, the mean effective pressure being 9.2 kg/cm^2.

It was, however, the shape of this new vehicle that was of such outstanding interest. To some it was ungainly, almost bizarre; to others, it simply seemed modernistic; to others again it had a strong appeal as an elegant, almost opulent grand tourer. It has to be remembered that at that time, whilst station wagons and estate cars were fairly common (and the Renault 4 came into that category), the type that is now known as the hatchback had not arrived. In fact, the Renault 16 was the first hatchback of the lift-up tailgate type.

The bonnet was of an interesting and entirely practical shape in that it gave great strength and very good sight lines for judging position, and the same applied to the rear of the body. The roof of the car was a great novelty. In cross section it had a lower face which was relatively flat and an upper face concave in form. In other words, the longitudinal member over the doors was higher than the door and not lower, as was more usual. This served to provide two strong stiffening members from screen to tailgate. It also served to infuriate people who wanted to fit conventional roof-racks.

The interior arrangements of the body allowed for seven variations in the use of the rear compartment, as follows:

1. Normal position, with five or even six people sitting comfortably, the rear seat being pushed back as far as possible. Incidentally, the rear floors had wells for the passengers' feet, under the front seats.

2. The 'holiday' position. By moving the rear seat and its squab on its locating links, it could be moved 6 in forward, thus increasing the depth of the goods compartment by 2 cu ft, the space for the rear passengers still being reasonable.

3. Position for carrying bulky goods. This was obtained by folding the rear seat cushion forwards then lifting the squab to a horizontal position where it could be secured with straps. This gave a cargo space of 26.5 cu ft.

4. Shooting brake position. This involved removing the rear seat and squab, also the rear window shelf.

Additional position on GL model:

5. Mother and child position—pushing rear seat forward and front passenger seat back so as to provide a 'capsule' for a child.

Additional positions on GL (reclining seat) model:

6. Rally position. When the car had only two occupants and the rear seat was in its normal position, the squab could be brought forward at about 45° and rested on the door armrests. If the passenger seat was then pushed back and the squab inclined, the occupant could rest in a half-lying position.

7. Travel bed position. With the front seats fully forward, the squabs could be lowered and would be at the same level as the rear seat, and not resting on it, as with most other recliners. This would give a flat double bed.

To ensure a body which was rigid, strong and moderate in weight, Renault engineers retained the principle of the chassis platform with deep side and cross members. This punt structure could be driven without the bodywork, although obviously it was not intended that this should be done.

The stiffness of the body sides themselves was exceptional because the outer panel of each side was pressed in one piece and fully lined by an inner wall panel forming a box section enclosed around its periphery.

The floor section consisted of two side members joined by three strong cross members, the first under the sloping toe-board, the second under the front seats and the third under the rear seats. This chassis was completed by two projecting members at the front and two at the rear. Thus the whole structure, whilst of integral, welded-up type, had a virtual chassis frame.

The front projecting members carrying the engine were tied by a front-end cross member, another under the engine and another removable one passing over the gearbox and supporting the steering gear. The rear projecting members were tied by a floor panel under the fuel tank and a cross member at their rear ends. The body was spot-welded to this chassis structure.

The body itself consisted, in its essentials, of the two double-skin sides, welded along their complete peripheries, both internal and external, and a roof spot-welded in position along the upper edges of the body sides. The shallow rear wings were formed by part of the single-piece body sides. The front wings were bolted in place and their inner panels welded both to the front chassis members and the scuttle, to add to the rigidity of the overall assembly.

Making the body sides from a single pressing extending from scuttle to rear bumpers undoubtedly presented difficulties from the press shop's point of view, but it also ensured that the door apertures were dimensionally accurate, whilst it simplified assembly operations. This simplification was aided by the peripheral weld line round the edges of the two panels, for the roof could be fixed by welding its raised edge to the raised joint line along the tops of the body sides.

The face-to-face seams formed by this method of construction were covered along the roof line by two chromium plated beads and inside the door apertures by the weatherproofing seal. This method of assembly meant that the members serving as the door cant rails were, in fact, box section in form and this gave added strength. The whole plan made for a very rigid assembly without any form of partitioning between the luggage compartment and the passenger space. This is what made it possible to fit a removable rear parcel shelf and to have the versatile seating arrangements. Renault were truly trendsetters with the R 16, other manufacturers following suit and the hatchback with removable parcel shelf and folding seating becoming as universal a format as the saloon or estate, as it still is today.

Renault went to great trouble to make the new car quiet as well as exceptionally comfortable. From my many tests of various models of the 16 through the years I can confirm that it has been one of the most successful of all cars in most respects and particularly on account of its smoothness and quietness. It was understandable that when it went out of production recently there should have been such a wave of regret, despite the introduction of admirable replacements in the form of the 18 and 20.

The suspension was, like that of the Renault 4, based on simple, strong torsion bars, although those at the rear were also enclosed in steel tubes. The suspension travel was considerable (300 mm or 11.8 inches at the rear and 200 mm or 7.8 inches at the front) and the oscillation period approached one cycle per second when the car was loaded, which was exceptional for any European design.

Renault, at the time, stated: 'The use of radially braced cord tyres was kept in mind when the whole design was started. The special qualities of this type of tyre are well known, but they are often suspected of setting up noisy vibrations, particularly at slow speed over rough road surfaces.' Certainly raidals, and particularly steel radials, are noisy and some Renaults make more road noise than others but the R 16 was always quieter than most.

The steering of the new car was, of course, of rack-and-pinion type, as on every post-war Renault. It is interesting to reflect that since Lefaucheux's day, the firm has been ahead of the game in some way or another, eg, independent springing, rack-and-pinion steering, sealed cooling, alternators, front-wheel drive, etc. Louis Renault was never really ahead of the game, after his illustrious direct drive, although the firm occasionally introduced oddities and bits of moderately advanced engineering.

The rack and pinion did not this time have the famous return spring, which was a crude device for overcoming inherently heavy steering on the rear-engined cars which should have had the most naturally light steering imaginable. As to the 16, Renault explained the absence of a self-centring spring in the following terms, almost as though they were apologising: 'But on a front-wheel-drive vehicle, the suspension angles of which include a caster angle of 2–4° and a kingpin inclination of 30°, the wheels automatically assure their own caster action.'

The steering column had a universal joint at the scuttle enabling the wheel to be placed parallel to the centre line of the vehicle and directly in front of the driver. Despite the relatively long wheelbase, the turning circle was still reasonable at 32.8

Like many another Renault, the 16 was a favourite with celebrities. Lulu poses with Wyn Calvin, broadcaster-owner of the car.

ft. This was due to the double universal-joint arrangement at each wheel, which could turn an angle of almost 45° assisted by the slight backwards angle of the transmission shafts, permitting a very large lock angle to be obtained at the inner wheel. Incidentally, as on the Renault 4, the wheelbase was a couple of inches more on one side than the other because of the use of transverse torsion bars one in front of the other linking the suspension arms.

The use of the alternator was, as I have already implied, a trendsetter; hardly anybody uses anything else these days. Renault were astute enough to copy the commercial vehicle boys in this respect. An alternator is simpler than a dynamo because it does not have a composite segment commutator but just steel slip rings on which the carbon brushes run. It can run at high speed safely, in this case twice engine speed, yet charge at a little above idling.

A great deal of midnight oil had been spent over the planning of the heating and ventilation system of the 16. Instead of using the usual concentration of hot air, the Renault system utilised large volumes of warm air which were fed via a built-in radiator (actually a simple tube with masses of fins) occupying almost the entire width of the scuttle. In order to keep large volumes of air in circulation, the body had slots round the edges of the tailgate frame which extracted air by taking advantage of the low-pressure area in the slipstream of the car. There were also adjustable vents at each end of the fascia. It was all very sophisticated, but the average British motorist quite frankly likes a good blast of hot air and not so many owners appreciated the low-pressure large-volume system of the 16. The people at the Acton factory—always sensitive, always loyal to the point of obstinacy—refused to accept that the system could be faulted but somehow over the years it seemed to get better.

In fact, in 1967, the Régie itself commented, with naive reluctance: 'After a few months of operation it appeared that all the potential embodied in the initial arrangement was not being entirely exploited from the very start and this is why the 1967 model of the Renault 16 has been equipped with a heating and ventilation system which operates on the same principle but is considerably improved in performance.'

Expanding on the theme with growing enthusiasm, they added: 'Physiological studies which have been carried out in external temperatures of between 30° and 35° have shown that ventilation by means of a large flow low-speed air stream passing over the entire upper part of the body provides considerable improvement in comfort when compared with the former automobile practice of a concentrated high velocity draught . . .. This violent draught cannot be tolerated for a long period and the local cooling of the body which results cannot be good from the medical point of view. Contrary to this, the air flow that the flaps on the distributor grille permit a person to direct towards his head continually dissipates the excess calories produced by the human heat mechanism and diminishes the impression of being in a steam bath and also the effect of perspiration along the contact area with the seat.'

So the Renault 16 was a success; the Régie at last had a big car which was not a white elephant as the 45 or the Frégate had been. By 1971, as many as 800,000 would have been sold. It is human nature never to be quite satisfied, however. A man gets a nice new little house on an estate; he soon wants the detached four-bedroom town house on the 'exclusive development'. He buys a little motorised dinghy but soon has his eye on a smart blue cabin cruiser with chrome fittings. His wife is 'satisified' with the twin-tub but wants an automatic washing machine when they can afford it. The kids want bigger bicycles, but of course they have an excuse—they are growing out of the old ones. The man and his wife are not growing out of anything (except perhaps careless rapture) but they have a normal healthy desire to be something better and get something better.

It appeared that many people, who might or might not already have a Renault 16 and who might love it very much, wanted something better—in this case *even* better, for nobody anywhere or at any time was suggesting that the Renault 16 TL was not an admirable, lovable, reliable and economical machine. 'Here is a chance' said Dreyfus, 'masses of these people seem to want to go over the top a bit. Let's come up with a super version of the same car. I'm prepared to bet it'll sell like hot cakes. Make it more powerful. Make it go faster, but still do its eight litres to 100 kilometres.'

Thus was born the Renault 16 TS in March 1968. The new car had all the acknowledged charms of the 16, plus over 35 per cent more power and a maximum speed of over the magic 'ton'—at a time, of course, when there was no speed limit on motorways. The 16 TS had a new 1,565 cc engine and, to match the performance, powerful progressive brakes with servo assistance.

It was, of course, pure coincidence that the introduction of the new car came at a time when seething, corrosive and finally explosive industrial unrest sent French industry, and the automotive industry in particular, reeling from one body blow after another. The workers of the Régie were not interested in any particular model. They just made motorcars and took the money for their sweat and toil and whatever motorcars they themselves had at the time—probably 4 CVs or Dauphines if not a battered Peugeot or Citroën—had no relation to industrial politics.

Neither had Dreyfus planned a new franc-, dollar- and pound-earning new model as a weapon to fight the inevitable losses of revenue. The 16 TS was simply a part of the new policy of widening the Renault range, and reflected the classic comment of Yves Georges, Director of Research and Development—'Look upon me as a kind of grocer with a range of goods from which you can select the product that suits you'.

It was in the Renault factories that the signal was, in effect, given for a general strike that gave the French economy a rain of karate punches. 'If Renault sneezes, France catches a cold', it has been said with some foundation. The resultant turmoil hit Renault as hard as anybody—probably harder—but the excellent new products and the cool but steely direction of Dreyfus saved the day and the years for the Régie. But for the strikes, 1968 might have been a record year for Renault. As it was, they were lucky to improve on the previous year's production.

In 1967, production had been 775,000 vehicles against 740,000 in 1966. Of these, 700,000 were cars, the rest being commercials. The R 4 was the best-selling French car in all markets, whilst the R 16 confirmed its position among medium-priced cars, taking 18 per cent of the domestic market. Half the production was exported, mostly to EEC and EFTA countries, and Renaults sold particularly well in Germany, and not at all badly in the UK.

Amazingly, production in this strike-ridden year of 1968 turned out to be 807,000, plus Saviem's 30,000. Renault went ahead, hand-in-hand with Peugeot, as I have already described.

The 16 TS (Tourisme Spéciale) with its up-rated engine, was a honey. Because of its increased power—87.5 bhp at 5,750 rpm—the front disc brakes were increased to 10 inch diameter and a 6 inch servo was fitted. Larger radial tyres (155 × 14) were specified, to give the safest possible handling at the higher cornering speeds likely to be used, as well as to aid the braking performance.

The interior of the car was the subject of improvements, including a snazzy new fascia, incorporating a newly-designed panel of instruments set in circular dials, with a console of tumbler switches. Other features of the TS included a tachometer, scaled temperature gauge, trip recorder, two-speed screen wipers, reading lamp for the front seat passenger, steering wheel with rim and spokes covered in foam-padded leathercloth, and extra loud twin-tone horns. The seats, even better than the splendid GL seats, were covered in best quality bronze grained leathercloth, to

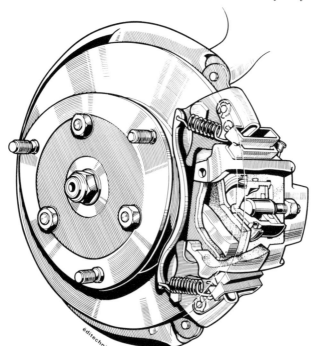

Disc front brake of the R 16.

match the general interior finish. An electrically heated rear window set a precedent for all Renaults of a later date.

As far as the exterior was concerned, there was no difference between the TS and the GL apart from TS motifs on wings and rear door. The car was offered in a choice of three special metallic finishes—blue, green and bronze, with trim in bronze leathercloth in all cases. As Renault quite rightly said: 'All this adds up to a luxuriously-appointed grand touring car having the ability to cover long distances safely, rapidly and effortlessly'. They had said it before and they will doubtless say it again, and mean it.

Renault were at some pains to emphasise that the TS was not a 'souped up' version of the 16. To this end they published a detailed treatise on their philosophy of obtaining extra power. In effect they were disclaiming any idea of power without responsibility.

Renault pointed out that there are three basic methods which can be used to increase engine power, ie, increasing the engine efficiency by raising the compression ratio; increasing the engine speed and thus performing a greater amount of work for a given unit of time; increasing the gas charge entering the cylinder during each cycle.

Increasing the compression ratio.

Everything else being equal, an increase in compression ratio automatically increases the power. The advantage gained by this method becomes smaller as the ratio rises. There is a tendency to pinking and detonation and this must be compensated by using fuel of a higher octane rating and, within certain limits, changing the shape of the chamber.

In the case of the Renault 16 TS the compression ratio has been retained at 8.6:1— the same as the 16 GL—because importance has been attached to the possibility of using the car with low octane fuel in certain markets.

Because the engine breathing has been improved, however, there is an effective slight increase in the compression ratio and for this reason the shape of the combustion chamber has been improved, to induce turbulence and counteract detonation.

Increasing the engine speed.

This obviously means increasing the speed at which maximum power is developed. We know that the power increases in proportion to the speed up to a certain point, when the increase suddenly ceases. This is because the cylinders are no longer being fully charged because the engine cannot breathe effectively at this speed. One way of increasing the speed at which maximum power is produced is, therefore, to improve engine breathing, as has been done on the 16 TS.

Another factor which limits the speed is the inertia of the various moving components. This is proportional not only to the mass, but to the square of their angular and linear velocities. The 16 TS engine produces its maximum power at 5,750 rpm whilst the 16 produces it at 5,000 rpm.

Increasing the intake charge.

Increasing the capacity of the engine seems the simplest and most obvious method. If nothing else is modified, the power increase is mainly noticeable in the slow and middle speed ranges because at high speeds the components through which the gas mixture passes become incapable of accommodating the increased flow. Increasing the capacity therefore gives a more flexible engine with higher torque at low speeds. Also, an increase in bore or stroke automatically increases the weight of the moving parts, and, in the case of the stroke, the acceleration to which these parts are subjected.

In the 16 TS, both bore and stroke were increased. There was never any question of increasing the overall dimensions of the existing block so the cylinder liners had to be machined on the outside as well as the inside to permit adequate water circulation between them, now that they were closer together. A second benefit from this machining operation was a more uniform liner thickness, thus distributing the thermal strains more evenly along the length of the barrel.

Improved engine breathing.

The parts that have a direct influence on this are the air filter, the pipe connecting it to the carburettor, the carburettor itself, the inlet manifold, the ducting in the cylinder head, and the valves. Of all those, only the ducts and valves are fundamental engine parts.

To increase valve size and cross-section area of inlet and exhaust ducting meant using inclined valves, with the angles of inclination converging. One side of the head accommodates the inlet ducting and the other side the exhaust ducting, producing a combustion chamber approximately hemispherical, but asymetrically shaped to promote turbulence, thus cooling the spark plug and burning the charge more evenly.

On the 16 TS unit, the time during which the valves remain open has been slightly increased compared with that on the 16. This improves high-speed engine breathing but a power loss at low speeds is compensated by the higher capacity.

The problem of resonance in the air filter hose—a long one—was solved by a resonance cavity in the filter body. The carburettor fitted to the TS had to be equipped with a much greater intake cross-sectional area than on the 16 but it took the form of a two-barrelled instrument with differential throttles.

So much for measures to increase power. There was also the matter of measures to reduce *power loss*. The exhaust manifold and silencer were the two largest sources of parasite power absorption, but it is impossible to do without them. Furthermore, the power they absorb increases, with an increase in engine power, out of all proportion. For example, the exhaust system fitted to the 16 absorbed approximately 5 hp when its engine was developing maximum power, but if it were fitted without any modification in the engine of the 16 TS it would absorb 13–14 hp. The exhaust system was accordingly completely redesigned, with the assistance of Peugeot engineers, and absorbed only 4.5 hp.

There remained the matter of taking measures to resist the increased loads imposed by the power increase. Although there was no increase in crankshaft bearing areas (this would have added to the power losses) measures were taken to assist the shaft and its bearings to resist the loads. They were coated with an alloy of 80 per cent aluminium and 20 per cent tin, which can take very high loads but has certain drawbacks. It has a much lower tolerance to dirt than many other materials and assembly must be carried out under conditions of absolute cleanliness and the oil must be particularly well filtered. It is intolerant to finish defects on the bearing areas and this involves superlapping the bearing areas after grinding. The bearing area on the shaft must also be hardened. Induction hardening is used for this purpose.

Pistons with a more rigid skirt and a reduced clearance between piston and cylinder, on the section above the upper ring, were fitted. It was also barrel machined from the bottom of the skirt up to the top of the area in which the grooves are machined. The effect of these modifications was to make heat transfer from the piston to the liner more effective, to reduce the gas flow onto the rings and prevent ring grooves spreading and the firing ring breaking.

To improve the operating life of the firing ring and reduce the inertia of the ring assembly, the thickness of the former was reduced from 2 to 1.75 mm. The use of a narrow ring also tends to scrape off any oil deposit on the cylinder walls and assist in reducing oil consumption. The piston rings used in the 16 TS were lapped so that they had a convex outer surface. To reduce oil consumption at high speeds the steel oil scraper ring was replaced by a cast iron one held in tension by a coil spring.

The load to which the cylinder block was subjected had been increased, so it was stiffened at various points such as the cylinder head attachment bolts and the starter mounting points. The slight increase in the weight of the valves and the increase in engine speed involved fitting double valve springs and chilled cast iron tappets in place of the former steel tappets, to resist the force of the springs.

One could certainly feel the difference in power of the new car at once, and the performance was sharpened considerably, compared with the 16 with its 'little' 1,470 engine. Personally I felt that the TS was very slightly harsh compared with the GL, but there is usually some small penalty with increased performance unless it is obtained by fitting a 'big softy' engine, in other words a technically low-efficiency unit but of large capacity—the sort of thing the Americans excel in. But in any case, everybody in the great Renault 'family' appreciated the little extras in the specification and the general air of luxury about the new car—not that the GL in any way lost its entitlement to the Grand Luxe tag.

It is worth divagating here, perhaps, to comment on this business of the 'Renault family'. The marque has always had a following which has amounted almost to a cult, although, as with all marques which proliferate enormously, this tends to diminish in inverse ratio to production figures. For three decades or more there has been a vigorous Renault Owners' Club which has fostered an already burgeoning enthusiasm among owners of all classes, and Renault UK for many years gave their support to the annual family event known as Rallye Renault where fellow enthusiasts and their families could meet and take part in *concours* and sporting events. There were, however, millions of less gregarious, less extrovert owners who expressed their enthusiasm simply among a group of friends and/or fellow owners and many of whom wrote letters of lavish praise for the marque to the motoring Press or to *Autoworld*, the bi-monthly glossy magazine for Renault owners, then published by PSL Publications Ltd, and which I edited for ten years. Many of the countless letters I received were almost embarrassing in their praise for the various models, but particularly the 16s.

An important and newsworthy debutante at the Geneva Motor Show in March 1969 was the Renault 16 TA, a version of the 16 with a completely new automatic transmission. It was everything that the Frégate Transfluide of 1960 should have been and wasn't.

The new system, which had an entirely original electronic control unit, was designed and produced by the Régie's research and design department and was the model for all the Renault automatics used today. It was for specific use on the 16 TA (Transmission Automatique) only and was not at that time fitted to any other model.

The 16 TA had the same general specification as the GL or TS and used the 1,565 cc engine but with the basic parallel valving. In other words it was an up-rated 1,470 or a detuned 1,565, whichever way you cared to look at it. There is always some power loss with automatics, so the extra capacity made up for this. With this 71 bhp engine, the performance came out at about the same as the standard 16 with four-speed manual box.

The three-speed auto box followed the conventional clutchless hydraulic torque converter coupling and epicyclic gearbox formula. Its novelty lay in the use of an electronic computer to decide which gear was needed for any set of conditions. The small 'black box' computer acted on static data supplied by the position of the gear shift, and variable data supplied by road speed and engine loading. There was a tiny alternator driven off the speedometer worm, engine speed varying its voltage output. It operated two solenoid valves, and upward or downward gear selection was then effected through the torque converter.

The gear lever was originally column-mounted and had six positions—marked 1, 2, A, N, R and P. Placed in 1 or 2, held the box in those speeds, whilst in A the automatic was in full control. N was for neutral, R for reverse and P for park, which was conventional. The ratios of the three speeds were 2.4:1 for first, 1.48:1 for second and 1.03:1 for top, compared with 3.65:1, 2.25:1, 1.48:1 and 1.03:1 on the manual 16 GL. Final drive ratio was 3.77:1.

The new transmission was contained together with the differential in a pressure

The TS version took the 16 into a higher performance bracket.

diecast aluminium alloy housing holding 10½ pints of oil (for special specification) compared with three pints in the 16 gearbox.

Other special features on the 16 TA included an electrically-heated rear window, dipping rear-view mirror and foam floor-padding front and rear. Kerb weight of the car was 110 lb heavier than the standard 16, at 2,271 lb compared with 2,161 lb, but the bigger engine made up for this.

The car came to the UK a year later, but it was not until early 1972 that I got my hands on one for a proper road test. What I call a proper road test is a week with a car—to do what I like with it. Even that is not long enough to judge a car fairly, but it is as much as most road testers get. For what it is worth, anyway, I quote my own words, which appeared in *Autoworld* under the title 'Who Needs a Left Foot?'

'Regular readers of this journal will be aware that I am almost morbidly interested in the matter of whether a motorcar is or is not easy to park on a dime or to wiggle its way through the dog's leg of a chicane in my bungaloid driveway. This obsession is bound to be beneficial to others, because sooner or later, even for a man who lived in the middle of Salisbury Plain or Thetford Heath, there would come a time to slot a car into a kerchief-sized space, or extract it therefrom.

In summer, with the Renault 16 TS Automatic, there would be no problem about this. The car has a good lock, a smooth throttle action and first-class see-out and the steering, if not finger-light, requires less effort than many we know.

In temperatures below about 5°C, however, there appears to be a marked change, and since I like to get adverse criticisms off my chest early on, and not hide them somewhere in the back end of a road test report, I may as well say that sometimes I had a bit of a time with this admirable car in the purlieus of my modest abode, on frosty mornings.

Most automatics tend to creep under those conditions, until warmed up after a mile or two and the Renault, although a better automatic than many, seemed to suffer just as much as most from torque-converter drag. The effect is that as soon as you get into R, 1, 2 or D from neutral, the car either jumps backwards or forward or, if you have the brake on, stalls. What you have to learn to do, with automatics, is to drive on the brake for the first few yards—or it could be further if the car needs a lot of choke.

In the case of the particular car I tried—a very new one, which possibly had not settled down yet, in the manner of many Renaults—a good deal of choke was needed, which meant that it ran fast, so that the "surge or stall" syndrome was aggravated. You cannot use an umbrella-handle handbrake for driving on the brake and neither can you use footbrake and accelerator with the same foot, so the only answer is left-foot braking, which comes naturally to Americans, but to few Britons. If the car I tried was typical, I think one would have to cultivate this technique for cold starts at any rate, but some drivers in this country are in any case beginning to emulate their transatlantic brothers and sisters.

Let it be clearly understood that I am being deliberately super-critical on this matter, because existing and potential Renault owners tend to expect something so good that it cannot be faulted in the most minor degree, so I am saying there is something about this form of transmission that might seem less than perfect to people who park in confined spaces and make lots of short journeys every day.

I am going to come right out and say that the eternal squeaky brakes annoyed me too. Now, I know that this can be cured, but I do not see why the design should not have been improved on by now, so I will join with doubtless numerous owners in making an impassioned appeal to Paris to do something about it, just as they must do something more about that handbrake, because now that it has been lengthened, I remove skin from my knuckles. This is an example of how an improvement can have side effects.

Now I can get on and say with great sincerity that this is a fantastic car for what is a very small sum of money for fantastic cars, when you come to think of it. [NB: £1,600 at that time.]

For the benefit of those who are not familiar with the Renault range, I should point out that automatic transmission is an optional extra on both the 16 TL and 16 TS . . .. [NB: This option was introduced soon after the introduction of the TA, which ceased to be a model in its own right.]

There is no doubt that the transmission does its job extremely well. It is uncannily smooth in operation, so much so that it is almost impossible to tell when it changes gear under normal conditions of driving, either upwards or downwards. Apart from the exceptional cold morning conditions I have mentioned, the take-off from rest is always as smooth as silk and there is no trace of creep in "drive" once warmed up, provided that throttle and choke are initially properly set.

The kick-down worked very well. In case the reader is not familiar with this provision, I should say that on automatic transmissions there is a means of obtaining extra acceleration in emergencies by pushing the accelerator pedal down hard and quickly so as to over-ride the normal brisk but not violent acceleration. My only reservation is that I would prefer the kick-down to be operative in the higher speed ranges; on the car tested it did not apply much above an indicated 40 mph but would be very useful at up to 50 or 55.

In effect, of course, the transmission can be used as a manual three-speed box which is sometimes more useful than the kick-down. The fascia indicator is not ideal—a small slot of a window, with figures which are not really large enough—but one soon learns to use the column lever as much by feel as by sight, so that it is possible to start off in 1, move quickly to 2, then up to D, which is top gear automatic. The surprising thing—or perhaps not all that surprising to those familiar with the TS in manual form—is that the second gear ratio of 5.6 will take the car up to the legal maximum, without stress. It is about the same ratio as third gear on the manual car, of course.

I believe the early production cars in France had a system whereby the engine could be started by pressing the gear shift lever in P (parked, or locked wheels) position, and I can see the point of such a thing, because if you get a tick-over stall, as sometimes happens with automatics, you would just waggle the lever. As it is, you have to come out of gear, select N or P, then restart with a double movement of the ignition key, then select D again, which all takes time.

Acceleration is very good for an automatic, but not quite as dramatic as on the manual cars. My 0–50 figure at 10 seconds is probably 1½ seconds slower than for the three-pedal TS, and 0–60, at 14.2 seconds, is maybe two seconds slower. Where you lose time is on the take-off, which is so mild that wheelspin is practically impossible. This, I think, may be a marked advantage especially on wet roads, for wheelspin is rather easily provoked with the manual car when in a hurry, which may mean loss of lateral adhesion. With the automatic, it is almost impossible to "lose it" even with full throttle and the wheels locked hard over.

Rolling acceleration is excellent, however, and becomes outstanding in the higher speed ranges. One of the prominent motoring magazines gave 5.2 seconds as the 30–

Extra luxury as well as performance characterised the 16 TX.

50 figure for the 16 TS automatic, compared with 10.1 seconds for the manual. My own efforts gave 6.4 seconds—as always the average of several attempts in opposite directions, to cancel out the effects of gradient and windage. I was so interested in this rolling acceleration that I took figures for 20-50, 40-60 and 50-70 mph too, and these respectively came out at 8 seconds, 7.2 seconds and 10.1 seconds. I tried all figures in 2 as well as in D but there was very little difference. This implies that there is not much point in using manual gears except in a kick-down above 45 mph, when a slight advantage can be gained.

As regards maximum speed, Renault claim 97 mph as against 100 mph for the manual TS. Certainly these automatics will do an indicated 100–105 mph, so I would think that allowing for the common speedometer error, 97 mph is about right, and at speeds like that the car is still comparatively quiet and restful.'

It will be noted that I was comparatively harsh in my criticism of the car. It was the policy of the British company at that time to allow me to be honest in my road test reports; later this attitude hardened and I considered myself lucky to be testing Renaults, because there was very seldom any need to make adverse criticisms, compared with other cars which I was testing for a different magazine. It is true, however, that most road test reports in marque magazines are of dubious value, as they are usually in the category of promotional material.

The 16 reached the summit of sophistication with the TX version, introduced in 1973 and of which the British company, who launched it in April 1974, said: 'Designated the Renault 16 TX, this new model offers an outstanding degree of comfort and equipment and the performance of a 2-litre from an engine of 1,647 cc'.

To get the extra capacity, the engine had been linered out to 79 mm bore, in the familiar way. It now gave 93 bhp at 6,000 rpm with a maximum torque of 93 lb ft at 4,000 rpm, and was teamed with a five-speed box giving excellent economy and a long motorway stride. At the legal UK limit the motor was lazily turning at a mere 3,200 rpm but the car had a top speed of 106 mph, with an engine speed of 5,500 rpm.

The main exterior distinguishing features of the TX were the four iodine head-lights, special sports wheels, wheelarch embellishers, an aerodynamic spoiler above the rear window, and a rear wipe/wash. The standard specification, even more comprehensive than that of the 16 TS, included electric front windows, tinted glass, electromagnetic locking, laminated screen and even better seats.

Nicely chosen gear ratios gave the creditable acceleration figure of 12 seconds for 0–60 mph and at a steady speed of 70 mph the car would do 35 miles on a gallon of fuel.

The power of the 1,647 engine, pulling a higher final drive ratio, allowed the excellent fuel economy characteristics of the 16 TX to be maintained in the automatic version, which gave 32.5 mpg at a steady 65 mph compared with 31.4 for the Renault 16 TS manual.

8: The widening Renault range

Three score years and ten, far from marking the 'evening of life' for Renault, seemed to be a kind of rebirth and the Régie celebrated it in 1968 with a pageant of Renault history on wheels—predictably and naturally enough down the Champs Elysées. The quiet, rather studious Dreyfus was no razzmatazz man himself, but he knew the value of trumpet blowing and, anyway, Renault had something to blow about. So all the stops were pulled out for this bit of nostalgia, and half of Paris seemed to cheer the motorcade along. The parade was led, of course, by the 1898 voiturette, whilst the stars of the more modern models were the new Renault 16 TS, 8 S and 6.

In the same year, the Régie introduced the Renault 16 TS, as we have seen, whilst at the lower end of the range, the R 6 was brought in to take the place of the R 8, soon to be phased out. Its world première was at the Paris Motor Show on October 3, but it did not reach the UK market until mid-1969.

With reasonable justification, people were calling it the 'little 16'. It had the same six-window five-door fastback body style as the larger car. The design formula was very similar, with platform chassis, front wheel drive and four-cylinder wet-liner ohv motor with sealed cooling.

Although later to become an 1100, the car was for three years an 850, the engine being a development of the Dauphine–Gordini unit but differing in the use of a single chain to drive the camshaft, different rocker arms and stronger valve springs. (It seems to me that timing chains, possibly rockers and certainly valves and springs were often the subject of trouble, or at any rate premature deterioration, on 750/850 engines but neither the Régie nor Acton were ever prepared to admit it.)

With a compression ratio of 8:1 and a single Solex carburettor type 32 PDIS 3, with manual choke, the new unit put out 38 bhp at 5,000 rpm compared with the 30 bhp of the R 4.

Personally I always felt that the R 6 was a grown-up R 4 rather than a junior 16, but at the introduction of the car, when I put this view to Renault executives, they sulked a little.

In the late summer of '68 I had the good fortune to try an early example of the car in the Camargue—that beloved and now a little spoiled region famed for its rice-fields, flamingoes, white horses, gipsies, bullfights and, of course, Manitas de Plata, the flamboyant guitarist. As a matter of fact, in the course of this Press event we were entertained by members of Manitas's family, including miniscule gipsy toddlers who stamped their heels and twirled their skirts as to the manner born. We

Above *The original R 6, as presented to the Press in Provence.*

Below *The 850 cc Renault 6 engine.*

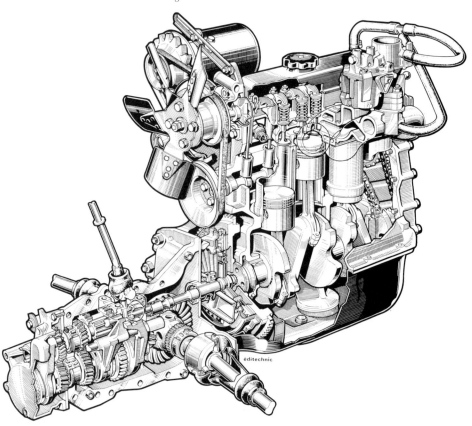

also attended one of those fascinating cow fights, at Les Stes Maries de la Mer—celebrating the birthday of a national newspaper man by pushing him into the ring where he acquitted himself well but went extremely white.

The following are extracts from my subsequent road test report: 'It is clearly no empty boast on the part of Renault that they have set new standards of safety with this lovable small, yet not so small, car. I was particularly impressed by the excellent visibility, the great comfort and the logical placing of all controls, handles, switches, etc. There is a general feeling of restfulness about the car, aided in a large measure by the generous sound-proofing. All these add up to safety as well as convenience and there are the many additional preventive safety features. . ..

It is true that I more than once found myself comparing the Renault 6 with the 4s that I have owned and with my new Renault 8 . . . but the 6 is a model in its own right with more of its elder sister, the 16, about it. Certainly the 6 has brisker acceleration than the baby of the range and I was particularly impressed by the third-gear punch. We checked acceleration up to a speedometer 70 kph several times with a stopwatch from standing start and the average result worked out at as near 15 seconds for 0–50 mph as makes no difference. Renault themselves give the acceleration figures in relation to distance, not time, eg, 400 metres (437 yards) in 23 seconds—and I see no reason to dispute them.

What is certain is that no matter how hard you push this engine—even to the point of valve bounce—it never feels stressed. The SAE maximum bhp figure of 38 comes in at 5,000 but valve bounce is well above that speed. The motor is uncannily quiet, not simply because of good basic design and generous insulation but because of the chain driven camshaft and effective exhaust system.

The roads in the Hérault region are often narrow, tortuous and rock-girt, with the strong possibility of mad dogs, haycarts and *camionettes* round every or any bend and I was delighted with the brilliant controlability of the sophisticated 6, which kept us out of trouble even deep in the bowels of the fantastic Cirque de Navacelles where we lost our way in this king-size devil's punchbowl and finished up in a farmyard . . ..

Steering is light—lighter, perhaps, than on the 16 and a shade heavier than on the Renault 1100 at low speeds. The new car does not have any centralising spring on the rack, and in this respect follows the design of the 16. There is not too much of a roll factor, although you have to be ready for a change of attitudes on sharp bends or gradual ones taken really fast. Braking is superb—and we needed it more than once for thought-provoking circumstances. . ..

The Renault 6 has the type of gearbox and gear-shift used on the 4 for more than a year, and already well proven, but I am still not sold on it. Admittedly I have never used this box for more than a few days at a time, even on 4s, and I am prepared to be convinced that one could come to love it. For me, however, there always seems an element of uncertainty on the downshifts if I am in a hurry, although one can soon become familiar with the 'laissez-faire' technique for up-shifts. But then again, I know that Renault boxes and shifts tend to improve and become more free with age. Certainly the diaphragm-spring clutch is smooth and light, and the action is assisted by the ball-bearing thrust which I regard as an important feature.

Petrol consumption worked out at 40.3 mpg for the whole of our trip and in case lean and frugal fanatics of 4, 8 and 10 consider this extravagant, let it be clearly understood that this was no turnpike tour.'

The Renault 6 came out at a time when vehicle safety—or lack of safety—had come into an almost dazzling limelight, partly because of steeply rising accident figures and partly on account of the (some say) hysterical accusations, condemnations and demands of Ralph Nader, the American consumer protectionist. It is therefore understandable that Renault should make much of the safety qualities of the new car and they were to a large extent justified in so doing because they really had gone to a great deal of trouble to maximise passive security—that is, safety concerned with factors disassociated from the driver's actions. For example, on any car the steering and braking are very much under the control of the driver, whether they are by nature good or bad, but the position and shape of steering wheel or brake pedal are established and unalterable and can be safe or unsafe.

Renault, in their press material for the new car, actually spotlighted a changing attitude which altered the course of automotive design and indeed motorists' thinking, thenceforth. They put the proposition in the following terms:

'Public opinion experts the world over agree that on the whole, European cars have excellent active safety qualities. European clientele have, in fact, always been very interested, even passionately interested, in the solution of road holding problems, braking, manoeuvrability, visibility. This is not surprising if one looks at the configuration of the European network and the density of its traffic.

But this does not necessarily signify that Europe neglected the problems of passive security. The fact is simply that the European and Latin clientele in particular found it repugnant to even consider the possibility of an accident and that, consequently, passive security qualities could not be discussed in manufacturers' publicity, as enquiries proved that these would have constituted a negative rather than a positive argument.

Now the situation has changed and many European motorists are now convinced that whatever are their personal qualities as drivers and the active safety quality of their vehicle, they are still liable to have an accident and, consequently, they want to know what measures have been taken by the manufacturer to limit the consequences.'

They somewhat plaintively added: 'Unfortunately, this publicity effort has not yet gone far enough and has not succeeded in convincing the majority of European drivers of the primordial necessity of using safety belts'. (Although seat belts had become compulsory on new vehicles, there was no obligation to use them.)

In the areas of active security, or what other designers often call primary safety, Renault said that the 6 benefited from all the experiences accumulated with previous models and notably the 16. As in the case of the 16, studies were carried out in two distinct but equally important spheres—the comfort and well-being of the driver and the manoeuvrability and 'docility' of the vehicle.

Well-being of the driver depended on seating quality, visibility, 'abundant and silent ventilation' and 'well-dispersed heating without hot blasts'. Noise, a considerable contributory element both to the driver's and passengers' fatigue, had been the subject of particular study. 'Finally', they stated, 'the type of suspension comfort is that resulting from the use of long torsion bars allowing large vertical movement, and the example of the Renault 16 and the Renault 4 make any further commentary on this subject unnecessary'.

In the areas of manoeuvrability and responsiveness, they stated, the Renault 6 had been the object of special studies which had resulted in the adoption of very direct steering which, combined with the road holding and steering qualities of radial

General format of the R 6 engine-gearbox unit was similar to that of the R 4.

corded tyres and very supple suspension, and the braking qualities resulting from the compensator for load on the rear wheels, 'ensured the vehicle's road holding and response to the driver's command—in a word, a safety margin in all circumstances very much above average'.

As far as passive security (secondary safety) is concerned, efforts were successfully made, as in all subsequent Renaults, to avoid any protruding elements on the bodywork which could cause serious injury or could hook on to the clothing of anyone hit by the car. This is why the bumper ends were turned inwards and rounded. This kind of attention was quite significant and historic, really; one has only to think of the bumpers and wings of early cars to call to mind Boadicea's chariot with its scimitar-hubbed wheels . . .'

Interior passive security was given new attention. The steering wheel was plastic strengthened with metal, not metal decorated with plastic. Extensive tests ensured that if hit by the driver's chest, it could not cause serious injury. The boss was surrounded by a thick block of polyurethane foam.

All switches were recessed or made of a substance which would give, in the event of impact. For example, the handle of the heating regulator vent, under the fascia, was made of a long strip of plastic which under a weak impact would break and not injure the driver's lower limbs. The ignition switch was 'embedded' in the polypropylene box surrounding the steering column.

The fascia itself was made of polypropylene, that wonder material so tough that hinges can be made from strips which will bend a million times or more. It is shatterproof and flexible enough to take great impact without injury. The interior door handles, of plastic strengthened with metal, were recessed into the doors and the window winding handles were of supple but tough plastic. The backs of the

Fascia treatment of the Renault 6 was ahead of its time.

front seats were completely padded so as to avoid injury to rear passengers thrown forward in the event of a shunt.

One thing that I personally never considered a safety feature was the umbrella-handle-type handbrake tucked under the fascia to the left of the steering wheel. I think all umbrella-handle handbrakes are an abomination and, except on the R 4, Renault gave them up after many years of protest by owners. Nevertheless this was at the expense of the centre armrest, thus creating more protests!

The 'very direct steering', which I mentioned earlier, had a reduction ratio of 17 to 1, this corresponding with 3¼ turns of the steering wheel from stop to stop, permitting the inner road wheel to turn through more than 36°. The castor angle on the front wheels was 13°, and the famous centralising spring of the R 4 was no longer needed.

As has been the case with the R 16, there was soon a clamour for more power. motor manufacturers have always been suckers for this kind of thing—it is part of their stock in trade anyway; if there is a demand and it can be met without too much risk, it makes commercial sense to meet it. Renault did this very easily in the case of the 6 by dropping in the 1,100 cc unit—the 48 bhp Sierra. In 1970, daily production rate of the 850 and 1100 Renault 6 was 900 and by 1971 the Regie had made 350,000.

With the 1,100 cc engine went the appropriate gearbox and this was an improvement. Testing the new car at the time, I said: 'I liked the new gear shift arrangement very much indeed; to me, it is much preferable to the kinky (!) shift on the 850. For some reason which may lie deep in the psyche, I have always felt that one should pull *back* into top gear and not push forward. To have to twist and push, as on the 4 and 6, is to me a minor aggro.'

Of this car, which proved a great success to Renault, I said the following:

'If I did not fall head over heels in love with the 6-1100, to the extent of being disloyal to the rest of the "famille Renault", I nevertheless believed that many people would. The car is a right little charmer and the only thing that really bothered me was that the steering seemed heavier than on the 850 version. It is perfectly natural that this should be the case, because the power unit and the gearbox are heavier, and their weight more or less straddles the front axle.

Mostly this is only noticeable at parking speeds, but a different kind of steering characteristic is noticeable on sharp bends at low or moderate speeds. This is an effect caused by the high torque of this engine tending to push the (driven) front wheels straight ahead, and it is very marked if one has the power well on and not too firm a grip of the wheel . . ..'

I found the performance one of 'eager vigour' compared with the 850 and even with other makes of car of the same capacity. On the speedometer readings (admittedly usually a little high on Renaults) I could get a 0 to 60 acceleration figure of just over 17 seconds. A reputable motoring magazine gave the car a figure of 19 seconds for 0 to 60 and presumably that would be for a corrected speedometer figure.

I noted that most of the time the car was quite quiet and less strident than the R 8/10 series. There was a different sound and feel and, performance apart, one could hardly tell that it was not the modified Dauphine unit used on the 6-850. Also there was a small occasional noise, a ticking sound, which was unfamiliar to Renault owners and this was the make-and-break of the electric petrol pump. As far as I know, this was the only time Renault had ever used an electric instead of mechanical fuel pump and it was situated in a ridiculous place under the rear nearside of the body. Later models had an improved system.

As with the 4 and the 6-850, I found the pedals annoying at first, because you had to lift your feet and put them down again—you could not just swivel your heels. Testing the car, *Motor* said 'heeling and toeing' was difficult. If by this they meant the old-fashioned and rather mythical business of trying to operate brake and throttle pedals with toe and heel in some clumsy endeavour to do 'racing changes' I was glad it was not possible, because I cannot think of a more dangerous perfor-mance, although we used to do it in the old days of double declutching.

I found that the car had many praiseworthy minor features. Thus, the armrests on the doors were not mere scratching posts; they really worked. The ashtray was a stout sensible one. A door-fitted exterior mirror, additional to the day/night interior mirror made for extra safety, in days when people regarded them as fripperies. The roof lining had some semblance of padding, which was a welcome change, and it was good to know that one could have a sun roof for a mere £40.

A fuel computation gave an overall figure of about 37 mpg and the reasonably aerodynamic body allowed the car to do about 45 mpg on long high-speed runs if there were not too many hills.

With many minor modifications, but basically as the same car, the Renault 6 stayed successfully in production until a few years ago. In France, there was a Rodeo version—a kind of beach car or buggy-type open version like the R 4 Rodeo, but few of these were seen in the UK. The Renault 6 was intended, of course, to replace the rear-engined R 8/10 series but this did not happen for a year or two. It was a fairly gradual process and somewhat secretive, as usual, and when it did finally happen, there was much weeping and wailing and gnashing of enthusiasts' teeth. There is no reason to suppose that Dreyfus, or anybody else at Billancourt, was particularly moved by such outbursts; Renault was in top gear, in front-wheel drive and really going places, and when the Renault 12 came out, in September 1969 the 'supermarket range of products' idea was at last a reality.

Over a million vehicles were produced by the Régie in 1969. It was the first time the magic figure had been attained in a year and it made Renault the third largest motor manufacturer in Europe. This achievement represented an increase of 25 per cent over 1968 and brought a record export figure of 530,000. The million was made up of 911,000 cars and 98,000 light commercials and accounted for 40 per cent of France's automotive production and 45 per cent of all car exports. The ghost of 'Louis le collaborateur' must have been doing an utterly gleeful *danse macabre* somewhere out there.

All this was happening when the R 12 had not yet had any effect on sales and when the R 6 had not even got into its stride. It was the established models that were selling like hot brioche—the 4, 8, 10, 16 and 16 TS. Of exports, the R 4 was best seller with 194,000 global. The R 8/10 accounted for 160,000, and R 16 and TS for 90,000 and the R 6 for 40,000. Great Britain took 19,000 cars.

In addition to their production record in France, Renault assembly and manufacturing plants in 28 countries also developed richly, with a total production of 295,000 for 1969 compared with 248,000 in 1968, an increase of 19 per cent. Renault sales in Eastern European countries were up by as much as 78 per cent.

Just when everybody thought that the Régie had decided to go hook, line and sinker for the hatchback format—to offer the 4, 6 and 16, with the R 8/10 series already a dead duck—out they came with the Renault 12. It was almost as though a conscious decision had been made to surprise the motoring public, regardless of policy and sales strategy. Dreyfus was not that sort of animal, however. Very much into motorcars now, and being carried along quite excitedly by the design programme, he was no whit less the financier and industrialist, who was seldom far from a balance sheet and a computer, seldom inaccessible to his valued advisers. The advisers he often sought most were the market research boys, and this was a time when they convinced him, at first against his own judgement, that there was not only room for, but a crying need for, a plain and simple family saloon. In the event it turned out to be simple enough, in the mechanical sense, but by no means plain. Many people considered it a beauty; certainly it was more than merely a *joli minois*.

Introducing the car as the R 1170, of 7 CV Fiscale, the Régie said the following:

'The unveiling of a new model is always an important occasion for a motorcar manufacturer. This is especially true when the vehicle in question is destined to be produced in large numbers and appears to differ, at least in certain respects, from the manufacturer's previous concepts.

Since the appearance of the R 4, R 6 and R 16, the Régie Renault has accustomed public opinion to the idea of so-called functional vehicles—functional insofar as they possess a fifth door and front wheel drive. The Renault 12 retains the front wheel drive but has no fifth door. It is available in two versions—TL (Tourisme Luxe) and L (Luxe).'

'Does this mean', asked Dreyfus, 'that the Régie is abandoning the style and techniques which have made the Renault 4 the most widely sold French car in the world and the Renault 16, with its TS variant, the biggest selling 1,500 cc car in Europe?' Answering his own question he was able to say 'There is no question of this, and without unveiling the future projects of the Renault marque, there is no

Modernistic but restrained body design characterised the Renault 12 front-wheel-drive 1300 cc saloon.

doubt that the future will see many models closely related to the R 4, 6 and 16'.

Nevertheless, he and his publicists pointed out that a company such as Renault, with expansion in full swing and determined to widen its range, must aim at satisfying the maximum number of people. Market research had shown that in the '70s the category in which the new car would fall (4–5 seater, 1,300 cc) would be one of the focal points of the main European markets, and it was important that the company should establish itself in that class.

To be competitive in the main Euro market, a car must satisfy a great variety of requirements. There must be plenty of room for all passengers and their luggage and it must allow untiring long-distance travel. It must also answer the needs of each member of the family—business, pleasure, shopping, ferrying the kids, etc. (French women were among the slowest to take up driving; now the floodgates were open and the second car was becoming commonplace.)

A family saloon car, reasoned Dreyfus and his designers, must be safe and tough enough to be driven by anyone, economical enough for moderate family means and sufficiently manoeuverable for dense urban conditions. The result was necessarily a compromise. 'Moreover', stated the Régie, 'the designers also had to take into account the changes in motorists' demands marking the start of the 1970s, eg, a

Luxurious interior of the Renault 12 TS. Head restraints were just becoming accepted.

desire for greater comfort and a greater emphasis on aesthetic appearance and finish'.

'From a technical point of view', said Billancourt, 'this vehicle was designed for a clientele predominantly interested in driving qualities and reliability rather than in avant-garde techniques. The vehicle has to have a sufficiently modern appearance and to express all its qualities, but without excessive conformism which quickly dates, so that there can be no uncertainty as to its length of life. This is the balance which the Renault 12 has tried to achieve—a high-class, medium-sized car of the 1970s.'

In keeping with the new American, Japanese and European preoccupation with death and injury on the roads, the Régie spared no pains to make the new car as safe as possible, both primarily and with regard to passive security.

Renault claimed exceptional road-holding characteristics, due to front-wheel drive and the rather unusual suspension, also the use of radial tyres as standard. Independent road tests and the use of the car for rallying and saloon car racing showed that the claim was justified. The braking system was, as on all Renaults, above reproach if adequately maintained. The seating was comfortable, the driver's view of the road excellent and the heating and ventilation system very good, although not perfect, since the car could get too hot in warm weather.

In matters of secondary safety there was no room for complaint. As Renault said 'Firstly, there is the relative length of the bonnet and the impact absorbing front and rear structures. Provided that the occupants are restrained by safety belts, this design feature gives them maximum protection in the case of front or rear collision by allowing the progressive distortion of a large quantity of sheet steel.' The steering column was jointed behind the front axle and the wheel padded, whilst the whole fascia assembly was of a material which would give way progressively in the event of a violent blow.

The 12 TS was distinguished by special sports wheels.

Without being in any way bizarre, like some Citroëns or the Renault 14 to be introduced years later, the 12 had lines which anticipated many later designs. The shape, which just happened to look a little futuristic, was evolved with the aim of giving a body which would be as roomy for the people in the back as those in the front, at the same time allowing good visibility and a capacious (12½ cu ft) boot. The nose of the car drooped more than was conventional and both front and rear screens were well raked. The roof line rose to a point above the rear seat, where the line was broken abruptly by an unusual step-down to the concave rear screen. It was claimed that the lines gave a good aerodynamic form but also minimised aerodynamic lift at high speeds.

Stating that it was a comparatively long car (14 ft 3 in) the Régie suggested that this made it look elegant and allowed lower, more comfortable seating. They claimed it was easy to park because of the set-back front wheels. In practice I doubt if this made much difference, but it was easier to park than the R 16.

The body construction was technically very interesting. Although of unitary construction, it had an integral chassis of great strength yet with frontal impact-absorption, the side members ahead of the suspension being curved outwards so as to 'give' progressively in a collision. Two parallel side members at the front formed part of the body and supported the engine and front suspension; the rear also included two side members more widely spaced and forming a carrier fork for the fuel tank and boot floor.

On each side of the floor there were two more outer side members of considerable strength (0.059 in thick) running below the door sills and ensuring protection in the event of a lateral impact. There were four box-section cross members. The floor panel embodied foot wells. Behind the rear bench seat there was a cross bracing element which strengthened the assembly against torsion by transmitting forces acting at roof level to the rest of the body shell.

Paint processes on the 12 were above average for the era, and there are still a lot of old 12s about which do not show the ravages of rust as much as their contemporaries. The shell was pressure washed and degreased, then phosphated to prevent rust and key the paint. It was then immersed in an epoxy resin base which, in theory at any rate, reached all internal areas of box sections, etc. Panel surfaces which were spot-welded were first treated with zinc-based paint.

The body then received two coats of synthetic-resin-based primer which were stoved. After careful rubbing down, two coats of glyceropthalic finish were sprayed on and stoved. The wheel arches were sprayed with thick bituminous sound-deadening compound.

A novelty was the system of front engine mountings of inertia type, and I quote: 'During the vibration cycle, the engine bears down on one of the mounting blocks and therefore on the side member of the same side. As a result, it imparts motion in the same direction to the tip of the pivot member to which it is attached. The inertia of the weight in the centre of the pivot member is sufficient to form a sort of floating fulcrum so that a pressure in the opposite direction to that applied by the engine is simultaneously applied to the chassis by the other end of the pivot member. This pressure is equal to between 60 and 70 per cent of that exerted by the engine.'

Presumably Renault knew what they meant. For my part, when I tested the car, I was content to register that the engine seemed to throb and chunter a fair amount at tickover speeds, and presumably without this strange device it would have been more than just mildly irritating at traffic speeds. At any speeds above tickover it was sweet and smooth as a peach.

The 1,300 cc engine was a new version of the basic design used in the Renault 8 (956 cc), Renault 1100 and Estafette (1,108 cc) and R 8 Gordini (1,255 cc). Maximum bhp was 60 (SAE) at 5,250 rpm, equivalent to 54 bhp (DIN). The carburettor was a Solex 32 EISA with manual choke. Compression ratio was 8.5:1. The gearbox was a slightly modified version of that fitted to the Renault 16 and 16 TS.

The suspension of the 12 was fairly ordinary at the front, but somewhat more interesting at the rear. The frontal system comprised a transverse variable parallelo-gram layout with big coil springs, telescopic shock absorbers and an anti-roll torsion bar as well as oblique tie bars, between side members and stub-axle carriers.

Of the rear suspension, sticking their necks out quite impudently, Renault said 'Because of gyroscopic forces, the independent suspension of the front wheels of a car is a vital road holding and safety factor. In the case of the rear wheels, however, independent suspension is not an imperative condition for good road holding'. This was perfectly reasonable, of course, and the use of a 'dead beam' rear axle was not simply justifiable but mandatory, since the 12 had coil springs instead of the long torsion bars used on the other front-wheel-drive cars, which imparted their own rigidity as well as having an anti-roll bar to assist.

So the 12 had a robust, pressed steel axle, guided by two tie-bars and a central triangular member. There were two large coil springs which enclosed teledraulics, and an anti-roll torsion bar anchored at both ends to the tie bars.

Renault made public their reasoning about the adoption of this type of suspension, pointing out that the main advantage of torsion-bar rear springing is that it gives you a flat, low rear floor, but it is relatively expensive. Moreover, the roll centre is very low, which means that the car sways rather a lot on corners. With the beam type suspension, the floor can still be reasonably low and flat, but the roll centre is higher and the wheels are always perpendicular to the ground.

You can always tell when a vehicle has intrinsically good handling, for if it has, the motor sport enthusiasts will fall upon it and do great things on roads, tracks and circuits, and so it was with the Renault 12, even before it became 'Gordinified'. Certainly I was always happy with this model as far as handling is concerned, even when alarming myself at Silverstone, Donington, etc. In fact I liked the 12 on all counts and would have bought one if I had had the money. Although I was editing Renault's magazine by then, it brought no special concessions. When the R 12 came to Britain, in May 1970, it was priced at £870 and slotted between the R 10 at £790 and the R 16 at £990. Production of the car at Flins was already up to 800 a day and this soon rose to 1,000 units, taking it into second place behind the R 4 in Renault production.

My first experience of the new car was in late September 1969. Renault flew us out to Basle and we stepped out of the aircraft and straight into barely run-in left-hand-drive cars, in the dark and sleety rain. But my co-driver and I hummed happily enough up the motorway to Mulhouse, this being one of those cars you get into and feel at home in right away.

The plan was to share 400 km of Alsatian driving—up through Colmar on to a kidney-shaped route in the Vosges mountains, starting at the lush Trois Epis mountain hotel and with a lunch stop at Wangenburg on the edge of the Engenthal Forest then down to Selestat and Ribeauville.

Driving up the narrow switchback road to the Trois Epis—the floodlit chateau seeming to float up there in the sky miles ahead—the R 12 gave the immensely comforting feeling that any misjudgement of one of those crazy hairpins could be covered by a reserve of steerability pulled out of the bag. At night, on a strange road with a left-hand-drive car, I was not pushing my luck, not hustling. My co-driver later confirmed this feeling when he took over and gave the 12 every chance to hurl itself into the forest off a corkscrew mountain road and although it broke away once or twice, its forgiving nature kept us safely on course.

Between us, we tried the car under a fair variety of conditions and loved it for its fine handling and great comfort. The stylish, somewhat modernistic machine, could be urged from standstill to 50 mph in 9.4 seconds and from 0 to 60 mph in 14.5 seconds. Maximum speeds indicated in the gears were 34 mph (1st), 52.7 mph (2nd) and 77.6 mph (3rd). Time after time I got a maximum top gear indicated speed of 95 mph.

The low-speed torque was unusually good and one could drive with minimal use of the gears, but so smooth and free-revving was the motor that there was a great temptation to zoom up through the ratios. In traffic, a well-chosen second gear and willing engine allowed one to get about smartly with the minimum of effort and the steering was beautifully light and positive, except at parking speeds, when there was some advantage in having strong wrists.

I recall not being so enthusiastic about the gear shift itself. The lever movement was both 'longer and wider' than I liked and there was a rubbery feel about shifts, although the movements were positive enough and there was little likelihood of missing a gear, either up or down. Renault have always made good, tough, reliable gearboxes, but precision has not always been a characteristic of the selection arrangements.

The brakes were excellent—another consistent Renault feature in my experience. They were powerful, smooth and progressive in action. There was a faint rumble on high-speed application, probably due to microscopic run-out on the discs of such an early production model, but there was no fade or squealing on long mountainous descents.

The umbrella handbrake was less of an inconvenience than I had expected, but I still registered dislike of that piece of apparatus. All minor controls worked wonderfully well and the two-speed wipers were highly effective, but irritatingly noisy.

I felt safe in this car at all times—even when my co-driver was having his wild moments—and I found it a very easy car to 'place' by night or day, despite the fact that in the dark I could have done with quartz halogens.

I gave full marks for all the trimming and appointments and especially the big glove box with its automatic light. Every facet of the car showed great attention to detail.

Odd things often happen on Press trips of this kind. Thus, we unintentionally 'exported' our 12 by taking it back (very reluctantly) to Basle instead of leaving it at the big Renault depot at St Louis. Nobody at Basle's Alban Ambassador luxury hotel seemed in the least interested, so it was a case of back to St. Louis, where Renault's men chased our blues away with Biere d'Alsace, then gave us transport to Basle. We must have irritated the Franco–Swiss border officials with our comings and goings, but everyone kept their cool.

Renault got a very good press from the launch of the 12, and some journalists thought it the best car the Régie had ever made. Some people got very good fuel consumption figures, Renault having checked each team's mpg by topping up the tanks carefully on return. Our own figure was not particularly good, because we had been pushing the car pretty hard most of the time, but it was still creditable at 7.9 gallons (36 l) for 250.9 m (404 km), representing 31 mpg.

I was not able to test and report on the UK version of the car until May of the same year, but I was still jumping the gun, because other Press men had not had the car. Renault's PR people had asked me to do a special test for their magazine *Autoworld*. There was, in fact, an awful row with the sales people, who for some reason felt that this would offend the dealers. There has always been a good deal of this prima donna attitude on the part of the marketing people.

A curious situation existed in those years, whereby the PR people allowed me to be quite critical but the marketing people, on seeing anything even mildly derogatory in the magazine, would become hysterical with rage.

I belted the UK car up and down the M1 and used it in town and country conditions, and my general impression was again of an exceptionally good car, but I grumbled about a few small things, saying that the steering was stiff and the car too warm in summer. On the other hand I found the gear-shift decidedly better than on the left-hand-drive car.

I went to a lot of trouble to obtain accurate acceleration figures as we had done in France, although this time I went for a 0 to 70 mph figure also. In each case I made several runs in each direction and took an average of figures. From standstill to 50 mph took 10 seconds exactly, and it was not, of course, necessary to use top gear, as the car would do an easy 70 in third. The figure for 0 to 60 worked out at 14.25 seconds, and again I did not use top gear. To reach the legal maximum from standstill using first, second and third gear ratios, took 21.25 seconds and when I did similar runs using top, having changed up at about 60 mph, the figure was almost exactly a second slower.

The Renault 12 estate was remarkable value for money, with its impressive load capacity, and economical performance.

Maximum speeds in the gears were about the same as we had registered on the Alsace car, ie, 34, 53 and 77.6 mph—but of course one would seldom if ever use those for normal motoring.

My report included the following comment: 'Third ratio is a real life saver for high-speed overtaking, when sometimes it is more difficult to judge how long it will take to pass the vehicle in front than to estimate how quickly the oncoming traffic is approaching. The ability to snick into such a useful ratio at short notice can be a valuable safety factor, but then this Renault 12 is a remarkably safe car in so many ways.'

There were strong cross winds on the M1 when I did this test, and it rained heavily at times, but the 12 was absolutely unswerving and adhesion of both front and rear ends was exceptionally good.

The Renault 12 was an instant success, and like so many Renault new models, a baby without teething troubles. This, of course, was no accident. Perhaps because he was not an engineer, Dreyfus was almost obsessed with the idea of having a product exhaustively tried and tested until it could reach the customer as nearly perfect as possible. Engineers are apt, perhaps, to regard motor production as a continual development of prototypes, the unfortunate consumer being privileged to join the ranks of the testers.

As Dreyfus had stated in 1969, there was no intention to abandon the obligation to 'five-doorists' as well as to those interested primarily in family saloon cars, and the promise was honoured almost immediately by the introduction of the 12 Estate in 1971. It was another winner.

The Estate was derived directly from the saloon, but incorporated important mechanical modifications and offered unusually generous carrying capacity in the rear compartment—up to 60 cu ft with rear seat folded and a flat space 65 inches

Above *Ultimate Renault 12—the Gordini version in French racing blue.*

Below *The automatic version of the R 12 had a T-bar control.*

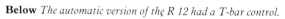

long. I remember noting that a large-wheeled bicycle could be carried without dismantling.

The rear suspension was specially strengthened and the flexibility modified to suit the weight distribution, laden or unladen. Diameter of the anti-roll bar was increased from 14 to 16 mm. There was greater braking power, the rear drums being 9 inches as compared with 7 inches diameter. Bigger tyres were fitted.

The rear quarters of the saloon lent themselves well to the substitution of a new panel assembly with two big windows, which gave exceptional rear visibility. Although the new model looked substantially larger than the saloon, it was, in fact, only 2¼ inches longer. Kerb weight of the car was 2,094 lb compared with 1,940 for the saloon, so there was no great penalty in performance, particularly as the gear ratios were suitably adjusted. For some reason or other, the only ratio that could be faulted was reverse, which seemed high, and in fact many owners complained about this to the factory.

It was not long before the French, full of the usual rationalised euphoria, clamoured for a hot version of the 12. The *enfants terribles* of Paris, Lyon, Le Mans, Clermont Ferrand, Nice, Juan, Tropez wanted something brash for the Saturday evening thrash. More serious minded but little less *terribles enfants* wanted a challenger for the greater and lesser rallies, hill climbs, circuit races. The Régie would provide something and sit in the pits or on the special sections watching what happened and wondering whether to have works cars . . ..

The result was theRenault 12 Gordini, in French racing blue with extrovert white go-faster stripes along the sides and across bonnet and boot. It looked good and it went fast. The standard version used the Renault 16's 1,565 cc motor, up-rated to produced 125 bhp with the use of twin Webers. The standard car was suitable for Group 1 events, but there was a hotter version (145 bhp) available to special order, whilst a tuning kit offered by La Sociéte Renault-Gordini of Viry-Châtillon was reputed to boost the power to 160. Naturally, the car was eligible for the Coupe Gordini.

For ordinary people with a taste for performance, and for the UK market, the Renault 12 TS was a more practical proposition, even if it did not shout so loud, nor dart and swoop to quite the same effect. Judicious tuning gave the 1,300 cc engine 60 bhp (DIN) compared with the 54 of the 12 TL. The car had Gordini type wheels and front seats with integral headrests. It sold extremely well and proved to be economical as well as brisk and reliable. There are still plenty of them about.

The 12 TS engine was used in an automatic version of the Renault 12 which was introduced in 1974. Designated the 12 TR, this new model was fitted with Renault's own three-speed epicyclic/electronic box which had been created for the R 16 as described earlier. I tested this model when it was launched in the UK and found it much to my liking, although not by any means a fireball.

9: New ideas, new shapes, greater safety . . .

For a long time there had been rumours that Renault were coming out with a sports car. It seemed at least half-logical. A certain sector of the motoring public had always clamoured for Alpines—those elusive exotica in blue fibreglass that rent the air with their barely-silenced exhausts and were gone in a flash, hugging the ground like guilty fleeing cats. But production was small, prices were daunting and the Régie regarded the whole Alpine ethos as a prestige exercise.

Could a mass producer afford to play around with sports cars at all? Was not the sports car itself an anachronism? There would always be people with enough money and enthusiasm to buy Porsches, Aston-Martins, Alpines, E-type Jaguars at three to six times the price of a family car, but even the inexpensive Jag did not make a lot of money for its fabricators and production figures were not in the big league. The answer was to make something that looked sporty but was frankly not a sports car. The idea was not new. Sunbeam Talbot had done that kind of thing since the early post-war years and were still doing it; ironically, one of their sports saloons was called the Alpine. Ford had made a lasting success of their Capri, the cheapest, really sporty and glamorous looking saloon ever. Or were these coupés? The term is imprecise. It simply means 'cut'. If you cut a bit too much off a saloon, to make it sporty, you are more or less obliged to call it a coupé.

Even the hard-headed Dreyfus had to admit that there would be a sales potential for a pretty, but practical and fairly rapid, sporty saloon and he had given the go-ahead in 1967, although finding it difficult to divert himself from the excitement of the gestation of the R 12 and R 5, and the still shadowy plans for a really big car.

In the spring of 1971, the Régie 'leaked' the new car by circulating a very simple and unadorned picture—a side view with plain background. It showed a somewhat angular but undeniably sporty-looking machine, with an obvious dihedral along the waistline, unusual louvred rear quarters and curious road wheels which looked somewhat as though they belonged to a moon buggy, or some other piece of extra-terrestrial exotica. The car was called the Renault 17 and it was powered by the 16 TS engine.

The car was launched at the Paris Show in October 1971, in TL and TS forms, and was the subject of a great deal of favourable comment and the placing of many orders—a feedback from the policy of proving new models thoroughly enough to prevent any adverse reputation for introducing new models which turned out to be bum steers. If there were any teething troubles at all, they were with the fuel injection system of the TS version, but the firm and its dealers were at great pains to

A little on the macho side, the 17 TS was nevertheless sweet to drive.

establish good relations with any complainants, and to get their motorcars into good kilter.

The TL version had the 'moon buggy' wheels and the TS had the same fancy cast wheels as the 12 and 16 TS. The engine of the TL pushed out 102 bhp whilst the slightly tuned unit of the TS gave 120 bhp and had a flatter torque curve. The more powerful car also had a five-speed gearbox. Bosch injection was used on this model. Chassis specification of both cars was similar to that of the Renault 12.

A pleasant surprise for many people was that a Renault 15, in much the same image, was released at the same time. This was virtually a Renault 12 with the same pleasing shell as the 17, except that it had rectangular headlamps and long rear windows to take the place of the admittedly rather pointless louvres of the latter. There were TL and TS versions, the former with the Renault 12 TS unit and the latter with the 26 TS motor, as on the R 17 TL. The 15 TL had the slotted wheels of the R 12 but the 15 TS had the 'moon buggy' wheels. Prices of the 15/17 range in the UK were from £1,325 to £2,000, so there was no shortage of prospective buyers, but delivery delays were not excessive.

Despite their sporting appearance (which, as always, made them appeal strongly to the ladies) the cars were true four seaters and had large luggage boots with easy access through a big tailgate.

The 15 TS and 17 TL were available with Renault's automatic transmission. Cloth upholstery was offered as an extra on all models, whilst electrically operated front windows were standard equipment on the 17 TS and optional on the 17 TL. All models had a heated rear window as standard.

The R 15/17 range were extremely well-built cars with a high degree of built-in safety. The motoring world and the industry in particular were becoming more and more safety conscious each year, as the fatality and casualty figures escalated in proportion to increasing traffic density and higher levels of performance.

It was all very well to congratulate ourselves on being into the space age—to think of the wonder of Russia's space docking station Salute, and of America's 1971 lunar landings and to wallow in the technology and flashing speed of the modern car—but man's progress in mastering the weather on his little planet was, and is, limited to making shadowy satellite pictures of cloud formations. The calibre of the modern kind of motoring accident in these years was represented by a 'shunt' in fog on the M1 motorway in November 1971, when ten people were killed and many injured. Fog accidents were almost unavoidable and still are. Sometimes some irresponsible or cretinous people cause them, sometimes they just happen. Other types of accident, in wet, snowy or perfectly clear summer conditions, can be just as lethal and their causes can be determined fairly accurately. Again, sometimes idiots are the perpetrators of this murderous folly, sometimes it is just a case of misjudgement or inexperience or both. Most accidents are avoidable but it is very difficult to persuade people to go to that trouble, particularly if they are not interested in cars or driving. There are others who are so passionately interested that they take all kinds of moronic risks.

Accordingly, the industry continues to think and act in terms of passive or secondary safety, as well as active and primary safety. In the case of the R 15/17 range, Renault quoted front-wheel-drive handling characteristics, dual-circuit servo braking and good all-round vision as primary safety features. On passive safety, they quoted as follows:

'*Impact absorbing strength of the passenger compartment:* The central framework is

One of the prettiest of modern Renaults—the 15 GTL.

strong and particularly resistant to buckling. Conversely, the engine compartment is designed to absorb an appreciable amount of shock, but buckles under impact.

Safe, clean lines of the interior: 1. padded, collapsible dashboard; 2. universal-jointed steering column mounted on a collapsible support; 3. collapsible window winders; 4. padded seat backs, locking in any position.

The bumper arrangements were unusual. The front bumper was a perimeter frame in metal, with rubber insert. It was in two parts, the lower having the property of progressive collapse and there were also rubber overriders. The rear bumper was made of pre-impregnated polyester, to some extent anticipating the design to be used on the Renault 5 and which has since been copied by other manufacturers.

I was able to test the new cars in my beloved Provence. It is a 'prerequisite of office' of motoring journalism (a notoriously ill-paid profession) that one should be able from time to time to live luxuriously for a few days, often in continental sunspots, while gaining brief experience of new models.

To a reasonable degree a Francophile, I could not resist paying tribute to the Midi in the following terms in my report in *Autoworld*, December 1971:

'Provence is not just a pretty place—it is also a demanding one for motors and drivers. Incidentally, just to provide the living proof of the familiarity-breeds-contempt tag, a maiden sitting next to me in the Nice-bound 727 jet mentioned that she lived in Antibes and found it all so dull . . ..

But Provence is always different, to those who do not know it so well as to take it for granted, and our test base, the Hôtellerie du Piol at St. Paul de Vence, seemed in a lovely little world of its own, remote from crowded end-of-season Nice and Cannes.

St Paul is on its way to the Alpine regions and the great rally country, so its location was ideal for a quick but intensive foray into the hills and the southerly

Standard seats on the 17 TS were exceptionally luxurious and beautifully upholstered.

sections of the great Route Napoleon. Renault had invited top motoring journalists from all over Europe, and a fleet of the new cars was at their disposal.'

I drove a 17 TL first, and commented in the following terms: 'placing the car with centimetres to spare, in congested Nice and Cannes, presented no hardship, despite the relatively unfamiliar left-hand drive, because visibility is unusually good and the bonnet line sensible.

Sniffing through my open windows the perfumed effluents of Grasse—surely the world's most lovely "pollution"—I was soon on the tortuous roads of the N 85, the scenic switchback road which follows the journey taken by the Emperor of France when he returned from Elba in 1815, and is touristically known as the Route Napoleon. Our lunch stop was to be at the Auberge Provençale at a place surprisingly called Mons on the N 563; between Grasse and Mons the road was ideal for very fast motoring—not on mountain passes, but on the highway that turns and twists round many sharp bends and hairpins, with heights rising to 1,200 ft . . ..

It now became obvious that the performance of the Renault 17, even in the TL version, was exceptional for its modest 1½-litre capacity and on the short straights between bends, I was often able to flash past other cars with a reassuring safety margin, in second or third according to conditions. Later I was to find the same gratifying sense of power in top gear on fast highways. At the same time I must admit that I could have wished for a faster gear change, and particularly with the shift from third to second, as I had anticipated.

After the lunch stop, which embraced a memorable bucolic repast in a spot commanding a fine view of the valleys, another tough spell of motoring followed, the route taking us via Fayence across the Lac de St. Cassien, then joining the RN 7 to take us in a southerly direction to Fréjus along the fringe of the Massif de L'Esterel. Just north of deeply-historic Fréjus we turned north again, up D 37 and on to the A8 toll road—that fine motorway to Nice, although we turned off a few miles short of that town for the road to St. Paul de Vence, for the night stop . . ..

On the day after our out-of-this-world night stop at the Hôtellerie du Piol at St. Paul, I tried the 17 TS and was able to make useful comparisons. The unit fitted in the Renault 17 TL pushes out 102 bhp, as compared with 120 bhp in the case of the R 17 TS, but it has a slightly different torque curve and this, combined with the fact that the intermediate gear ratios as well as final drive ratios are different, seems to make competitive point-to-point performance possible for the less powerful car. They are both very free-revving engines, like all Renaults I have ever known, and it is never any hardship to make enterprising use of the gears, except for that sticky third-to-second movement, which is best accomplished with a quick double declutch (veterans please note!) . . ..

The extra "steam" of the 17 TS is obtained not only by using a higher compression ratio, high-lift cams, etc, but also, of course, by virtue of the Bosch fuel injection system. I found that this system gave a rough idle from cold, but this corrected itself after about the same time as an automatic choke. Acceleration was clean and smooth (although hardly tigerish) up to about 4,500 rpm, then came in thrillingly to send the needle surging up well beyond the safe limit if one was not prudent.

On motorways, both cars gave a refined high-speed performance, taking their place comfortably in the high speed lane. It is on the steep, winding hill roads that the 17 TL feels at its best, perhaps, whilst the dramatic acceleration of the fuel-injection car is ideally suited to autoroutes, expressways and those incredibly dangerous three-lane 'highways' where high-speed overtaking ability often makes for greater safety than hanging about behind the curious breed of creature that is neither hare nor tortoise but has the characteristics, perhaps, of an elderly cockroach . . ..

Road holding is brilliant—it is the only word—and handling can be justly described as neutral, because without knowing the specification, one would hardly in any circumstances be able to tell, from inside the car, whether this was a front or rear drive design. There is no front-drive effect on steering or on the feel of the transmission, with the single exception of slight wheelspin on the heavy-throttle take off with the wheels locked over.'

The new cars were an unqualified success, apart from the little niggly problems with the fuel injection system, which were cured after a short while. Production soon rose to 300 and more units a day. In August 1974, the 17 TS was renamed the Renault Gordini, as a mark of respect to Amédée Gordini, 'The Sorcerer', who now seemed to be on Renault's payroll fairly firmly after years of uncertainty and indeterminate relationships. By April 1976, however, the injection car was taken out of production and a new 'carburettor' TS was introduced. Production went on until the 15/17 were replaced by the Fuego series.

Renault were now launched into a total committment to front-wheel drive in their series production cars. There was no turning back. From all 'mechanicals' at the back, they had gone to all mechanicals at the front. It was time to bring to stage another star—a small, rather pert, almost impudent prima ballerina to follow the leggy, somewhat haughty showgirls, the 15 and 17. The newcomer was the R 5, still a star today.

Before we look at this little lady's career, however, let us see how Renault was getting on in the wider industrial sense, ie, as what is now called a multi-national.

Seventy-five years earlier, Renault had been simply Renault—the man—with a garden shed and a bench and a buggy. Now it was a vast industrial complex bordering the Seine at salients from Paris to Le Havre (Sandouville) and also with factories on the banks of the Loire and in the region of Le Mans, as well as at Douai and at Annecy. To this native network must be added a world network of construction factories and of sales and service centres, containing a whole range of different industries—steelworks, foundries, heavy and light vehicle plants, machine tool factories, bearing works and general engineering firms.

Nationalised at the end of the war, the company paid dividends to the State and received nothing in return until 1963. By 1972, advances from the government at high interest rates totalled £50m. Progress since 1968 made Renault bigger than British Leyland, faster growing than Fiat, and sitting on Volkswagen's tail.

By virtue of its commercial results and its position as a public undertaking, the Régie plays an important part in the total French economy. Although nationalised, it is controlled as though it was a private enterprise concern by its president director general, who is appointed by the government. He is aided by an administrative council including representatives of the ministries and the workforce. His decisions and their implementation do not need the prior approval of the government but the accounts must be submitted to them. Since 1969, shares in the company have been made available to the employees.

By now, surprisingly, 40 years old, the Renault plant in Belgium was thriving and had produced over 120,000 cars. The Pitesti plant in Rumania was now assembling cars at the rate of 40,000 a year, and production was starting at the IMV works in Yugoslavia. In Spain, FASA Renault, with four factories at Valladolid and one at Seville, produced 128,000 vehicles in 1972. A new assembly plant in Mexico was getting into gear and Renaults were being produced by various Renault or affiliated concerns in Argentina, Venezuela and Colombia.

Renault had co-operated with the Soviets since 1953, when electromagnetic heads for machine tools were supplied. In 1966 the Régie signed an agreement concerning the supply of equipment for the modernisation and development of the Soviet automobile industry. This was primarily concerned with the Moskvich 412 car. The Régie may in some ways prefer to forget it—the car was monolithic and unpredictable, although cheap enough in European markets—but it was a piece of industrial history. The programme involved the construction of two bodywork factories with a capacity of 350,000 vehicles, and a mechanical unit factory for which Renault supplied all the automation lines. There was a considerable exchange of technicians between France and Russia.

In 1970 a new agreement was signed, with the aim of widening the participation of Renault in the supply of equipment for the Soviet automobile and commercial vehicles industries; and, by an agreement of 28 October 1971, for the Kama truck programme in particular.

Late in 1971, Dreyfus was a worried man, but he showed some of his finest qualities when worried, and he was an incurable optimist. In a progress report, he said that after having known a somewhat spectacular expansion in 1969 and 1970, French car exports had slackened in 1971. He went so far as to say, not cheerfully, but with calm and confidence: 'We can't expect important rates of progress during the coming years'.

They were making progress, he said, in West Germany, England and Spain, but were losing ground in Belgium, Holland, Italy and the Scandinavian countries. As for the Algerian market, they had purely and simply lost it. If they had been able to maintain their sales in volume in the east, they owed this to the increase in CKD (completely knocked down) kits to Rumania, whereas sales had fallen back in other areas. He quoted the following figures for completely and partly knocked down vehicles:

Country	1970	1971
E. Germany	5	2
Bulgaria	311	389
Hungary	617	238
Poland	206	4
Rumania	16,925	19,744
Czechoslovakia	2,165	2,036
Yugoslavia	7,063	6,039
Russia	19	18
	27,311	28,470

One of their fundamental problems continued to be the increase in production costs. For this reason, and following a strike in May, their 1971 results would be bad. In 1972 they would have to engage in a policy of strict austerity. Meanwhile—and the confident half-smile came again—they had certain assets, including good production plant, well-established networks and good models, new or old. (In the event, Renault total production in 1971 reached 1,170,000—a figure similar to that of 1970—despite losing over 60,000 cars during the May strike.)

Dreyfus remarked that the enthusiasm of existing and potential customers for the R 4 and 12 had in no way abated. There were 'certain difficulties' as far as the R 6 was concerned, 'no doubt provisional'. As for the R 16 and 16 TS, they were maintaining their popularity in spite of more and more lively competition. The R 15 and 17, for their part, were likely to interest a clientele which did not consist of habitual buyers of their ranges, and this seemed to be happening.

Finally, said Dreyfus—and his shrewd but humorous eyes seemed to light up—the new Renault 5 should enable them to regain lost ground in percentage, in a national market of which he could see no limit in the coming months. With the R 5 and other new models he hoped they would improve their position in France as well as in Europe, Great Britain and Germany, although the situation was less certain in most of the other markets. Perhaps even he was not to know how much the Régie would owe to the Renault 5 in its march towards prosperity.

An interesting sidelight on the Régie's economic structure was provided at this time, in the following terms:

'Each time the Régie receives 100 fr, it uses it in the following manner—55.27 per cent is taken up with the purchase of raw materials, energy, accessories, sub-contracted work and goods; 23 per cent is distributed to the personnel in salaries, appointments, bonuses and social charges; 12.56 per cent goes to transport costs (including transport of raw materials and finished goods in France and abroad), and administrative costs; 2.04 per cent in financial costs; 2.93 per cent is set aside as reserve against immobilised goods (materials, buildings, installations), risks, reserves and result, before any distribution.'

In Britain, a very different story was being told by Basiliou, the Renault UK managing director, in January 1972, in the following terms:

'We have increased our sales from 31,159 in 1970 to just about 41,000 in 1971—

Above *Small car with a great future—the original Renault 5.*

Below *Playtime for Renault 5 drivers at a rally.*

that is a 32 per cent rise and a market share of 3.2 per cent. It is very good indeed, but it does not reflect the true potential, because whilst already in a tight supply position we had to suffer a loss of about 4,000 cars following our May strike in France.

As it seems that we are now getting more support from our parent company, I am confident that during 1972 our progress will be even more significant and that 60,000 will be a realistic target. It must be remembered that during 1972 we will receive three important new models—the Renault 15 and 17 and, later in the year, the Renault 5.

As to our longer term prospects, we are developing our UK organisation to handle still more cars and the 100,000 mark does seem to be within our reach in the not too distant future. We, as Renault Ltd., are going to invest, in 1971–72, over one million pounds. Furthermore, as part of our five-year plan, we provide for investments of similar magnitude—that is half a million pounds a year.'

The Renault 5 was given its international launch in January 1972, against the industrial and economic background already described. The substance of its sales potential and technical conception resided in the wide and growing demand for a car of greater stature and presence than the Mini, more refined than the Renault 4, certainly more sophisticated than the Dyane or DAF, and 'trendier' than the Morris 1000 or Toyota Corolla. The shadowy image in the public mind was of a smallish, luxurious, peppy hatchback—or rather estate car, since the term hatchback was not at that time current in Europe. There was also the vague notion of a 'big Mini'—not such a contradiction in terms as might be supposed.

Renault were actually pipped to the post by Fiat, who launched their 127 in October 1971, but that car was not the subject of such massive promotion, nor did its design catch the imagination in quite the same way. Nevertheless it has always been competitive in the 'big Mini' league which was later to include the VW Polo and Ford Fiesta.

The new car made its UK debut at the Earls Court, London Motor Show in October, and was instantly acclaimed. Far more than simply a model slotting between the R 4 and R 6, it was in its own right a transportation unit of the new age—the epitome, in fact, of the environmental motorcar. (As Renault France had said, 'La Renault 5 apparaîtra comme une voiture à l'image de notre civilisation d'aesthetique industrielle, "voiture-design" jolie, originale, attachante. Une voiture functionelle mais plaisante—"sympa" et "marrante" comme diraient les jeunes— qui jettera un pont entre deux générations, et facilitera l'union de la ville d'hier avec l'automobile de demain.')

For Renault and particularly the UK company, it was gratifying that the car had already had conferred upon it the title of Car of the Year in the *Daily Telegraph*/BBC TV 'Honours list'. The R 5 was winner of the low-price category of these awards, but was also voted overall runner-up (to the Jaguar XJ 12!). It was also voted overall Car of the Year by *Car* magazine.

At that time, and even more so now, the compact car could be seen as a most desirable concept, if not yet quite a vital necessity, bearing in mind the increasing density of traffic not only in city centres but in the suburbs, and at peak touring times, even on the highways.

The Renault 5 was certainly a compact car, and being only 11 ft 6 in long, it was a true city and commuter car. At the same time it earned itself a place in the next higher class, as an unusually comfortable 4–5 seater with a top speed—over 80 mph for the 956 cc version—and general performance little below that of many medium-sized and priced saloons. As a bonus, it had the estate car facility giving rear-door access to 9½ cu ft of luggage space, or a generous 31¾ cu ft with rear seat folded.

The L version of the car had the classic 850 cc three-bearing engine and this gave it a performance much the same as the Renault 4—no sluggard, as any owner would confirm. It had drum brakes all round, and a dynamo, whilst the 5 TL not only had a five-bearing engine similar to that of the Renault 8 but also front discs and an alternator type of generator.

But was the TL engine that of the R 8? To say so to the factory smacked of heresy, for the marketing people, as always, regarded it as failure if anything was admitted to be 'old'. Let it be sufficient to say, perhaps, that it had the same bore and stroke (therefore the same capacity) and the same general design as the original R 8 engine. Renault claimed a DIN horsepower figure of 43 at 5,500 rpm and they said that this power was achieved by using a lower-capacity version of the 1,100 engine but with compression raised to 8.3 by machining the cylinder head. But the R 8 engine had a compression ratio of 8.5, moreover its SAE bhp figure was 47, so it seems odd to have reworked the 1,100 engine. All the small five-bearing engines were siblings of the R 8 in any case. The changes have always been rung by altering the bores, cam lift, valve diameter, compression ratio, carburettor, etc. Only when the R 14 arrived was there a radical change, the engine then being a Renault-Peugeot unit.

The 850 version of the car had the normal belt-driven cooling fan, but the 956 had the luxury of an automatic electric fan, operated by the thermostat and relay, so it only wasted power when the engine got really hot. Both engines had a Solex 32 SE1 carburettor with manual choke.

The gearbox was a normal four-speed all-synchromesh with the familiar umbrella-handle fascia shift. Later, a floor shift was used, but it never seemed to me to be as good as the dashboard lever.

The neat 'capsule' body of the R 5 was a highly scientific structure of monocoque type, mainly welded, although the bonnet, front wings, bumpers, doors, etc, were bolted in the usual way. Thickness of main outer panels was 0.7 mm but the sill members, which take a great deal of punishment on any car, were of 1 mm steel. The front wings were of unusually stiff calibre. They also permitted the fitting of 145 × 13 inch tyres and provided sufficient clearance for snow chains, but if that clearance was sacrificed, 155 × 13 inch tyres could be fitted.

Front and rear bumpers were innovative and interesting, being moulded from a pre-impregnated glass-fibre and polyester mat material. As far as I know, this was the first application of this process on mass-production car assembly lines but within a few years others had started copying. Now the idea is almost commonplace but no less effective. Such bumpers had already been used on the rear of the 15/17 series. The material is as tough as steel but more resilient.

A French chemical company delivered the material in 1,500 kg rolls to Renault's Dreux factory in watertight containers so as to keep it fresh. The material contained 35 per cent glass fibre and 65 per cent impregnation paste. The stuff was unrolled, and the rough shapes were cut out. These were then put in the presses and moulded at a pressure of 70 kg/cm^2. The operation was carried out at 150°C to cure the material. The bumpers, or shields, as Renault called them, were self-coloured in a neutral grey shade. One of their great merits was their unusually large area, whereby they gave extra protection to the bodywork.

Above *Cutaway promotional car demonstrates innovative space-saving design with many safety features.*

Right *Moulded reinforced plastic front bumper of the R 5.*

I had practical experience of the efficacy of these bumpers when navigating with a Press colleague. He was driving us at a brisk pace—probably 50 mph—when another motorist shot out of a side turning in front of us without warning. Braking hard, we still could not avoid the offender and hit his offside front with our nearside front at what must have been 10–15 mph. He was pushed into the passenger seat by his buckled door but managed to continue driving a few yards into a small river. We stayed where we were, and indeed could not have done otherwise, because the front bumper of the R 5 had broken off, obviously reluctantly, but the panelling of the front mudguard had crumpled backwards into the tyre and the suspension had been bent backwards more than a little. Nobody was hurt. The bumper must have taken a severe impact before bending and breaking.

Safety had been a primary factor in the design of the R 5. Active safety features included the inherent qualities of the front-wheel drive, good visibility, large head-lights, high comfort factor and excellent braking—although even the last-mentioned was not able to prevent collision in the incident I have mentioned above. Passive safety features included progressive crushability of the structure, embodying a very rigid central area; seat belt anchor points for rear as well as front; many interior safety features including padded and collapsible parts, universally-jointed steering column, safety glass, non-injurious switches, handles, etc.

The fascia was of a scientific design, plastics being used creatively and not in imitation of traditional materials. The casing, which was shallow for good visibility, was made from ABS plastic with a soft coating. The instrument panel was connected to the electrical harness by a single multi-pin connector. A printed circuit on flexible plastic was used, and all warning bulbs were easily detachable. The speedometer cable had a bayonet fixing and everything was easily removable.

The seating was not blatantly luxurious, although the car shown at Earls Court had seats upholstered in somewhat garish orange PVC—looking very much like what used to be called patent leather. I had ordered one of the new cars and was terrified in case mine should turn up with the same trim, especially as I was told (take it or leave it) that the car would be in orange paintwork. Fortunately it came with grained black trim.

The seats were supposed to be anatomically designed. Maybe they were, but whose anatomy did they use? It has always been agreed that the seat backs were too short and that for some people, the thighs were not supported adequately. But they were good seats in every other way, and the back bench seat was very good. The 5 was not a true five-seater but one could squeeze three moderate-sized people into the back. The two side doors were very wide and gave relatively easy access to the rear compartment.

The head lining was said to be technically advanced, in being a compressed-fibre sheet glued direct to the roof panel—applied, in fact by a kind of robot. It was a sandwich of several materials with high damping properties; mechanically, acoustically and thermally. But a folding sun roof was an optional extra. I myself specified a proprietary one which I considered a better proposition.

The new cars, in both L and TL form, were well equipped. Even the 850 had the full heating/ventilation equipment, interior courtesy light, two-speed wipers, electric washers, anti-theft steering lock, headlamp flasher, twin sun visors, underbody protective spray, rubber boot mat, etc. In addition, the 5 TL had the heated rear window, individual reclining front seats, front armrests, rear ashtrays and a vanity mirror for the front passenger. The heating system was not the car's best feature; to keep warm on a cold day, one had to keep the fan on the faster of the two ratings for a fair time, then on the lower rating. If the fan was not switched on, the car never became very warm. Some owners even went to the extent of fabricating a small air-ram to fix on the bonnet air inlet.

A new plant for the R 5 was set up at Flins. One of the most important features was a mechanical robot, situated experimentally in the general assembly line. It was the forerunner of many such devices to be used in Renault factories. One senses that the workmen feeding the thing were undecided whether it was friend or foe— whether they should or should not allow the triffid-like device to become a success . . ..

Basically it was a turret which could turn and tilt and which carried an extensible arm, at the end of which was a kind of mechanical hand. This hand could carry any required welding electrode and its movements were controlled through hydraulic servo mechanisms which took their orders from memory tapes in the console of the turret. The thing had to be set up and programmed by a specialist or two; thereafter it got on with the job itself.

I was able to try the car in France early in 1972; as I was thinking of buying one, I was particularly interested in this test. Renault flew us to Brittany and the cheeky little cars were on the airport apron waiting for us and garnished with a few smart uniformed Renault hostesses.

I introduced my test report in the following terms:

'Unlike its British counterpart Cornwall, the French province of Morbihan does not abound in steep hills, so I am unable to unfold gripping accounts of downland forays, let alone mountain or alpine ones, in the course of my comments on the Renault 5.

This is a tough, eager, powerful little car, however and there is little room for doubt that it would acquit itself well even in the Himalayas . . ..

Following my usual practice of getting my grouches off my chest first, I would mention something that I am sure had some connection with the characteristics of the region. This was a habit of misting up slightly every time one dropped below about 10 mph.

Our base of operations was the Sofitel luxury hotel on the tip of the Quiberon peninsula, so that we might almost just as well have been on a great liner, being almost surrounded by sea. Sea is damp stuff, and this must have been the reason for misting and sweating of the car's screens and windows.'

I was wrong, of course. The R 5 always had a tendency to mist up, like many small saloons and particularly hatchbacks, and it would be just as likely to happen in Morden as in Morbihan.

I went on:

'I and my co-driver colleague unanimously decided that this was a well-mannered, sprightly, safe and decidedly comfortable small car. It is good for me to have this kind of second opinion, because I might otherwise mistrust my own judgement, which always tends to make Renault ducklings into cygnets and geese into swans, I suppose.

For a 1-litre car, the R 5 is not outstandingly fast for today, but it is not much good having a racy engine if it wears out quickly or throws a rod in the middle of the Autoroute du Sud, and the smaller five-bearing-crankshaft Renault motors are renowned for their fantastic toughness.

The performance may not feel urgent, but the cobby little car gets along quicker

Sophisticated travelbag. With rear seat folded, the R 5 gave 32 cu ft of load space.

than one would think from its fussless feel. It never for an instant feels strained, even when one is winding it up to its maximum indicated speed of 110 kph (68 mph) in third, which means well over 6,000 rpm even allowing for speedometer error. Our maximum indicated speed, on a slight downhill stretch of highway, was 145 kph or 90 mph but the true speed would probably be nearer the claimed 84–85 mph, as one would expect from the 956 cc unit.

Kerb weight of the car is 1,730 lb compared with 1,568 lb for the original 956 cc Renault 8, 1,687 lb for the R 8-1100, 1,654 lb for the R 6-850 and 1,808 lb for the R 6-1100. One would not expect "thrust in the back" acceleration, but the car is no snail. We were not in a position to check the speedometers on any of the cars, but at least we double and treble-checked our stop-watch times by making repeated attempts. The average figure for 0–50 mph was 12.8 seconds and that for 0–60 mph was 16.4 seconds based on the indicated speeds. At the time when I tested the 6-1100 I did not do much better, and the speedometer error, if any, would probably have been about the same . . ..'

For the 40–60 mph bracket, we chose nearly equivalent readings of 70 and 100 on the somewhat vaguely-marked but easily legible speedometer and the average figure came out at 22.8 seconds. Again, this is not going to cause anybody to have a 'high-g' blackout but so good is the handling and so effective are the brakes of the 5 TL that one would not have to try at all hard to make a magnificent average speed over a long give-and-take run.

'As we made our way towards Vannes, through a variety of country lanes, there was very much an 'all-square' feeling about the 5, as though it disdained to be affected in the slightest degree by ridges, potholes or other irregularities. It is not intended to be a true maid-of-all-work like the R 4, which really started life as a sort of farmer's hack, but stopping to inspect an interesting monolithic war memorial in a remote part, we could not resist making a foray up the narrow woodland track by its side. Via a route that would have made a good rally section, this took us to a great old farmstead, and the almost copybook scene of the Breton farmer in dark beret, faded blue overalls and muddy gumboots, reciting his story of the horrors of war.

. . . The R 5 got us up that long winding trail and back like a scout car—agile, sure-footed and without the slightest protest at being treated as a cross-country vehicle. Later in the test, we did the same kind of thing again, when each of us in turn played around in fairly deep hummocky sand with the car, satisfying ourselves that it had ant-like qualities in making instant directional changes without loss of adhesion. Farmers, as well as housewives, trendy young folk, up-and-coming executives, shopfloor workers and you-name-it, are going to fall for this car as we did.

When I was not driving, I assessed the passenger's reactions and again the bill came out on the credit side, for the car is astonishingly spacious and the ride is soft and flat, without too much roll on corners. I noticed, in fact, that the roof-mounted grab handles were almost superfluous except on rough tracks. During normal fast cornering, articles on the back seat would slide across due to high sideways 'g' but as a passenger I did not get flung about, as can happen in an enthusiastically conducted R 4. The driver, of course, automatically braces himself. For such a short car, there is quite reasonable fore-and-aft space in the back and the seat is comfy for two, if not quite wide enough for three.'

(Note that I later conceded that there was room for three not too large people.)

Left *In TS form, the Renault 5 had a very brisk performance. Note see-through high-back seats.*

Left *Limousine in miniature—the Renault 5 automatic 1400.*

Below *An instant success—the cheeky little R 5 Gordini.*

I continued:

'Driving the car back around the Gulf of Morbihan, from charming little Port Navalo which must be a sailing man's delight, I was further impressed by its rock-steady feeling, and I mean steady without ever feeling heavy or lumpish. In fact the Renault 5 has the lightness of a true minicar, although it is far from being a miniature in its load capacity and capability. A thing that particularly delighted me was the finger-light steering, and regular readers will perhaps recall that I am almost ultra-sensitive about this aspect of a car's design. Even at a creep, the action is light and positive—reminiscent in a way of the old 4 CV, the first true minicar of them all.

On the wide dual carriageway between Vannes and Hennebont, on the return leg of the test circuit, the 5 TL was untiring and not obtrusively noisy at an indicated 120 kph (75 mph) which seemed to be its happiest cruising speed, although it would go quite effortlessly to the 140 kph mentioned earlier, albeit with a raised noise level. How noisy? Certainly much quieter than a Renault 4 in full song, and perhaps quieter than an R 6 but not in the same class as the whispering R 12 nor the hush-hush 16—in other words very much what one would expect.

At all times, with the new car, you get this feeling of rugged rigidity, as you do with the Renault 12, 15 and 17 and I think this is due to the monocoque construction. The R 4 and 6 series are chassis cars with bolted-on bodies, and there is a different feel about them, although they are very rugged indeed. Since the new car's panelling is stress-bearing, it is somewhat thicker—from 0.7 to 1 mm.

The complete appearance of this car is made distinctive by its unusual bumpers, or what Renault call shields, in the latest idiom. These are made from pre-impregnated glass-reinforced plastic (GRP) mouldings and it is claimed that there will be no appreciable deformation even in an impact of up to 5 mph.

Because of the quite high performance, disc brakes are used at the front and drums at the rear, and there is the usual limiting valve. It will please many potential purchasers to know that the handbrake is a "proper" one . . .

. . . Although reclining front seats are fitted, they are not quite as luxurious as those used on the Renault 6-1100, although anatomically good, and pleasant in appearance . . ..'

I never had much cause to modify my initial reactions to the Renault 5. I would write very much the same about my own 5 TL, which I still had at the time of writing this book, after nearly 10 years, although it had a mere 30,000 miles on the odometer. It has served me well beyond the call of duty, despite irregular and sometimes indifferent servicing. I never had any preferential treatment from Renault as regards servicing or anything else, except that they gave me a trade discount of 12½ per cent on the original price. The paper value of the car is about the same as my original purchase price, so in theory it has not depreciated. In practice, of course, inflation makes a nonsense of such values. The R 5 cost £930 when introduced in the UK and it now costs £3,600, although it has been improved in many ways.

The Renault 5 went on to be a best seller for the Régie, and it still is. Various variants have been introduced—the 1.3 litre TS, the 1.3 GTL, the 5-speed GTX, the 5 Automatic and the Gordini (5 Alpine in France). The 'ultimate' 5 is the Turbo, a limited production saloon racer, but there is a Gordini Turbo series car too.

10: Renault's first Six since '39

Astute motoring journalists knew about the Renault 30 TS a year before it appeared. Journalists with big expense accounts make a habit of interviewing and wining and dining top executives regularly. Top executives will often talk—in confidence. They know that breaches of confidence or the breaking of embargoes work both ways. Writers and reporters can lose their jobs, or at any rate valuable connections, if they betray a confidence, especially on paper. If an embargo is broken, advertising worth half a million pounds could be withdrawn. Newspaper proprietors are not happy about such things. Fortunately they do not often happen, so top executives and sometimes even underlings can reveal secrets—in strict confidence.

The deliberate leak is another matter. Manufacturers sometimes find it convenient to be careless with photographs, brief details, cars driven publicly without camouflage. Occasionally they contrive a 'scoop' in their house magazine.

Outside the intimate circles of communication and professional and social inter-course in the motor business, journalists lean heavily on hearsay, spin-offs from high-level confidences, authoritative or other reports in trade or foreign papers, and intelligent guesswork. They also keep their eyes open.

There was no deliberate leak on the R 30 but one newspaper man sniffed it out and obtained a photo. Another used that wonderful stand-by, an artist's impression. Most were content to know that Dreyfus had something up his now voluminous conjurer's sleeve. Many connected it with something called the BRV, which Renault publicised widely in the middle of 1974, and which was a Basic Research Vehicle conceived by Renault and Peugeot. They were right and they were wrong.

The BRV was a French government backed project aimed at the development of safer motorcars. The Régie pointed out that it was neither a prototype nor a pre-production vehicle, nor even a styling exercise and least of all a 'dream car'. It actually looked more like the Renault 18 than the R 30 and in any case it had the Renault 16 TS engine. Nevertheless, features of the BRV were progressively introduced in original or modified form into all future models including the R 30, and whilst its styling could not be directly related to production models, it was an interesting and on-going exercise.

The year 1974 brought the Renault 12 automatic and the five-speed Renault 16 TX, whilst it was also notable for the successful introduction of Renault 5 circuit racing, which provided valuable promotional impetus for the precocious small car and probably helped to make it a best seller for years.

Above *Flagship of the Renault range—the big V 6 Renault 30 TS.*

Below *Special equipment luxury version of the 30, with TX designation.*

World wide trading figures released by the Régie at the end of June showed that despite problems in the world's motor industry in 1974, the company achieved higher production, sales and exports than in 1973. Turnover increased by 16.3 per cent. Profits had declined but nevertheless reached £3.6m. Renault continued to top the French domestic car market, with 36 per cent of registrations, as well as being the leading French exporter. Total production for the year was 1,487,528 vehicles (5.2 per cent above 1973). In November, for the first time Renault became the best-selling marque throughout the nine Common Market countries—a position previously held by Fiat.

In the UK, Renault's performance was satisfactory to the Régie, too, although not quite up to the expectations of the Acton people themselves. For many years they had been the leading importers in Britain, but latterly the Japanese Datsun concern had been a thorn in the flesh. In the autumn of '73 Datsun actually outsold Renault (as they were to do many times in the years to come) although in November Renault achieved their highest-ever penetration, at 4.79 per cent. During '74 they sold 57,026 cars and 1,440 vans and although this was less than in '73, it represented 4.5 per cent penetration. Renault were doing well on all fronts and this was undoubtedly in a large measure due to the widening range of models which they offered. All they needed was something to compete with the Ford Granada, the big Citroens, the Mercedes 280 and smaller Jaguars perhaps, the Rover, the Volvo, etc. Dreyfus had the answer. The new car—immediately dubbed 'flagship' of the Renault range—was unveiled at the Geneva Show in March 1975 and appeared at Earls Court in October. It turned out to be everything that the Frégate had never been. In fact it more than made up for Lefaucheux's mistake—a quarter of a century later . . ..

The car bristled with technically interesting features, but the most important one was undoubtedly the use of a 2.6-litre V6 engine. The idea of a V6-cylinder arrangement was not new; the Lancia had one in their Aurelia, contemporary with the Frégate. But this new Renault engine was something rather special.

For some years, the Régie had somewhat stealthily been courting Volvo and it was perhaps characteristic that long before the R 30 was introduced, Renault, Peugeot and Volvo had come to an agreement to construct an entire factory at Douvrin, for the mass production of a new engine—the 90-degree V6 of the Renault-Peugeot-Volvo Franco-Swedish Engine Company, and the result of intensive technical co-operation between the three companies. This unit is used in cars of the three marques, with slightly different specifications and different auxiliaries. It was the first V6 with a light alloy cylinder block to be made in France. Its conformation, with three cylinders on each side, was chosen to give the minimum overall engine volume. The inlet manifolds were inside the V and the exhausts on the side. The alloy heads had hemispherical chambers and each bank had an overhead camshaft.

The crankshaft of the fascinating new engine had four bearings and three throws spaced at 120°, each with two con-rods. This was the arrangement considered the best compromise for good balance—always a problem with V6 engines, but far less so than in earlier days when it was not possible to construct and machine engine components to such fine limits and when metal technology still had a long way to go.

The carburation system was based on a tubular inlet manifold and there were two Solex carburettors—a single-choke unit of 1.34 inches (34 mm) the opening of which was controlled by the accelerator, and a twin-choke unit of 1.38 inches

(35 mm) which opened automatically by the action of a diaphragm sensitive to engine vacuum. There was a twin ignition system with independent circuits for the two cylinder blocks. Each circuit had a coil and condenser, but there was only one twin circuit breaker for the two circuits. The engine being a 6-cylinder 90° V type, the angular gaps between ignition were alternately 150° and 90°, the firing order being 1-6-3-5-2-4. (In its arrangement of cylinders, crankshaft and firing, in fact, the new design reminded one of the somewhat advanced Buick V6 of ten years earlier.)

The R 30 was from the start designed to take automatic transmission as an option. Because the 139 box used on other Renault automatics could not transmit the power of the 2.6-litre engine, a new unit, the Type 141, was designed and put into production by the Société de Transmissions Automatiques, the Renault–Peugeot subsidiary, at its factory at Ruitz, in northern France.

The 141 consisted of gearbox and differential located longitudinally with the components in three main casings containing a hydraulic torque converter linked to the crankshaft, a differential and final-drive unit, and the gearbox itself—an epicyclic unit giving three forward speeds and reverse. As on the 139 box, there was a hydraulic control system which could be compared to the 'nervous system'. All functions such as vehicle-speed sensing, engine-load sensing and information processing took place in the 'black box' called the governor comparator.

Front suspension of the R 30 TS was of double-wishbone type with a substantial anti-roll bar. The rear suspension was of a new design called the three-articulated-bar type. The transverse bar—the main load bar—carried the vehicle weight and transverse load on bends, via the coil springs. The longitudinal bar carried most of the longitudinal loads, particularly those involved in braking. The vertical bar was actually the telescopic damper on each side. What the British Renault company called 'three-bar suspension' actually meant 'three-member suspension'. It is often the case that things are translated literally and do not convey quite the original meaning. Owners of Renaults and other imported cars were not always entirely happy with their drivers' handbooks and service instructions. The translators were often at fault. To translate technical matters requires not only a knowledge of the language but also of the subject.

An important contribution to the built-in safety, both active and passive, of the new car was the power-assisted rack and pinion steering. With the car moving straight, the degree of actual power assistance was relatively small, but it increased progressively in relation to the force against which it was acting. A permanent mechanical link ensured that there was function of the steering whether or not the hydraulic aid system was working.

Brakes were discs all round—ventilated at the front and with two calliper cylinders for each front wheel, allowing splitting of the brake circuits for each wheel. Thus there were two independent brake circuits, one for the front and one for the front and rear. Power assistance was provided by a Master Vac servo unit.

This was a top-of-the-market car for Renault and they had made sure that interior appointments and furnishings were of the highest standard. The front seats had a wide range of settings, reclinable backs and adjustable built-in head rests/restraints. In the back, following the example set by the R 16, there were as many as seven variations of positioning for both seats and squabs, giving luggage space for 11 cu ft in the normal position and almost 50 cu ft in the exceptional load position.

There was, of course, a comprehensive heating and ventilation system of constant fresh-air-circulation type. All controls were illuminated at night—a feature which is more important than it sounds. All controls, major and minor, were said to be ergonomically designed. This is an expression which is bandied about somewhat recklessly in the motor industry and it derives from the jargon of method study. What it means, of course, is simply the design of things so that they work to the best advantage and as easily as possible, bearing in mind the human physiology and its limitations. In the old days of motoring journalism, it was regarded as an unpardonable cliché to say that a particular control 'came readily to hand' but it expressed what is now described as 'ergonomic', by publicists inebriated by technology.

Renault, like other car manufacturers, were now into safety in a big way, and with the influences of the BRV in addition to normal contemporary techniques, they were able quite justifiably to claim that the new car was exceptionally safe.

The body was developed particularly so as to give the passenger compartment strength on all three axes, with progressive deformation for other parts of the vehicle, so as to get the greatest possible cushioning effect in the event of collision. At the front, rigidity was ensured by longitudinal members, avoiding any folding of the floor, with heavy gauge material under the windscreen and linked with the corresponding zone of the engine compartment.

A hollow-section cross member under the scuttle prevented wheel intrusion into the passenger compartment under front impact. Its effectiveness was verified many times by the research department. At the rear, the fuel tank was well protected by a hollow ring structure surrounding the tail door and incorporating a complete reinforcement of the rear skirt area. The fuel tank location, well forward and as low as possible, was not only safe but it lowered the centre of gravity and made for good road holding.

The front and central pillars were of ample dimensions and well integrated with the structure. The front and rear doors incorporated waist-level longitudinal members in heavy gauge steel and the upper parts of the front doors also had a similar longitudinal reinforcing member. Longitudinal members at the front diverged and included specially weakened zones which allowed any deformation to be localised. Cut-outs in the front sections and holes in the transverse steering member lessened the rigidity of the front part in the event of impact, whilst the rear floor could deform under heavy impact without causing any crushing of the fuel tank.

The steering column, rigidly fixed to resist forces coming through the scuttle, had a double universal joint which, in the event of heavy impact, allowed a backward movement of the steering gear without steering movement. The one-piece, foam-padded fascia was free from projections and the lower part smoothly shaped.

The upper side-anchorage points for the inertia-reel safety belts were mounted as far back as possible and the central points as far forward as possible, with a webbing width of 2.63 inches, giving the best distribution of body loading under impact. The safety door locks were stated to eliminate any danger of occupant ejection whilst the electro-magnetic locking had a fail-safe device which automatically unlocked all four doors in the event of impact. Electric locking, incidentally, was considered very advanced at that time, and Renault were ahead of the pack with this now quite popular feature.

I tested the 30 TS in August 1975 when Renault took selected motoring Pressmen to the Cotswolds for a few days. They announced the UK price—£3,950—which was realistic for a luxury car of this calibre.

I said:

'Not only does the driver feel immediately at ease in the car but its impeccable manners and behaviour become his own. Although the 30 TS is almost a foot longer than the Renault 16 or 17, at 14 ft 10 in, it both looks and feels if anything shorter and in fact it has a compact feel about it in all circumstances, and is a very easy car to place and manoeuvre, not least on account of its power-assisted steering. It was the power steering, as a matter of fact, that made the first marked impression on me on taking the car over, because other Renault models, except the smallest, tend to require a firm pressure when applying lock, but this certainly does not apply to the R 30. The degree of assistance is perfect. I have known some systems which were positively hazardous because there was too much power and almost no 'feel' but the engineers have certainly got it right with the Renault.

At the time of the test the manual version only was obtainable in the UK. On the two cars which I tried, the shift was sweet as honey; a short, stubby stick gives a silky but positive movement for all changes. The ratios are, as on all Renaults, perfectly suited to the engine speed and torque characteristics. Top gear is an ideal motorway ratio, allowing a comfortable maximum of 115 mph. At 100 mph the Renault 30 TS feels unstressed, quiet and ready to cruise all day. Third gear is ideal for emergency high-speed overtaking.

I have an open mind on the question of whether the V6 motor is any smoother than Renault's four-cylinder aluminium engines, which all who know them agree are exceptional. Certainly, however, it is free from any idiosyncratic vibrations, and with such a short stiff bottom end, the four-bearing crankshaft is no handicap. What is certain is that the unit gives a gutsy but effortless performance throughout its speed range.

One expects excellent steering, road holding and suspension from any Renault, but the latest addition to the range shows even greater virtuosity. One of several ways in which this was demonstrated to us was in a "phenomenal avoidance" on the M4, when the driver had to make a sudden swerve at 70 mph on account of the inconvenient presence of a baulk of timber. Since the "victim" was the wife of *Country Life*'s motoring correspondent and we had elected her to assess the car from the woman's point of view, this seemed a somewhat savage way of proving a point, but we were all able to carry out tests in more normal ways, and agreed that the 30 TS is an exceptionally good car to handle at all speeds. One thing that did not altogether please this lady, and I am inclined to agree, was the shape of the head restraints on the front seats, and from a rear seat passenger's point of view I think I prefer the tapering see-through type used on the R 5 TS. On the other hand as a head *rest* I found those on the R 30 TS better for driving, and they would probably be better for cat-napping on a long run.

I tried the rear seat ride for a fair period and found it extremely restful; moreover, although this is such a compact car, it is comfortably spacious regardless of the position of the front seats. The ride is unusually quiet in front or rear. There are no engine resonance phases and wind noise is minimal.

The new rear suspension, coupled with the well-established coil-and-strut front system, gives a relatively soft ride without even a trace of wallowing, although there is a slow pitching motion on rough roads. The roll factor is much the same as on the Renault 16 series, although it seems greater if the power steering leads one into exuberance, as can sometimes be the case. In other words, it is very easy to corner faster than you normally would—in complete safety, but with the car heeling more than would otherwise be the case.

The power braking is superb. Warning my passengers, I did a panic stop from cruising speed and there was no trace of wheel lock, grab, or veering from the straight. Later, one of the ladies repeated the same process and found that progressive emergency braking needed only moderate pedal pressure.

All minor controls and interior appointments are easy to use and designed for safety and comfort. The inertia reel safety belts are particularly good, the combined door pulls and armrests (front and rear) serve their purpose admirably and the seating is of the high order one has come to expect from the French manufacturer. We all found the heating and ventilation system to be uncomplicated and effective and it is worthy of note that there are console-mounted air vents as well as those at the ends of the fascia.'

If the praise which I was bestowing upon this car seemed rather fulsome, it should be remembered that I was writing for the Renault magazine *Autoworld*, which was given free to every buyer of a new Renault for two years. I was not expected to say anything very nasty about any of their products although I went as far as I dared. Fortunately my conscience was seldom troubled, for most of the cars were good, and I was myself a satisfied owner.

Realising that they were beginning to compete with several kinds of top-of-the-market motorcars, including the cheaper Mercedes and possibly the Jaguar, although there was a considerable price differential in their favour, the Régie, in October 1978, introduced an even more prestigious machine—the Renault 30 TX, which at the time was something of a bargain at a little under £8,000. It came to Britain in April 1979.

The 30 TX had more power, several technical refinements and a still higher equipment specification. It was available, like the 30 TS, with manual or automatic transmission, but the manual was a five-speed box. There was just one optional extra—leather upholstery, at £350. The main features of the car were fuel injection, electronic ignition, a headlamp wash/wipe system, combined electro-magnetic central locking for doors and filler-cap flap, heating ducts to both front and rear compartments, and special wheels, with a kind of Maltese cross motif, and perhaps not to everyone's taste although 'high fashion'.

Top speed of the manual version of the 30 TX was claimed as 117 mph and that of the automatic car as 113 mph. Equipped with the Bosch K-Jetronic fuel injection system in place of carburettors, the V 6 motor thrust out a useful 142 bhp at 5,500 rpm, and a maximum torque of 161 lb/ft at 3,000 rpm. Principal advantages of the injection system were, perhaps reasonably, stated to be lower fuel consumption, reduction of unburnt gases in the exhaust system, high torque at lower rpm, and greater smoothness of power delivery. 'On the road', said Renault, 'the most notable technical feature of the TX is its engine flexibility, comparable to many bigger-engined, more powerful cars in the American vogue'. They were, of course, getting a little carried away, for there was really very little of the American vogue about the R 30 in any of its forms, although it was a good, smooth and rather beefy French car, it resembled, if anything, a big British car like a Rover or a Ford Granada.

In summary, said Renault, the 30 TX crystallised their current model philosophy of spreading their range across the entire car-buying market, from the R 4 and the R 5 up through the middle-range models. Their marketing director said: 'Up to now we have only touched the surface of this top-flight segment of the market with the

With the same spacious shell as the 30, but with 4-cylinder engine—the Renault 20 TL.

Renault 20 TS and the 30 TS. The 30 TX could be called the apex of the pyramid and with a sales target of 83,000 Renaults in Britain this year, that amounts to a very big pyramid'.

At the same time as the R 30 TS went on sale in Britain, in November 1975, the Renault 20 was launched in France. The new car had the same shell as the 30, but had the well-proven 1,647 cc, 90 bhp four-cylinder motor. At this time, it filled the gap between the 16 TX at £2,700 and the 30 TS at £4,000, without replacing any model. Renault now had model ranges of 17–20 cars, according to the particular market.

Offered in four-speed manual and three-speed automatic versions (five speeds came later) the 20 TL had a top speed of 102.5 mph, 0–60 mph acceleration of 12 seconds and fuel consumption in the 25–30 mpg range, according to the Régie.

Renault had no hesitation in claiming that the 20 was much superior to its competitors. This was the time when, in matters of product promotion, a barrier and a convention had been broken down. Quite suddenly it was no longer

Ghosted drawing of the Renault 20 TL.

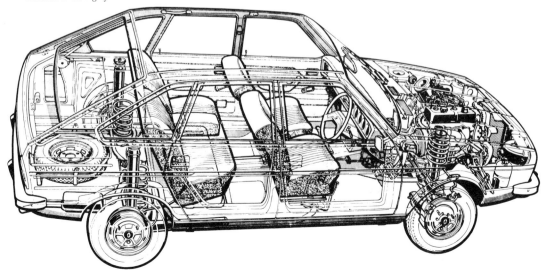

considered improper—hardly cricket, old chap—to make direct comparisons and name names. It happened slowly at first, but it took a hold. Today, it is almost *de rigeur* to denigrate one's competitors even in advertising. What the ad. man once called 'knocking copy' with a sneer of distaste on his face, is not simply accepted but celebrated.

So Renault asked, publicly, 'How does the Renault 20 TL compare with other cars in its class?' and answered its own question in the following terms:

'A detailed study, covering the ten closest rivals—Audi 100 LS, Citroën CX 2000, Ford Granada 2000 GL, Lancia Beta 2000 ES, Saab 99 GL, Peugeot 504 GL, Princess 2200 HLS, Rover 2200 SC, Volvo 244 DL, Triumph 2500 TC—shows that it is competitive in speed, acceleration and fuel consumption; shorter than all except the Lancia, Saab, Peugeot and Princess; has the tightest turning circle (33 ft 1 in) of all except the Volvo; is the only model except the Citroën to have ventilated front disc brakes; offers the biggest luggage capacity of the whole group, and is the only model with five doors. Only the 20 TL and Lancia have internal headlamp adjustment and optional electric window operation. Only the 20 TL offers optional electro-magnetic door locks.'

Renault's market research people were cockahoop about the 20—so much so that they bared their souls and told the Press how they had seen the car's chances and its potential buyers long before it progressed from the mock-up stage.

Careful qualitative research, it was stated, had shown that it would be considered

The 20 TS, with 2-litre overhead-camshaft engine.

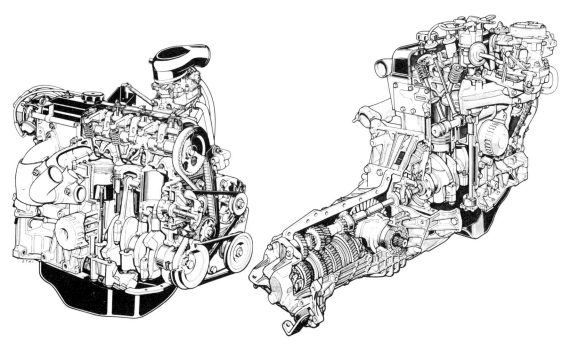

Left *Power unit of the 20 TS—a compact 110 bhp engine.* **Right** *Renault 20 TL power unit—the well-tried 1,647 cc 4-cylinder.*

attractive in looks ('long and low, with sporty connotations') and spaciousness for luggage as well as passengers. It 'equated with what was expected from an expensive car'. It would be considered particularly comfortable, not only in its seating but in smoothness and quietness of ride. It was seen as appealing to the active family man—particularly the sportsman—and rising young executive looking for a car to reflect his lifestyle as well as fulfil his practical family requirements of space and comfort.

The firm's study showed that the 20 TL buyer could be expected to have above-average income and size of household, be upwards of 35 years old and come into one of four distinct occupational categories, ie, professional, executive manager in industry or commerce, small business owner, company director. Business usage would be high—about 65 per cent against the market average of 45 per cent—and annual mileage about 13,000.

The 20 TL buyer, it was claimed, would be motivated by reliability, styling, accessibility, interior space and comfort, whilst secondary factors would include operating costs, performance, luggage capacity and safety.

Safety, said the market research gurus, would be a feature receiving special consideration from buyers in this market sector. The highest source of sales for the 20 could be expected among previous owners of Renault, Volvo, Rover and Triumph cars in this class, and some 90 per cent of principal drivers and 95 per cent of buyers would be men.

Renault, as usual, gave me a car to take away and live with for a few days. Looking back at my report, in August 1976, I realised that I went over the top again a bit, but I truly did like the car. Among other things, I said: 'We may not have reached the days of the flawless diamond yet, but this was certainly the best, most balanced Renault I have yet tried. I use the word "balanced" deliberately because in

Renault 20 with more muscle—the 2.2-litre TX version.

so many ways the Renault 20 offers magnificent compromises, eg, that the performance is competitive without being in the least alarming; that the road holding is superb and the ride soft, yet roll is minimal (three normally incompatible features); that the steering is positive yet light; that the brakes are immensely powerful yet progressive to the last degree.' (My seemingly irrelevant reference to diamonds is a somewhat corny play on the diamond logo of the marque.)

In August 1977, the Régie introduced the Renault 20 TS, saying that its new power unit, produced in the Renault-Volvo-Peugeot plant at Douvrin, was significant as the first all-new Renault-designed engine since that of the Renault 16. It was a 2-litre overhead-camshaft, light-alloy unit developing 110 bhp. By powering the car with this new 1,995 cc super-square engine, said Renault, they were the first of the three associates to use it 'as the dominant partner in the joint engine development group'.

In 1979 the 20 TS was fitted with a five-speed manual gearbox as standard equipment, the three-speed automatic box remaining an optional extra. This was an important year for the UK arm of Renault with the introduction also of the 30 TX and the 5 Gordini, whilst the sales figures soared and Renault UK overtook Datsun once more, in their ding-dong battle.

At the start of 1981 the R 20 gained the accolade of the 'TX' suffix, emerging as a 2.2-litre 'motorway cruiser' by virtue of a 7 mm increase in piston stroke, and several modifications to take the extra power. A significant novelty was that the car was offered with the optional extra of cruise control, ie, a facility for automatic speed hold or speed limit.

11: Cars in the age of economy

I well recall that when the Renault 14 was launched in the UK, the outspoken motoring correspondent George Bishop stood up at a question session and asked the Régie's head designer 'Why have you chosen to produce such an ugly looking car?' Nobody was particularly surprised, not just because they were accustomed to Bishop's brash outbursts, but because nobody was really sure whether the car was ugly or not. Even now nobody is sure. The designer's answer, in any case, was 'Sometimes it is a good idea to shock the market. It is a modern design and we wanted people to sit up and take notice.'

When I first saw the car, at its introduction in France, I hoped that all future Renaults would not be in the same image, but after a while I found it quite acceptable. The international launch was in May 1976, but it was almost another year before it came to the UK.

There was a hint of the apologetic in Renault's comment on the role of the new car, in the terms: 'In setting its target for the Renault 14 as the middle-range sector in Europe—the area with the greatest variety and widest choice of models—Renault recognises the need for a major constructor to offer several models having definite personalities. Hitherto, Renault's offering in this class was represented by the 12 and 16. The Renault 14 is therefore intended to reinforce the company's position by adding to its new generation of "functional" models, which began with the Renault 5 in 1972.'

Some people saw it as a kind of cover-up, too, when, in September 1976, the French Industrial Aesthetics Institute awarded its Grand Prix to the Régie, with the citation 'for the deliberate policy that it has asserted with respect to industrial aesthetics in the design of its products—the Renault 14 particularly materialising this effort'.

There is no doubt, however, that the shape of the car served well the purpose of maximising interior space whilst minimising external dimensions.

The Renault 14, said the Régie, sat squarely in the middle-range market, shoulder to shoulder with the R 12. By its very definition, however, the 14 was aimed at a clientele fundamentally different from that concerned with the R 12, and sales of both models would enable the Régie to improve their penetration in an important sector of the Euro market.

The new car was built at Douai, near Lille, in a purpose-built plant representing an investment of 1,400 million francs. At Douvrin the basic engine was made, along

More capsule than car? The Renault 14 TL.

with the V6. It was more a Peugeot than Renault engine, and the same applied to the gearbox.

The total production target for the new car was set at two and a half million over ten years.

The Renault designers broke with tradition and for the first time used a transverse engine. It was a 1,218 cc, 57 bhp unit with light alloy wet-liner block for the four 75 × 69 mm cylinders, and compression ratio was 9.3:1. The engine was inclined 72 degrees rearwards to allow a low bonnet line and room for the spare wheel, which simply lay in a tubular cradle—a typically French simplification and really a very good idea as the wheel kept clean, was easily accessible and did not take up luggage space. Renault had first done this with the spare wheel of the 16, although it was held down by a somewhat irritating metal strap in that case. A bonus with this idea is that the tyre can act as a buffer in frontal collision and I have seen one or two actual examples of this. It is not simply a theoretical advantage.

Renault said the 14 was a car conceived from the inside outwards and of course this is a very good way to design a car, especially in these days when computer services are available to the designers. This, said the Régie, was a car in which the family motorist did not have to over invest for size.

The car had an overall length of 13 ft 2 in, exactly mid-way between that of the R 5 and the R 30 but with a 'habitable length' to quote the Régie. That is to say, the distance from floor and seat-back was 1.74 m—the same as on the R 16, which was 8½ inches longer.

There is no doubt that the mechanical design and specification of the 14 were carefully studied, and at the same time, many chassis components common to other models in the range were used. The plan of having the gearbox under the engine, in unit of course, and the whole assembly ahead of the front axle, made for a low 'droop snoot' and good traction, whilst the assembly was on a cradle held by four

A limited edition 14 TS to celebrate the wedding of the Prince of Wales and Lady Diana.

bolts and the upper shock-absorber mountings, making for easy major servicing.

The power pack with gearbox weighed only 289 lb. The cross-flow cylinder head was in light alloy and there were the familiar Renault wet liners. A chain driven overhead camshaft bore a family resemblance to that of the R 30. The distributor was mounted horizontally and driven off the camshaft and the contact points could be adjusted outside the distributor body with the engine running. Units requiring the most frequent attention or adjustment, eg, carburettor, fuel pump, oil filter, water pump, alternator, starter and distributor, were on top of or in front of the engine.

The design of the front axle, using a sub-frame for the half-axles, simplified adjustments in that area. The car had a diagnostic socket for quick and accurate checking of basic ignition values, and the cylinder head was factory tightened 'for always'.

Suspension was by coils at the front and torsion bars at the rear and the steering was rack and pinion. The usual front disc and rear drum braking system was employed.

For some peculiar reason, Renault UK sent British motoring pressmen out to France in right-hand-drive 14s from Acton and back again. These were some of my comments:

'With the dawn coming up like thunder, followed by early morning fog, the omens for a jaunt to Lille and Douai in a Renault 14, via Dover–Calais, seemed unattractive. So powerful is the influence of Townsend-Thoresen public relations, however, that Dover came up all blue skies and white sun-kissed cliffs, and for two days even northern France pretended to be the Vendée . . .

First impressions of the 14, as I left the Acton plant of Renault Ltd., were of being in a capsule, module, space egg—something at any rate almost extra-terrestrial. This kind of feeling arises not only on account of the vehicle's slightly ovoid droop-snoot shape, but because of the technologically advanced interior, instantly characterised by the understated but fully informative fascia in soft reinforced plastic and the aircraft-type steering wheel with padded rim and cushioned centre.

Getting out of London in the rush hour on a Monday morning is a top test of any car's agility, never mind the driver. I give the Renault 14 the highest rating, apart from a slightly notchy gear shift which would almost certainly improve with a few more thousands of miles on the clock. The steering is lighter than on my own Renault 5 and few cars could be easier to place. All control and pedal positions are—to me at any rate—beyond criticism.

On the motorway I could just feel and check the slight sidewind twitch; few models of any make are free from it, but they do vary and the Renault 5, for example, is so exceptionally steady as to make anything else seem less than perfect. The old rear-engined cars could, of course, be quite alarming at times . . . .

As far as performance is concerned, Renault say "The jointly-developed Renault-Peugeot overhead camshaft engine of 1,218 cc, producing 57 bhp and teamed with a four-speed gearbox, provides effortless 70–80 mph cruising, a top speed of 88.9 mph and fuel consumption of around 35 mpg" and as far as I know, none of us on this press event had reason to dispute the claim. Fuel consumption was carefully checked on all cars by the refill-to-the-brim method and some people were getting as good as 37 mpg with quite hard driving, and with only a few miles of motorway involved. An indicated 90 mph was easily possible, I found, and at 70 mph the car was very quiet and completely unstressed. Low-speed torque was not particularly high, compared with larger-engined models, but for high-speed motoring this is largely offset by the mid-range and upper-range torque and high rev. capability, giving a useful maximum of 70 mph in third.'

Turning up *Autoworld* No: 62, to quote the foregoing, I was reminded that this was the 75th anniversary of the historic Paris–Vienna race won by Marcel Renault in 1902 and was also the 75th year of Renault Ltd. in Great Britain. Louis Renault was indeed a pioneer of the philosophy of high power-to-weight ratio in those days, even if he seemed to lose sight of the advantages in later years. The little 16 hp Renaults were Davids among the Goliaths of the vast Mercedes, Mors, Panhards, etc,. Now, 75 years later, the R 14 was offering proof that light weight and reasonable power make for an excellent basic specification.

Douai, the factory where the 14 is built, stands in open country, with plenty of room for future expansion. It is a model factory and is the fourth bodywork plant of the Régie. I found it impressive, as well as a little uncanny, because of its high degree of automation. Major construction of the 14 and the 5 goes on steadily and swiftly in vast immaculate shops and you often have to play a game of 'spot the human'. Great robots pick up, assemble and weld sides, roofs and floors of cars. Some of them bear boldly-lettered names like Alice, Theo, Fany. They are creatures to the human work force, some may see them as hostile; some love them for doing repetitive work so contentedly. All respect them.

About 7,300 people are employed at Douai. Modern, designed to meet all developments in method study and work study, it holds a prime position in the economic development of northern France, yet it respects environmental demands and even the little woodland of La Brayelle, which lies in a valley near the industrial complex, has been preserved.

Characteristically, Renault up-rated the 14 after a few years to make available the TS model in addition to the TL. Cylinder stroke went up from 69 to 77 mm, and

A 'three box' car of distinction—the Renault 18 GTS.

power from 57 to 70 bhp. A new frontal treatment and large plastic bumpers were features. Meanwhile a 14 GTL, additional to the TL, offered certain refinements on the basic model. In 1981, to celebrate the wedding of Prince Charles, there was a 'Regency' model of the 14—a limited edition car in dark red with gold lining.

When Renault introduced the 18 range—internationally in April 1978 and to the UK in February 1979—there was considerable fuss about it being a 'three-box' car. Most people had not heard this odd expression before. It is really a drawing office expression, which spilled out into marketing and was picked up by public relations, the way PR will gratefully pick up scraps of jargon when they are not quite sure what to say.

The PR people themselves explained: 'Most Renault models have been designed to be, above all, functional and practical, reflecting the demands of a large and growing number of motorists. But it is clear that this concept cannot appeal to everyone.

Today there is a dichotomy in every market—a split between the demands for two major categories of car: "three box" (engine, passenger compartment, luggage boot) and "two box" (hatchback), though the relative proportions of these two factions vary from country to country. Renault must therefore be geared to offer competitive cars in each category, both to satisfy a bigger clientele and to consolidate its marketing position.'

The Renault 12 had, of course, been a three-box car—a booted car. But the Régie seemed to be forgetting this, perhaps because they knew that the 12 was dated, and would soon be on its way out. When a car was becoming obsolete, they tended to keep very quiet about it and almost to play down the model.

The reintroduction of a booted car probably needed some explanation in the late 1970s, even though other manufacturers were experiencing this somewhat inexplicable swing to the three-box design, reminding them that you can carry out market research till the cows come home and some awkward whim of the consumers will upset all your calculations.

Renault continued to explain: 'The Renault 18, which was conceived from the outset to have an international appeal, has been cast in a more traditional mould to complete and complement a range in which the essence of the style was functionalism. Traditional it may be, but this car nevertheless embodies features that comply with the most modern requirements. The lines of the Renault 18 had to be attractive. But today the design of a car is no longer a pure and simple work of art. It is an extremely difficult and complex task, hedged about by all manner of constraints, for it must blend as harmoniously as possible the demands of safety,

The 'blower' returns to fashion. Renault's 18 turbo car.

strength and aerodynamics—this last having an important effect on fuel consumption. Bearing all this in mind, and taking into account all available competition, Renault wanted to give this new car something else as well—the extra attraction of greater value for money.'

The car cost from £3,300 to £4,500 on the British market, depending upon specification, so it certainly offered the usual Renault good value.

But Renault were not making the three-box concept the main point of their sales campaign. It was not enough, realised Dreyfus and his marketing teams, simply to say 'Look, people are asking for simple saloons again and we are providing one, only better than all the others'. Neither was it enough simply to do that thing. What came out of the think tank in Paris was actually what Ford had been doing for a long time, but never mind, it was new for Renault. This was the concept of launching a new model, known to be basically acceptable, in four versions right from the start, and no more of the business of introducing a TL, then a TS, then a GTL, then a GTS and so on. (At least that was the theory, although an estate version, then a turbo, came later.)

The 18 was aimed at such competitors as the Ford Cortina and Vauxhall Cavalier, as well as challenging the mid-range Fiat, BL, Chrysler and Japanese saloons. Production of the 18 was soon running at well over 1,200 cars a day at Flins and Sandouville.

The car was undoubtedly good looking, and utterly conservative compared with the 14. It was more conventional than the 12 and indeed seemed almost the archetype of the new European cars, although really it was planned alongside them several years earlier.

The range came with two engine options, a choice of manual or auto transmission on the beefier versions and four distinct equipment specifications—TL, GTL, TS and GTS. In TL and GTL form, the rather VW- or Audi-looking car was powered by the 1,397 motor giving 64 bhp at 5,500 rpm, whilst the TS and GTS had a 1,647 cc engine developing 79 bhp at 5,500 rpm. The engines were fore-and-aft aligned. Four-speed boxes were fitted on all the manual cars except the GTS, which had a five-speed. The TS and FTS could have automatic.

Diesel version of the R 18.

The 1,400 engine was basically an up-rated version of the unit used in the R 12 and the 1,650 was fundamentally that of the R 16, 17 and 20 TL. There was a lot of this 'proven component' philosophy about the new cars. For instance, the suspension was very much that used on the Renault 12, which had turned out so successful.

Renault claimed something new about the rust-protection. It was unusual for the Régie even to mention rust. They had been sensitive in this matter ever since the Dauphine era, although they had little need to be, for their processes thereafter were as good as those used by any manufacturers and better than some. Now, however, they said that the 18 series benefited from all the techniques normally used on Renaults but for further assurance and better protection of the most exposed areas—under the grille, door sills, wings, etc,—they were using pre-protected sheet steel. In this process the freshly rolled and cleansed steel is treated by a special electrolytic system which gives it a fine skin of zinc alloy.

All the Renault 18s turned out to be fine cars—a little lacking in character, perhaps, but were the days of cars of character perhaps already numbered? Who needs character when all they really want is reliable, comfortable, reasonably fast and very economical transport? The question is arguable, of course. There is a section of the motoring public devoted to cars with so-called character, in every developed country, and many pay dearly for the privilege, but there is a strong trend towards eliminating all quirks, eccentricities, whims and deviant behaviour of any kind in the mass-produced motorcar, so that it is as effective, safe and purposeful as a washing machine or central heating boiler. And why not? After all, there is little joy in programming a Bendix but there is still skill, fun and fair excitement in driving a motorcar. One should be able to revel in its performance without being distracted by peculiarities.

Whether turbocharging constitutes an aberration or a logical progression remains to be seen. Certainly the system lends character to a car, and demands some rethinking of driving techniques. Renault, possibly, were bowing to the demands of fashion in introducing a turbo version of the R 18 in October 1980. Before that, in 1980, the 18 and 20 were introduced in diesel form. This was also partly to meet a fashion demand, but was much more realistic, the fashion having been based on the harsh dictates of economy in European markets. It was of more limited but none-the-less significant interest on the UK market. The diesel gave character to the car but in a very different way from the turbo. The performance was relatively low, and driving technique had to be adjusted accordingly, just as it had to be adjusted for the high-revving-range power boost of the turbo.

With the introduction of the 18 range, Renault celebrated 80 years in motor manufacture. Dreyfus, engineer of the Régie's extraordinary ascent to multi-national status, had retired quietly and with essential dignity, his place as President Director General being taken by Bernard Vernier-Palliez, an astute, undemonstrative man who had been number two to Lefaucheux and Dreyfus and had been with the concern for 30 years. Vernier-Palliez at this time said: 'One of our tasks is to adapt ourselves to eventual changes in the structure of the world economic process.

We must find solutions, always more humane, to the confrontation of man with the machine.

We retain our confidence in the company because the past is a guarantee of the future and because the strength of material progress, about which Pierre Lefaucheux spoke shortly before his death as "the spiritual duty that we have to help to progress", are powerful stimulants; and because Renault, a national company, can count on those who work for her, especially so because they feel that the Régie is a creation of their own making.'

Bernard Vernier-Palliez was lucky as well as intelligent and hard-working. He did not have to create or re-create, like Louis Renault or Pierre Lefaucheux, nor did he have the dramatic problems of Pierre Dreyfus during his term of office. For him it was progress, progress all the way. He spent his time on the crest of a wave that rolled into the 1980s and he retired at the end of 1981. His successor was Bernard Hanon, like Dreyfus primarily a business man and indeed a doctor of economy at Columbia University in the early 1960s. 'Economy', in that sense, refers to the administration of community resources, but the turn of events, in the early 1980s, was such as to indicate that Hanon would spend a lot of time thinking about the economy of motorcars, as well as economies in the administration of the Régie.

Renault results for 1980 were excellent, and the group made more than two million vehicles for the first time; but the sound global performance was based on a good first six months and a second half of the year which was increasingly affected by falling markets and intensifying competition, particularly that from Japan. But Renault spokesmen were optimistic, voicing their hopes in the following terms:

'In the past two years, Renault has been able to continue to strengthen its financial structures. If the difficulties which affect the automobile industry and other mechanical industries in which the group is engaged do not worsen, there should be no change in the investment plans for the future, nor in the launch of new models.'

Hanon inherited from Vernier-Palliez the Renault 9 range, as an introduction to what was likely to be a challenging as well as agreeably stimulating term of office. He also inherited two significant projects—a new safety research vehicle and an economy research prototype. With typical Renault flair, these were respectively called EPURE (Étude de la Protection des Usagers de la Route et de l'Environment) and EVE (Économie Vehicule Éléments). Each of these imparted some features to the Renault 9 range, so it is worth briefly considering them.

Above *EPURE safety vehicle based on the Renault 5.*

Below *Main design points of the EPURE safety car.*

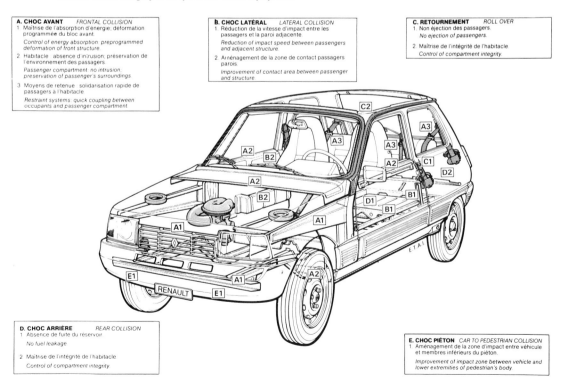

A. CHOC AVANT   *FRONTAL COLLISION*
1. Maîtrise de l'absorption d'énergie; déformation programmée du bloc avant.
   Control of energy absorption: preprogrammed deformation of front structure.
2. Habitacle : absence d'intrusion; préservation de l'environnement des passagers.
   Passenger compartment: no intrusion; preservation of passenger's surroundings.
3. Moyens de retenue : solidarisation rapide de passagers à l'habitacle.
   Restraint systems: quick coupling between occupants and passenger compartment.

B. CHOC LATÉRAL   *LATERAL COLLISION*
1. Réduction de la vitesse d'impact entre les passagers et la paroi adjacente.
   Reduction of impact speed between passengers and adjacent structure.
2. Aménagement de la zone de contact passagers parois.
   Improvement of contact area between passenger and structure.

C. RETOURNEMENT   *ROLL OVER*
1. Non éjection des passagers.
   No ejection of passengers.
2. Maîtrise de l'intégrité de l'habitacle.
   Control of compartment integrity.

D. CHOC ARRIÈRE   *REAR COLLISION*
1. Absence de fuite du réservoir.
   No fuel leakage.
2. Maîtrise de l'intégrité de l'habitacle.
   Control of compartment integrity.

E. CHOC PIÉTON   *CAR TO PEDESTRIAN COLLISION*
1. Aménagement de la zone d'impact entre véhicule et membres inférieurs du piéton.
   Improvement of impact zone between vehicle and lower extremities of pedestrian's body.

Normal Renault 18 and EVE—the economy project car seen below.

The Epure was proudly claimed as the world's smallest four-seater safety car, and it was presented at the International Safety Vehicle Conference in Paris in mid-1979. Simultaneously Renault entered a strong plea for a 'sensible, cost-effective and positive attitude' towards international regulations for passive safety, which 'still has little appeal for car buyers'.

Epure was based on the R 5 but the engine compartment was modified to take the R 14's transverse power pack. By virtue of a system of longerons and cross members, the front structure was designed to collapse progressively on impact without intrusion into the main compartment. Renault emphasised that where the nose structure was concerned, it was more important to meet safety requirements than to keep it short . . ..

Regarding side impacts, the heavy cross member under the front seats played an important part, as did the doors themselves and their latching arrangements. Padding was installed on doors, pillars and roof rails. Pillars and roof rails acted as a roll-over feature. The fuel tank was enclosed in a strong box structure, and the car was fitted with a new safety-belt system whereby an impact could be sensed in a hundredth of a second and the belts fully tightened a hundredth of a second later.

The bonnet had a 'shovel' aspect to reduce pedestrian injury, the screen was sharply raked and all protuberances shrouded. The lessons of the Epure, it was stated, would be applied to Renault models of the early 1980s.

The Eve project was a prototype which, it was stated, achieved nearly 50 per cent better fuel consumption 'with more to come'. Based on the R 18, the first phase of its programme was concentrated on better aerodynamics and on the use of advanced electronics to control engine and transmission, the power pack and final drive being left as standard initially. Having an all-up weight comparable with that of the R 18 TL, it had a lower-drag body shape to give a drag coefficient of 0.239—43 per cent better than that of the average European car. Good performance was thus achieved with a smaller engine, the Eve version of the 18 having a 5 TL engine of 1,100 cc. The second part of the programme was planned to embrace special economy engines and different types of transmission, at least one of which would conserve rather than waste energy when the car was slowing down. Renault officially passed the project over to the French Energy Saving Agency in June 1981.

The Renault 9 series was announced in the autumn of 1981. The basic car was a conventional, rather anonymous-looking saloon, just over 13 ft long and powered by a transverse engine of 1,100 or 1,400 cc driving the front wheels, but it gained the 'Car of the Year 1982' accolade.

Renault spokesmen said a three-box car with a boot was needed to meet the needs of the large number of middle-class motorists who for various reasons do not like two-box designs. Moreover, it was felt that the time had come to take advantage of recent technical developments and offer buyers in this class a better car than had previously been available, especially as regards fuel economy and running costs. Presumably they meant as a replacement for the R12 which had 'melted into the night' some months earlier. The 9 was additional to the 14, and did not replace it. In all, there were eleven models of the new car, arrived at by permutating the various engines, transmissions and equipment standards.

The engines were based on the familiar 1,108 and 1,397, but with modifications for transverse location and with more efficient top ends for better gas flow and combustion.

Renault stated: 'The 9 continues the already well-established Renault trend of using camshafts with reduced valve overlap to give a fatter torque curve which in turn permits the use of higher gearing for better economy'. This may sound

Ghosted drawing of the R 9 TSE.

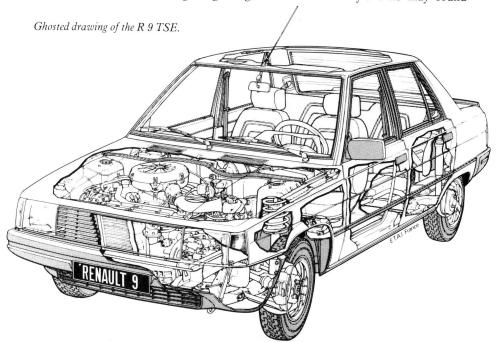

Renault 9 TSE.

abstruse but actually it is perfectly simple. Overlap is the time during which exhaust and inlet valves are both open, and the object is to use the momentum of the exhaust gases to help to draw the fresh fuel mixture into the engine. It is a kind of miniature turbo-charging effect, but it is mainly of use in high-performance, fast-revving engines. Renault were saying that they were deliberately avoiding using the engine's full performance potential. This, of course, is why speed freaks tended to pounce on Renault engines, knowing they could develop the power without anything bursting.

The smaller R 9 engine developed 47.5 bhp (DIN) at 5,250 rpm, giving the car a top speed of 86 mph. This was about the same power output as that of the old R 8-1100. The larger unit was produced in two forms, one with a single-choke carburettor, and developing 60 bhp (DIN) to make possible a top speed of 93 mph and the other with a twin-choke instrument to produce 72 bhp and give a maximum of 100 mph.

The transmission was essentially new, because the box was designed for the transverse engine. There were four- and five-speed versions. The R 9 automatic stood as a model in its own right, with a 68 bhp version of the engine.

As with the R 5 and 14, the Régie went in for plastic bumpers, but there was a new development in that they were mounted at four points on strong plastic springs which, they said, formed the next link in a 'safety chain' which ended with the main deformable parts of the front and rear ends of the car. This was claimed to mean survival of a 5 mph impact without damage.

There was a new seat design called Monotrace (Monotrack in English). It involved the use of closely-spaced front runners which, together with the smooth curve of the seat at the junction of cushion and squab, meant extra leg room for rear-seat passengers. A bonus feature was that, because the runners were so close together—in effect a single width runner—it was possible to arrange a linkage to tilt the seat around an axis through the occupant's hips.

In their publicity material, Renault said: 'In the eyes of today's motorist, hard-pressed by spiralling prices, a car needs to be economical in every sense' and went on to claim that the 9 was, on currently available figures, potentially the most

Car of the Year 1982—the Renault 9, in TC form.

economical car in its class in the world. They were certainly right about spiralling prices. The cheapest R 9 was costing about four times as much as a comparable car ten years earlier. It had been a decade of runaway inflation in Europe, with wage rises just keeping ahead of price increases because of the militancy of the unions.

Meanwhile another Renault new model was setting hearts and cheque books a-fluttering—the slightly tarty-looking but utterly respectable Fuego. 'Fuego' means firebird, and this bird turned heads as soon as it appeared in the showrooms.

Renault said about it: 'Superb aerodynamic styling from nose to tail is the dominant feature of this elegant newcomer to the coupé scene—a car to be rated unquestionably among the world's best lookers'. Not everyone agreed, perhaps, but it was unquestionably a striking car. It had a hint of status about it, and some people called it the poor man's Porsche. In my test report for a popular car magazine, I wrote: 'The droop-snooty going-downhill look, somewhat reminiscent of the Triumph TR 7, makes some people uneasy, vaguely dissatisfied. Others enthuse freely. You take it or leave it. I found the car so pleasing I gave up deciding whether I liked the look of it or not. Certainly it is different.' Incidentally this was the first Renault to have a name, instead of simply a designation, since the Caravelle of the 1960s.

The Fuego was a natural replacement for the Renault 15/17 range with its hatchback conformation, although it had a lift-up rear window rather than a door. There were three engine options, from 1,400 cc to 2-litres, manual or automatic transmission, and five distinct trim and equipment levels, with designations TL, GTL, TS, GTS, TX and GTX. All cars had the same shell, of course, giving dimensions of 14.3 ft length, 5 ft 6 in width and 4 ft 3 in height, and although this was very much a coupé concept, the car was a true four-seater with the feeling of a spacious, medium-sized saloon. A sensible feature was that the rear seat-backs folded forward individually and the seats could be removed to make even more occasional goods space.

In my test (of the GTS) I said: 'This was an extremely pleasant car to drive, with a smooth, willing engine and a useful performance. Maximum speed is quoted as 112 mph in the Renault technical material and I see no reason to doubt it. Certainly 100

Lovely to look at? In the eyes of some, certainly. The Renault Fuego.

mph indicated will come up without difficulty and at just under 5,000 rpm the aluminium engine (similar to that of the Renault 16 TX) is unstressed. The acceleration figure for 0–60 mph is about 12 seconds and one gets quite a satisfying push in the back when applying the "loud pedal".'

I said that I was not overjoyed by the gear shift and that unless one concentrated, there was always a possibility of selecting fourth instead of second, or third instead of top which, as I said, can be an embarrassment. I have found this with five-speed boxes on many cars, however.

I went on: 'Cornering and road holding were exceptionally good and the (optional) power steering on the car tested was a true benefit—finger-light at parking speeds but with progressive "feel" up the speed range. Braking was, as on all Renaults, smooth and powerful with the anti-lock feature provided by the rear pressure limiting valve.'

It is interesting to note that the Fuego was one of the first European mass-production cars to carry that piece of equipment contemporarily known as a 'funny' or 'skinny' spare wheel. The occasional spare wheel has been an object of contention ever since its introduction and I had no hesitation, in my test report, in saying 'Personally I object to the idea'. But at least Renault excused themselves in the driver's handbook, in the following terms: 'Both the emergency wheel and its tyre are designed purposely for a limited mileage life and restricted speed use. Speed must be restricted to below 80 mph (130 km/h) and driving attitude must at all times avoid hard acceleration, fierce braking and fast cornering when this emergency wheel is in use. You will notice a slight difference in car behaviour. Tyre noise is normal and intentional, and exists to remind you not to use it longer than necessary.'

As in all the more recent models, the Fuego showed unmistakeable evidence of Renault's preoccupation with safety, both primary and secondary. Perhaps the most immediately obvious safety features were the deep-underswept plastic bumpers or shields.

12: Renault in motor sport

Apart from the prohibitions of two world wars, Renault have never been far from the arenas of motor sport. Even the death of his 31-year-old brother Marcel in the 1903 Paris–Madrid road race did not put Louis Renault off for too long. When Renault did return to racing in 1906 it was a case of all or nothing. The result was the historic victory of Francois Szisz in the first-ever French Grand Prix. It was not nothing. It was all.

'Nothing but the greatest' was again the aim of the Régie Renault in the late 1970s and after 73 years, in 1979, Renault won the French Grand Prix at Dijon. Between the two prestigious and historic occasions, there were countless victories, many of them spectacular and of little less importance for the fortunes of the firm.

We have seen how Renault covered themselves in glory in the early road races— the days of what are now called veteran cars—and how, in 'vintage' days, they did great deeds with the mouselike 8.3 and the elephantine 45, then the more sophisticated Nervasport.

After the 1939–45 war, the impudent, lusty little 4 CV took up the cudgels, winning its class in the Monte Carlo Rally in 1949, whilst in 1952 came wins in the Rallye des Alpes, Liége–Rome–Liége and, of course, the awe-inspiring, notorious Mille Miglia. In 1955 a 4 CV won the general passenger car class of the Tour de France Automobile, whilst a special-bodied, souped-up version took the 1,000 km record for the 750 class at Montlhèry at more than 103 mph. Class wins were more than once secured in the great Le Mans 24-hour race and 4 CVs went on winning events some years after the introduction of the Dauphine. Moreover, the Alpine sports car was based on the 4 CV right up to 1960.

The 1956 four Dauphines took the first four places in the Mille Miglia and there were class wins in the same murderous race in 1957, 1958 and 1959. The Dauph' was, in fact, victor in its class until the race was erased from the calendar in 1959 after the tragic pile-up which killed the Marquis de Portago and ten spectators. Dauphines went on through the years to have outright or class wins in road races or rallies all over Europe as well as gaining honours in Sebring in the USA, the Mexican 24 hours, the Buenos Aires six hours, the Argentine Grand Prix, etc. The Dauphine was the only car to have won outright the three main rallies of its day—the Tulip, Alpine and Monte Carlo. One wonders how this car came to have an indifferent reputation for handling and road holding among certain sections of the motoring public. True, the works cars were specially prepared and usually had high performance engines, but the suspensions and steering were basically the same

Top *Quatresous and Lahaye with the 8-cylinder works Nervastella in which they won the 1935 Monte Carlo rally.*

Above *A Renault 8 Gordini in the 1967 Monte Carlo Rally.*

Left *Dealer Team Renault 5 TS serviced by Old Oak Motor Co and raced by Tom Mautner (left) and Neil Inigo Jones.*

Above *Lateral G force ... a 'bunch of Fives' at Croft circuit in Britain.*

Right *Group 2 Renault 5 Alpine.*

Right *Girl racer Juliette Slaughter with the R 5 which she drove in 1978, with considerable success.*

as on the standard product. True, the works drivers were trained men and women with special reactions and instincts, but they were going far faster than the ordinary motorist and therefore were prone to shunts and other incidents.

The R 8/10 series and the R 12 in its various forms continued to win motor sporting honours for the marque. The Coupe Gordini (Gordini 8 championship) was launched in 1966 and served not only to promote the Renault sporting image but as a training course for young drivers, such as Jabouille, aspiring to honours in the classic races and rallies and in particular in circuit events for formula cars, including Formula 1, although Renault had not yet entered the lists in that 'champion of champions' arena. The Coupe R 12 Gordini (Gordini 12 championship) served a similar purpose, and was followed by the R 5 championship. All of these one-make championships were primarily contested in France, but had their counterparts in other European countries including Britain, where, in particular, the R 5 Renault-Elf races were contested with great vigour and enthusiasm. Formula Renault races were also valuable promotional events in Europe.

In 1973 and 1974 Renault, Alpine and Elf collaborated in fielding a brace of special cars for the 2-litre prototype European Championship and were successful in the latter year. In the early 1970s, too, Renault fielded many a successful rally car, as did private owners, and Alpines won the World Rally Championship in 1973. Renault had by now taken a substantial shareholding in Alpine, incidentally. In 1975-6 the Régie introduced Formula Renault Europe in addition to Formula Renault. Originally intended as a promotional circus, dreamed up by Renault's PR people, it attracted French and foreign race-car makers of repute, all using the 1,600 cc Renault engine and it emerged as a remarkable breeding ground for Formula 1 drivers such as Laffitte, Tambay, Arnoux and Prost.

World speeds records are like mountains—people attack them 'because they are there'. But this is not by any means always the primary reason. It may be reason enough for the great individualists such as Cobb, Eyston, Segrave, the Campbells, Breedlove and Gebelich, but for an industrial enterprise there must be a profit motive as well, and since profit equates with publicity and world records create powerful publicity as well as prestige, it is understandable that a concern such as Renault should embrace the idea.

The commercial record breaker may also find profit and prestige in a less direct way by regarding the machine as a mobile test bed, whereby automotive techniques can be advanced and developed in an extreme way. When Renault broke the world 24-hour record in 1926 and the world 48-hour record in 1934, it is unlikely that they developed anything but their advertising and their order books, but their next world record attempt, in 1956, had more serious technological implications, although time has so far proved them to have been misjudged.

With the Étoile Filante, Renault saw themselves as pace setters in the development of the gas-turbine engined car, as did Rover and, in America, Chrysler. Unfortunately, the turbine car has never proved itself valid, although at least Ford have not entirely given up hope, and presumably Renault may have closed the file but will hardly have thrown it away. But Dreyfus was in the chair at the time and with his fine sense of publicity, he knew the money would not be wasted.

On 5 September 1956, the Shooting Star clocked 192 mph on the Salt Lake City Flats, to become the fastest gas turbine car of all time. It was (and is) a beautiful car, and had been wind-tunnel developed, so Renault must have learnt some useful

Renault Elf 30—1,500 cc turbocharged F1 car.

things in the field of aerodynamics and this information may have come in handy later on, even if the power unit was only of academic value. Some useful things may also have been learnt about control of a car in high-speed conditions, although the speed was not high if you compared it with that of racing piston-engined vehicles.

It was a time when Renault wanted to gain prestige in the United States, so that the Dauphine could be exported in quantity. The Dauphine was confirming its own good qualities and to some extent masking its inadequacies by gaining many road racing and rally successes, but a spectacular success by a Renault turbine could only strengthen the total regard for the diamond symbol.

The man who carried the Étoile Filante project through was Fernand Picard, head of the Bureau d'Études. The blue car, surprisingly small and prophetically reminiscent of the aerodynamic Alpine Renaults to come more than a decade later, was built by Albert Lory to Picard's plans. The Étoile was sleek and beautiful, with wheel-arch fairings and vertical stabilisers, but no ailerons or spoilers, which had not yet arrived, and were first to appear on grand prix cars many years later. The driver was Jean Hébert.

The power unit of the car was a 270 bhp Turbomeca. This firm were well known for their aircraft turbines which have, in fact, powered Renault private executive planes. The motor was fed by a gas-generator stage turning at 35,000 rpm and burning, of course, paraffin and not petrol. There was no gearbox, but a three-stage reduction gear system. The car had disc brakes and alloy wheels, and a fair amount of duralumin was used in its construction.

But Renault never went out for any more world records. They did not really need to, since the rally and circuit cars were carrying their colours so brilliantly, and the little Alpines were already becoming Renaults in the minds of the general motoring public as well as the enthusiasts.

The entire Alpine concept was founded on the respect of one man—Jean Rédélé—for the 4 CV. Many people have loved the 4 CV or, like me, had a love-hate

Alpine Renault 1500 Berlinette.

relationship, but this man was a fanatic. Rédélé had inherited his father's garage business and was a natural for success in some automotive sphere. He chose motor sport and it was his garage trade that financed him in the early days. In 1952 he developed his own car from the much-modified 4 CV which had given him his start in racing. In 1955 the first production version came on to the market.

The first Alpine was the A 106 and it had a glass-fibre body styled by Michelotti in a low-slung fastback format. It still had the familiar 4 CV spider-type wheels, in its original form. This was the basis for various Alpines with 750, 850, 900 and 1,000 cc engines in the Dauphine series, suitably up-rated. Almost all these cars went to enthusiasts who raced and rallied them. By 1960, Rédélé was making a machine that set the shape and form of Alpines for years to come—the A 108, at first Dauphine based. In 1961 came the A 109 Tour de France berlinette, a coupé which was virtually the model for all Alpines until the middle 1970s. The A 110 Tour de France berlinette of 1963 saw the Dauph' engine at last abandoned, to be substituted by derivatives of the R 8 and Caravelle. This series went on until the early 1970s, by which time Renault were giving substantial support to the Dieppe firm of Alpine, not just by sponsoring them in events but with technical and financial assistance, including Gordini's wizardry.

In the early 1960s, Rédélé became interested in formula racing and had evolved a successful Formula 3 race car by 1964, as well as racing successfully in Formula France. In the '60s, the company's most prestigious efforts were made in the prototype class, starting with the M 63 and then the M 64, which won the Index of Performance award at Le Mans—a victory which has been repeated numerous times since then. But Alpine—or Alpine Renault, as they now became known—were never outstandingly successful in Formula 2 or 3 racing and this presumably is why the French government (or De Gaulle and Pompidou, to name names) financed Matra for three years so that they could develop a national Formula 1 car.

Impudently, and, as it turned out, imprudently, Alpine tried for an all-out win at Le Mans in 1967, using a new 3-litre engine designed by Gordini. The car made its debut in the 1,000 km race at Montlhéry and gained seventh place. This and a second car won places in the Paris 1,000 km and Monza events. When it came to the great Le Mans race, however, Alpine managed only an eighth place with the 3-litre cars.

At Le Mans in 1969, there were numerous Alpines, both works and private, including the reworked 3-litre which was still underpowered, but they fell out one by one, leaving only a privately-owned A 210, 1,000 cc to uphold the honour of the firm by finishing twelfth.

At the start of 1970, Renault announced expansion plans for Alpine, whereby the small factory would produce 2,000 cars a year. At the same time, it was announced that the Régie's entire competition programme would be run by Rédélé. A special organisation would be set up for this purpose, and for the time being, motor sport activities would be restricted to rally events, including an entry in the RAC Rally for the first time. It was stated that Alpine would not appear at Le Mans for the following few years, 'as it was intended to concentrate on events in which cars developed directly from those models available to the public can be tested'.

At this time also, Renault announced that it had acquired a majority shareholding in the Société Gordini, whose new factory at Viry Chatillon would become the research department for competition activities.

In the meantime, there was news of the latest works rally car. This was a special version of the 1600 S, powered by an engine based on that of the Renault 16 TS, pushing out something like 155 bhp at 7,000 rpm, compared with the 83 bhp of the 16. With its aerodynamic glass fibre body, the potent little coupé should be capable of scuttling along at 150 mph, which might be useful in some of the hairier rallies.

The new car showed its paces in the Italian Rally, with Jean-Luc Therier gaining outright victory and Jean Vinatier taking third place. The accolade for the Régie, however, came in 1971, with a spectacular first three places in the great Monte Carlo Rally . . .. Justifiably, Renault shouted long and hard, and the effect on sales was dynamic. The Alpines went on to win rally after rally.

Jean-Claude Andruet won the Monte Carlo in 1973 and by then Renault had won five Montes—in 1925, 1935, 1958 and 1971. It was another ten years before the great classic was again won by the Régie, and a very different car won this event— the Renault 5 Turbo, driven by French rally aces Jean Ragnotti and Jean-Marc Andrie. The result was a boost to worldwide Renault sales although the Régie had just announced a record production of 2,055,000 cars as well as record turnover and export figures. Although the 5 Turbo did not bear the name Alpine, it was very much their concern as well as that of Renault, or rather Renault-Gordini.

In the race car, as opposed to the rally car field, everything in the early 1970s was gradually leading up to the biggest challenge of all—that of Formula 1. Renault approached this through Le Mans, Formula 2 and Formula 3 and they made no bones about the fact that they intended an overkill—that they would spend a great deal of money and employ all the technical and research facilities at their disposal, as well as the best drivers available.

It was not until 1976 that the hierarchy of the Régie gave their official blessing to the Formula 1 programme, but the campaign had really started stealthily as soon as Gordini had put together the V6 2-litre in 1973, with a Le Mans win in view. Already, in another year, there were experiments with a turbo-charger . . ..

In the meantime, Alpine and Renault were getting chassis as well as engine experience with Formula 2 and 3 cars, and in 1964 the firm won their first French Formula 3 championship. In those days the single-seater Formula 2 and Formula 3 cars had a twin-cam 998 cc motor—still virtually the old faithful Sierra with 115 bhp muscle. Ten years later, in 1974, Renault and Elf brought the motor sporting world to its toes by announcing an attack on the European 2-litre prototype championship. The two Alpine-Renault-Elf cars had a 2-litre V6 engine developing 300 bhp. It was right for the job but one needs brilliant drivers as well. Renault had shrewdly signed up Jabouille and Larousse. The championship was taken.

If Formula 2 and 3 were forcing grounds for both cars and drivers, Formula Renault also served its purpose in chassis and component development and the training of young would-be grand prix drivers. The cars had to be single-seaters to a particular specification and with Renault 12 Gordini power pack. At first purely French, this became a European formula, so it was of even greater value to potential grand prix drivers, and in particular, Renault's future star drivers.

In 1976, Renault seemed all set to win the World Championship for Sports Cars, with the big, deep-skirted, 2-litre V6 turbo cars pushing out well over 500 bhp at 10,000 rpm. Unfortunately both cars crashed on the second bend of the first race. Renault retired to lick their wounds and perhaps to ponder on the dangers of over-confidence . . .. At the end of the season, however, they occupied second place in the championship final results of the seven races. They had great hopes for Le Mans 1977. In the European Formula 2 Championship in the same year, Elf-Renault and Martini-Renault cars took first and fourth, and second and third places, respectively.

Le Mans was the big target for Renault for 1977. 'We are going to Le Mans with three or perhaps four cars, and we go there with the aim of winning' said Gerard Larrousse, the Régie's competitions director. For Formula 1, he said, they were continuing to develop the turbo-charged, 1.5-litre V6 which was something that nobody else had ever tried before. The Formula 1 driver would be Jean-Pierre Jabouille, who would also head the Le Mans team. Renault were now committed to the same basic engine for Formula 1, Formula 2 and sports prototype (eg, Le Mans) events. They had the foresight to see that turbo-charging would almost certainly be valid for rallying and for everyday road cars too, within a few years.

June 1977—the razzmatazz and carnival atmosphere of Le Mans—the smell of hot dogs and hot engines, the camp sites and bars and discos, the raucous song of engines and the orbiting glare of headlamps at night . . ..

The Renault-Elf team—three Renault Alpine A 442s entered by Renault and two Renault Mirages entered by Grand Touring Cars of Phoenix (Harley Cluxton) were reorganised and eager to do battle with Porsche, the title holders.

Porsche were the veterans. Everyone, including, perhaps, even Renault, expected them to set a killing pace and defend their title desperately. So they did, but fortune was against them. They had entered only three cars, confidently, but after only three hours two of them had cracked up. The remaining driver, Jacky Ickx was, in effect, told 'win or bust'. His drive through the night was historic and he broke the lap record repeatedly. To all intents and purposes he also broke three Renaults which, taking up the challenge, blew up one by one. Later, two more cars of the Renault team dropped out, leaving only the Mirage driven by Jarier and Schuppan to finish the killing 24 hours, but at least it finished second. Renault had led for more than two thirds of the race, so they did not disgrace themselves, but it was clear that broken pistons do not help to win races; even though the solitary Porsche finished with such a malady, the cylinder blanked off.

The same year, Renault mechanism fared better in Formula 2, Arnoux winning the European Championship with his Martini-Renault, Pironi being third in a similar car. Moreover, Alpine A 310 V6 models won the French Rally Championship, the French Rallycross Championship and the European Rallycross Trophy. The Renault Formula 1 car, designated RS 01, had made its debut in grand prix races, but there were teething troubles with the turbine. The Régie was nevertheless

Alpine Renault A 310.

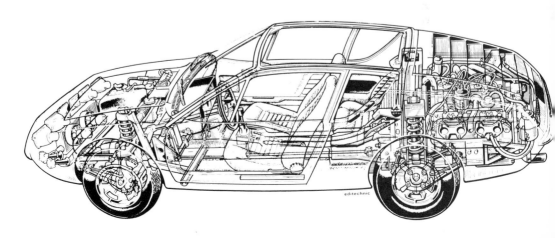

Above *René Arnoux (left) and Alain Prost—brilliant F1 drivers.*

Below *Renault Elf 30—1,500 cc turbocharged F1 car.*

Above *Ragnotti (left) and Jean-Marc Andrié.*

Below *Jean Ragnotti drifts a Renault 5 Turbo, on packed snow. Ragnotti and Andrié won the 1981 Monte Carlo Rally.*

Renault Gordini Formula 3 2-litre power unit.

satisfied that it was competitive, although concentration on Le Mans would take precedence again in 1978. Gerard Larrousse said 'While we did not win at Le Mans in 1977, we are aware of having been not entirely unsuccessful. For next year we have already taken our decision—our main aim being to study and resolve the very difficult problems imposed by the Hunaudieres straight . . ..' This was the long straight which had burnt up the pistons.

Again, in 1978, there were six turbo-charged cars in the Régie's team for Le Mans—four Alpines and two Mirages. One of the Alpines was the special A 443 for Jabouille-Depailler, which claimed 540 bhp. The others were A 442 cars. All were the subject of detail improvements to body and chassis, and there were deep side skirts.

Le Mans is a terribly punishing race, and both Porsche and Renault had depressing troubles which, of course, added to the excitement of the race. Porsche

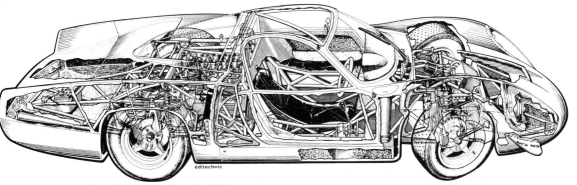

Type A 220 V 8 Alpine Renault 3000.

soon had only one car, and it went like a 'bat out of hell' all through the night, until gearbox trouble put it far back. For the first six hours of the race, the Pironi-Jussaud Renault led the field, but the Jabouille-Depailler A 443 then took the lead for 12 hours until another cooked piston put paid to their chances. Pironi and Jussaud went up front and stayed there without having to push the machine to risk point on the long straights. Renault had won Le Mans—perhaps with a slice of luck, but mainly by technical superiority, persistence and the skill and courage of their drivers. Jabouille and Depailler may have blown it, but they also blew the opposition. They also broke the lap record. The Ragnotti-Frequelin A 442 was fourth and the Lafitte-Schuppan Mirage Turbo tenth.

For 1979 Larrousse reorganised the competitions department, and combined the Dieppe and Viry-le-Chatillon premises under a new roof in Viry. The Le Mans effort had meant lost ground in Formula 1 activity in 1978 but now they were to go all out on the single seaters. Jabouille was retained as No. 1 driver. René Arnoux, like Jabouille a former European Formula 2 champion, was signed up as team mate. The RS 01 car remained basically the same as it was for the explorative outings in 1978, except that a few parts were remoulded in titanium. There was also a new car, the RS 10, and it was this car which took the Régie to its second French Grand Prix win in 1979. The first win had been in 1906, as all Renault *aficionados* will recall . . ..

The win at Dijon on 1 July 1979, was the culmination of the first stage of the Régie's plan to dominate Formula 1. In July 1977 the Renault turbo had qualified for its first Formula 1 circuit race, and in May 1978 it finished tenth in the Monaco Grand Prix. October of the same year saw a Renault turbo finish fourth in the USA Grand Prix and in 1979 came victory at Dijon, and second place in the British Grand Prix. In 1980 René Arnoux won the Brazilian and South African Grands Prix and Jean-Pierre Jabouille won the Austrian. In that year the thrusting young Alain Prost was showing great promise.

1981 saw victory for Prost in the French, Dutch and Italian Grands Prix. This was also the year in which Ragnotti and Andrié won the Monte with the R5 Turbo.

In 1982, as Gerard Larrousse outlined Renault's race plans for the year, he said: 'Renault Elf came very close to the target last year—just seven points short. In Formula 1, it is nothing, and yet it is enormous. The new page has now been turned and disappointment has given way to a new determination. The big adventure began in July 1977. It continues and it will continue, come what may, in 1982 and 1983'. His hopes for 1982 were not realised, although Renault had a 1-2 victory in the French Grand Prix, with Arnoux winning although he had been instructed to let Prost through for a vital three extra championship points. However, the cars had proved their potency and the omens looked good for 1983.

Conclusion:
Big plans and a little gadget

When, in mid-1982, the Renault Group released their consolidated accounts for 1981, they were utterly realistic, saying that '81 was a 'mediocre year, with record investments', which might sound paradoxical but makes financial sense, since they were losing money but also spending it on plans for the future. Pre-tax turnover, at Fr 87,700 m, was up 10 per cent, but there was a consolidated net loss of Fr 675 m, or 0.7 per cent of turnover.

Against what they called 'a very difficult background for the automobile industry, emphasised by a perceptible regression of world markets', they had to watch their production of cars and commercial vehicles diminish by nearly 12 per cent in 1981, compared with the record production in 1980 of 1,811,626 units. Nevertheless the group maintained a record level of investments with Fr 7,900 m—of which 75 per cent was in France.

The Régie itself realised a pre-tax turnover of Fr 53,600 m, an increase of 7.5 per cent. The balance sheet showed a loss of Fr 875 m compared with a new profit of Fr 303 m in 1980. Investment was down 3.8 per cent at Fr 4.5 m. Reimbursement to the State rose to Fr 136 m. These figures mean that the car side of Renault is having a relatively tough time, but whilst rigorous economies have been exercised in plant, production and administration, there have been no signs of cutbacks in improvement of designs or extension of ranges. The remarkable thing is that Renault seem to have been able to introduce new models which are cheaper to produce and at the same time offer the customer cheaper running, and all this without sacrifice of durability.

The Renault 9 range is exemplary in this respect and the secret seems to lie in weight reduction, allied with improved metal technology, notably the use of sheet steel coated with zinc at the foundry, the electro-plating of steel sheet in the body shops, the application of paints by cataphoresis and the use of special anti-corrosion processes. The Renault 9 may not look exciting, but there is quite a lot of exciting technology in it.

Renault underlined the policy of model diversification and advanced technology with the introduction of an automatic version of the R 9 with microprocessor-controlled transmission and described as 'the most electronic car in its class'. With an average fuel consumption figure of 37.9 mpg, it was also claimed as the best in its class.

Whilst the Régie Renault is very much a European undertaking, it is becoming increasingly a multi-national one and in the past few years it has been extending its

With a touch of surrealism, the Ile Seguin assembly plant at Billancourt took almost the shape of a ship.

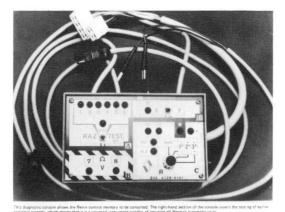

This diagnostic console allows the Renix control memory to be consulted. The right-hand section of the console covers the testing of earlier analogue systems, which means that it is a universal instrument capable of servicing all Renault automatic units.

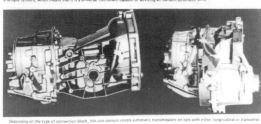

Depending on the type of connection block, this one console covers automatic transmissions on cars with either longitudinal or transverse mounted engines.

Right *'Car of the year 1982',* Renault 9.

links with companies around the globe. It now has a 46 per cent shareholding in American Motors Corporation and has initiated production of the Renault 9 on AMC assembly lines at Wisconsin.

Renault has co-operation agreements with Volvo (for car development and production), Peugeot (for engines and safety research), Volkswagen (for automatic transmissions), and joint marketing between Renault Industrial Vehicles and Mack Trucks USA. There are manufacturing agreements in Mexico, Argentina, Colombia and Portugal, whilst in Spain, FASA-Renault's three plants produce over 300,000 cars a year.

In the United Kingdom, Renault celebrated 80 years of trading in 1982. It is deeply involved in the British economy and most people realise that it is no less British than Ford, Vauxhall or Talbot if all factors are taken into account.

The company spends about £60 m with British suppliers; 20 per cent of its after-market purchases are made in the UK and it invests heavily in Britain—over £2 m in 1981, for example. It has a UK network of 500 direct dealers and satellites, plus 400 service points. In terms of employment, it plays an important role and in 1979–80 it created more than 1,100 new jobs for mechanics.

As an indication of its UK market success, it sold more than 260,000 units in the three years 1979–80–81 as against 187,000 in the previous three-year period. In 1981, sales totalled 75,000 units or just under five per cent of the market (itself down by some 11 per cent) compared with 72,000 three years earlier. Nevertheless, it is as an international group that Renault's capital growth and investments are so remarkable, when one recalls that it is a mere lifetime—85 years—since the eponymous hero (some said villain!) of this giant industrial undertaking filed and sawed and scraped in his little shed in a Paris garden.

From 1945 to 1963—the first 18 years after nationalisation—no government money went into Renault capital. The company was left to develop and perhaps prosper on its own.

Since 1963, its capital has been regularly increased to encourage growth. The arrangement was the outcome of talks—of arguments—between Dreyfus and Giscard d'Estaing, then Minister of Economy and Finance. In effect, Giscard said: 'Right, as shareholders, we should quite reasonably make a contribution to your capital, but we want to see our money back'. Dreyfus said: 'Well, of course, so we'll pay you dividends', and that was that.

In the seven years to 1980, Renault invested over Fr 18,000 m with a further Fr 8,000 m of its own money during 1981, Fr 5,900 m being put into new models and productivity, mainly in the Renault 9 plant at Douai.

The effect of this massive and continuing investment programme is seen in the Régie's progress, with 25 new models or major versions launched in two years, 27 million vehicles produced since 1945, production doubled over the past ten years, a workforce expanded by 3,500 in 1982 and a working year of 47 weeks with an average 36½-hour working week.

The year 1983 sees Renault going from strength to strength in the design and production of motor cars, commercial vehicles, industrial equipment, machine tools, military equipment, tractors and agricultural appliances, as well as in the fields of steel production and processing, civil engineering and allied industries, robotisation, etc.

A complete volume could be written on Renault's early and ongoing involvement with the aircraft industry and historians still revel in discussions on the concern's aeronautical and military contributions in two world wars. Currently, however, it is important to note the signing of an agreement between the French national undertaking Aerospatiale and the Régie Nationale des Usines Renault. This open-ended agreement will allow for a mutual exchange of information and techniques and, particularly, of transfers of technology between the two concerns.

As an example, the aerospace company will pass on to Renault, and thus to Renault owners, the benefits of its special know-how in new materials such as composite metals and special fibres and, of course, the fascinating new areas of specialised plastics and ceramics. More than one spin-off from spacecraft may enter the future Renault 1 or 2, or Renault 31 or 32, or Renault 'Scaramouche' or whatever it may be.

Renault in turn will bring to Aerospatiale its know-how in the field of automation and robots. This co-operation will be confirmed by specific agreements bearing as much on research and development together as on work effected by one of the companies on behalf of the other. If necessary, help may be sought from the public authorities.

Nothing has ever been too big or too small for Renault to contemplate or execute. When Louis Renault was, with an accomplice or two, working on the construction of those first few voiturettes in that draughty but somehow cosy little shed at Billancourt, he was concerned with immaculate and often original fabrication and design of even the smallest components, but he also already had visions of an automobile 'empire'.

Today, the Régie sees a future in which highly-mechanised, robotised production lines will turn out millions upon millions of safe, comfortable cars of utter reliability, dramatic economy and with an ability almost to drive themselves.

A life-size 'living montage' illustrates the history of Renault up to 1970, in terms of car design.

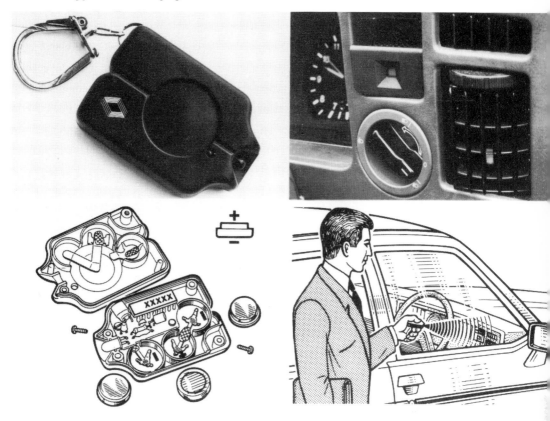

P.L.I.P. remote control locking system.

Renault thinks big, but it also thinks tiny, ingenious and meaningful. As an example, consider PLIP. The name is perhaps onomatopoeic but it is derived from that of a designer, Paul Lipschutz. Top-of-the-range Renault models now have this PLIP—remote control of the door locks by means of a tiny transmitter in the keyring carried by the driver. Renault has a big past and a big future, but little things mean a lot . . .

Index